D1242131

Survey Methodology and Missing Data

Seppo Laaksonen

Survey Methodology and Missing Data

Tools and Techniques for Practitioners

 Springer

Seppo Laaksonen
Social Research, Statistics
University of Helsinki
Helsinki, Finland

ISBN 978-3-319-79010-7   ISBN 978-3-319-79011-4   (eBook)
https://doi.org/10.1007/978-3-319-79011-4

Library of Congress Control Number: 2018939028

Printed on acid-free paper

This Springer imprint is published by the registered company Springer International Publishing AG part of Springer Nature.
The registered company address is: Gewerbestrasse 11, 6330 Cham, Switzerland

Preface

This book is a summary of my long and extensive research experiences in many forums, of which the following are probably the most important: Statistics Finland, the statistical office of the European Commission (Eurostat); the Social and Health Research Institute of Finland (Stakes); the University of Southampton; and the University of Helsinki.

At the same time, I have participated in many international networks and projects and have acted as a consultant on statistical issues in several places—most recently in Ethiopia—as noted in a few of the book's comments. One of the important networks is the Household Survey Nonresponse Network, which was founded in Stockholm in 1990 and continues to meet every year. I have often participated in these meetings. The other long-term group that I have been involved in is the expert sampling team of the European Social Survey (ESS); I have been a member since 2001. This book very much focusses on the ESS, which is a good framework for all social surveys, and I recommend that its standards are followed. Another useful network is the Programme for International Student Assessment (PISA). I was a member of the Finnish team that was responsible for the 2006 PISA survey. Thus, I learned quite a lot about it, and since then always have used the PISA data in my teaching and, to some extent, in my research.

For approximately 10 years around the year 2000, I was a Finnish coordinator of several European Union (EU) research projects, many concerning survey methods. In this book, the imputation methodology is based directly on two EU projects: Automatic Imputation Methods (AUTIMP) and Development and Evaluation of New Methods for Editing and Imputation (EUREDIT). The main data in Chap. 12 are derived from the second project, although greatly modified in the examples.

The impact of the EU's project, Data Quality of Complex Surveys within the New European Information Society (DACSEIS), on variance estimation also can be seen in this book, but not as explicitly. Later, around 2010, I was a member of the Finnish team that collated a representative data file on security and crime victimisation. We tested three survey modes, which is not a common approach. The findings were exciting, some of which are included here too.

I have presented short and long survey courses in all the institutions at which I have worked, and in other places as well, although the first comparatively complete version of this methodology was written in 1999 while I was at Stakes. It was the basis for the first course I taught at Helsinki University in 2002. Since then I have given survey courses there in various forms, including a recent one that covered all the main survey topics. Some of them, however, were at only a rather general level because it was anticipated that certain methods would be too difficult for students with not much background in statistical and/or other quantitative methods.

As a result, I also have given specialised courses on, for example, 'Advanced weighting and reweighting methods', 'Editing', 'Imputation methods' and 'Statistical disclosure limitation methods'. Course participants had a good background in statistical methods and informatics. The structure of this book is derived mostly from these experiences. That is, some parts are expected to be relatively easy for most social scientists, but the more sophisticated parts will be demanding for them, and for specialists as well, because the courses also include new methodologies.

Given that most students in general survey methodology courses have not been statisticians or mathematicians but have tended to be, for example, sociologists, social psychologists, economists, psychologists, demographers, geographers, and political scientists, the course is not formula-focussed. I have found that this can help when attempting to understand the main aspects of surveys. Another goal has been to ensure that students learn survey methodology well at a general level so that they are able to ask advice from specialists as early and knowledgeably as possible.

Often, I have found that a beginner may collect data but forget many important things when doing so. Some eventually understand that they need to contact a specialist for help. Unfortunately, the specialist then finds it difficult to make useful improvements because the mistakes made in the early stages frequently are fatal. This book should help to avoid such awkward situations, even if the reader does not completely understand everything in it. I believe that empirical, real data examples help to establish a basic understanding, if a participant has been paying attention sufficiently, before he or she started a survey. In addition, the students of my courses have done some of their own data handling and have reported on their outcomes. This book can be used for these purposes too.

Some years ago, I decided to write a full survey methodology book in Finnish. Its first version was published as an open access e-book by a Danish publisher, Ventus Publishing, in 2010. A new edition was issued in 2013. These books have helped with my teaching a great deal, although it was soon recommended that I use English more in teaching. When Springer contacted me in 2015, I suggested that I should write an English version as well. I have tested this version twice with my recent Helsinki University students. They have very much inspired my work, and some corrections have been made as a result. The comments of anonymous reviewers naturally have been taken into account as well.

I hope that readers will be pleased with my approach to survey methodology, with its focus on handling missing data. The history of sample surveys is not long, the first being implemented in the 1930s. Their use began to expand after the Second World War in the developed countries. Missing data at that time was not a great problem, but this issue has become increasingly worse as time has gone on.

This has led to the development of new research strategies and methods, many of which have been successful. Unfortunately, the strategies have not been able to solve everything. In particular, it is still difficult to obtain sufficiently accurate information about marginal groups. This is a nuisance that is evident in several examples in this book, the goal of which is to describe the newest methodologies for handling missing data. My focus here is more on post-survey adjustments; nevertheless, all the planning and fieldwork for surveys are just as important.

Helsinki, Finland   Seppo Laaksonen

Contents

Introduction

From the start road some steps forward

This textbook is on quantitative survey methodology, and it is written in such a way that survey beginners will be able to follow most of it. Nevertheless, they are expected to have some background knowledge about statistics and related issues, and to be interested in learning more about survey methods and practices. What is covered in this book is extensive. It includes fields such as advanced weighting, editing, and imputation, that are not covered well in corresponding survey books (cf. Bethlehem, 2009; Biemer & Lyberg, 2003; De Leeuw, Hox, & Dillman, 2008; Gideon, 2012; Groves et al., 2009; Valliant, Dever, & Kreuter, 2013; Wolf, Joye, Smith, & Fu, 2016). These subjects, naturally, are covered in specialized books and articles—see Chaps. 8, 11, and 12. On the other hand, we do not give much consideration here to statistical tools and methods relating to limitations caused by confidentiality, which are important in practice.

To help the reader without advanced statistical knowledge, we do not use many statistical formulas, but the necessary formulas are still included. This is possible because it does not take much space to explain the basic ideas in formulas. All of the more detailed and important formulas, however, can be found in the References included in this book. They are cited at the end of each chapter, but the Appendix entitled 'Further Reading' contains other bibliographical references on surveys in journals, books, and articles.

This book also will be useful for more experienced or even sophisticated users because some parts include methodologies that are not generally known even among survey experts. This is very much a result of the book's focus, which is on dealing with missing data. This focus is the result of survey practice, which has been becoming more awkward just because various types of missing data problems have been getting worse during recent decades. At the same time, new tools have been developed. Some of these tools and technologies are valuable, it is clear, but some are not, or their quality is not known. If the recommendations in this book are followed and implemented in a survey process, the outcome definitely will be good, or at least its quality will be known.

It is important to recognize that the book must be considered as a whole. In particular, this means that it will be beneficial to learn the terms used in each chapter, although Chap. 2 includes their core pattern. New terms are introduced later; thus, it might be difficult to go directly to the most sophisticated chapters—Chaps. 8 and 12. It should be noted that these authors' terms are not new, as they have been used earlier; however, terms seem to vary to some extent from one source to the next. It therefore would be useful to understand the terms in this book in order to understand its key points.

Survey Methodology and Missing Data presents many empirical examples that are, in most cases, from real surveys, particularly multinational ones. Two such surveys are used most generally. The first is the European Social Survey (ESS), which is an academically driven biannual survey (europeansocialsurvey.org). Its initial round was conducted in late 2002 or early 2003. The other survey, which has often been applied, is the Organization for Economic Cooperation and Development's (OECD) Program for International Student Assessment (PISA) that has been conducted every three years since 2000. The micro data from both surveys are publicly available and consequently are easy to use around the world, but they require adequate knowledge of survey methodology. We use much the same variables in examples throughout the book, which should help readers follow the methodology. Many examples have not been published elsewhere, as far as we know. The authors think that some results are also interesting from the subject matter point of view (e.g., Chap. 14).

Using examples just from one survey, either the ESS or the PISA, would not be reasonable in this textbook because these surveys are different. The ESS is used most commonly in the book's first part and the PISA is used toward the end, where we pay the most attention to survey analysis. The reason for this is that the public ESS files only include the survey weights, not two other important 'instruments'—stratum and cluster. Consequently, we cannot use the ESS in many examples, thus, the PISA is chosen when explaining the importance of other the instruments.

We are able to use examples that require the sampling data, given that the author had access to this material. Unfortunately, we cannot publish the related data file because it is confidential. We have passed over this problem by creating an artificial file that consists of two of the domains that have been used in almost all ESS countries. We include the description of this micro file in Chap. 6.

We use some additional survey data too. The Finnish Security Survey is used for two reasons: (1) some of its questions are special, and (2) it is based on three survey modes, which is not usual. We also use another special data file for imputation because neither the ESS nor the PISA survey is illustrative of this methodology. There are a few small-scale examples outside these main data files. In general, the examples are from social or human surveys, but some comparisons to business surveys are given.

An understanding of surveys and survey terms is demanding and takes time to gain such knowledge. It is not possible to write a book in a way that all terms will be immediately understood when they are explained. The authors use many 'graphical' and other schemes that we hope will facilitate understanding. The empirical examples are, then, for deeper comprehension. It would be beneficial if a user could use real data at the same time. This is possible in most cases since the ESS and the PISA files are publicly available.

Each survey should be conducted in the best way. This book is focused on the methods that help with the process so that the outcome is of as high a quality as possible. Second, the book's purpose is to give reasonable starting tools for using and analyzing a file once a survey has been conducted. This file should be reasonably well cleansed. The core of the book thus is focused on survey data collection and cleaning methods, which cover the following key steps:

- Designing the survey, which includes determining the target population
- Designing the questionnaire
- Designing the sample or samples
- Processing the fieldwork so that the data collection is productive, and the quality is high
- Entering data as much as possible during the fieldwork, or automatically
- Editing the raw data as much as possible during the fieldwork, with final editing afterward
- Inputing missing and implausible values, if this is believed will improve the results
- Including relevant auxiliary variables for the sampling design data file
- Creating the sampling design data file during and after the fieldwork
- Analysing nonresponse and other gaps found
- Weighting the micro data using the most advanced methods and the best possible auxiliary variables available and/or were gathered
- Documenting everything during the process, in a digital form to the extent that this is possible
- Adding other features into the data file that will help a user analyse it as easily as possible.

After creating the well cleaned survey micro file, it is possible to begin survey data analysis. Chapter 14 covers the basic methods for correctly performing the analysis so that the survey data 'instruments' are considered. More demanding survey analysis is not covered in this book.

The penultimate chapter, Chap. 13, contains a summary of all the key terms in the book. We recommend that readers look at this chapter from time to time, maybe after finishing each of the other chapters. It might be a good idea to read this whole chapter quite early, even though many of the concepts would not yet be understood.

The role of the photos at the beginning of each chapter are meant to give an image of the survey terms at a general level. They offer an opportunity to take a break between chapters and to start the next one without any prejudices. All the photos are from nature (not just from Finland) and are without people; they were taken by the author.

References

Bethlehem, J. (2009). *Applied survey methods: A statistical perspective* (p. 392). Hoboken: Wiley Survey Research Methods & Sampling.

Biemer, P. P., & Lyberg, L. E. (2003). *Introduction to survey quality*. Hoboken: Wiley.

De Leeuw, E., Hox, J., & Dillman, D. (2008). International handbook of survey methodology. Accessed October 2016, from http://joophox.net/papers/SurveyHandbookCRC.pdf

Gideon, L. (2012). *Handbook of survey methodology for the social sciences*. New York: Springer.

Groves, R. M., Fowler, F. J., Couper, M. P., Lepkowski, J. M., Singer, E., & Tourangeau, R. (2009). *Survey methodology* (2nd ed.). Hoboken: Wiley.

Valliant, R., Dever, J. A., & Kreuter, F. (2013). *Practical tools for designing and weighting survey samples*. New York: Springer.

Wolf, C., Joye, D., Smith, T. W., & Fu, Y.-C. (2016). *The SAGE handbook of survey methodology*. Los Angeles: Sage.

Concept of Survey and Key Survey Terms

2

Forest Mode and Garden Mode

2.1 What Is a Survey?

We determine the survey in its relatively short form, as follows, but it can be defined in many other forms as well (Laaksonen, 2012):

A survey is a methodology and a practical tool used to collect, handle, and analyse information from individuals in a systematic way. These individuals, or micro units, can be of various types (e.g., people, households, hospitals, schools, businesses, or other corporations). The units of a survey can be simultaneously available from two or more levels, such as from households and their members.

Information in surveys may be concerned with various topics such as people's personal characteristics, their behaviour, health, salary, attitudes and opinions, incomes, impoverishment, housing environments, or the characteristics and performance of businesses. Survey research is unavoidably interdisciplinary, although the role of statistics is extremely influential because the data for surveys is constructed in a quantitative form. Correspondingly, many survey methods are special statistical

© Springer International Publishing AG, part of Springer Nature 2018
S. Laaksonen, *Survey Methodology and Missing Data*,
https://doi.org/10.1007/978-3-319-79011-4_2

applications. Nevertheless, surveys substantially utilize many other sciences such as informatics, mathematics, cognitive psychology, and theories of subject-matter sciences of each survey topic.

A survey is a series of tasks that finally results in a statistical file of numerical units and their characteristics (variables); the units may be:

- Individual people
- Households and dwelling units ('register households' in registered countries)
- Families
- Schools and other public institutions
- Enterprises
- Plants (local units of enterprises)
- Local kinds-of-activity units of enterprises
- Villages, municipalities, and other administrations
- Other areas, including grid squares
- Societies, associations, and corporations

Such a data file may cover basically the entire desired population, or it can be based on a sample (i.e., the terms 'survey sampling' and 'survey statistics' are used, respectively). A survey often is considered to be only a sample survey, but similar methodologies and tools can be applied if a register or another administrative file has been created and handled.

Therefore, the authors use a relatively broad definition for surveys here; however, it is important to recognize that a final survey file may be a combination of various data collections, and several organizations may have participated in conducting it. Naturally, we concentrate mainly on surveys and their methods when collected and handled by one survey organization.

This chapter focusses on determining precisely five cross-sectional populations in surveys. We briefly continue to longitudinal and panel surveys, but our focus in this book is on cross-sectional studies. At the same time, we present other terms needed in later chapters. At this stage, they will not yet be understood thoroughly.

2.2   Five Populations in Surveys

A *population* is a key concept of statistics, as determined by Adolphe Quetelet in the 1820s. It is not just one population in surveys where we need even five. In addition, before the first one, *a target group* that the survey will be concerned with is in mind. That group is usually rather rough, but it may be close to one or more of the following five populations:

1. *Population of interest* is the population that a user would like to get or estimate ideally, but it is not always possible to completely reach; consequently, the researcher determines the second population—target.

2. *Target population* is a population that is realistic. Naturally, it should be exactly determined, including its reference period (i.e., a point in time or a time period).

> The following are examples of target populations used in this book. We do not mention any year because it varies in the first two cases.
>
> - The European Social Survey (ESS): 'Persons 15 years or older who are residents within private households in the country on the 1st of November'.
> - The European Finnish Security Survey (EFSS): Non-Swedish-speaking 15–74-year-old residents in Finland on the 1st of October.
> - The Programme for International Student Assessment (PISA) survey: 15-year-old school students (i.e., specified so that the full calendar year is covered).
> - The grid-based study of Finland: People from 25–74 years of age living in south Finland.

▶ **Discussion of the First Two Populations** We think that first it is better to try to find an ideal population (i.e., a population of interest). This is not possible in most cases. For instance, if the target is to get the voting population, it is not possible. Therefore, the population that is eligible to vote is reasonable, but it can be difficult to achieve as well because the survey institute may be using telephone interviewing with random digit dialing. Thus, it is not known in advance who will be willing to participate (e.g., vote). A good point is that people who do not participate in this survey do not vote well either. Consequently, the quality of such surveys is often satisfactory.

3. *Frame population and the frame* from which the statistical units for the survey can be found. Usually, the frame is not exactly from the same period as data from the target population. The delay in population surveys is rather short (i.e. 1–5 months), but enterprise surveys take much longer, even years. This frame is not always at the element level available, as in the case of the central population register-based surveys. Instead, the frame population can be created from several frames (multiframe), often from three—not all of which may be available when starting the survey fieldwork. Yet, the first frame is necessary to be able to begin. This often consists of the regions, or the areas, or the schools, or the addresses, but later other frames are needed. Fortunately, only the ones of those who were selected in the first stage.

A Multiframe Example

- *Stage 1:* List of the electoral sections (this number might be thousands).
- *Stage 2:* Lists of all household addresses of the units selected during the first stage. The address might be complex because there can be more than one dwelling at one address, and more than one household in one dwelling.
- *Stage 3:* One or more members at the selected household and/or address.

We thus observe that the Stage 1 frame should be available centrally, but the other frames are needed only for those units that are selected. This means that these frames need to be created at this stage. Sometimes this is possible using a local population register; however, from time to time it is created by the survey organization.

▶ **Comment** To get a realistic target population all important targets are not achieved, but because survey quality is crucial, a certain optimum is good to keep in mind. Respectively, it is advantageous to optimize the target population from the point of view of the availability of the frame or the frames. If the quality of the frames is inferior, the target population might be difficult to determine.

Any frame population is not completely up to date. Fortunately, when the survey fieldwork and the data collection are done some months later, it is possible to get a new frame, which is the fourth population.

4. *Updated frame population* is useful for better estimating the results. Usually, the initial frame population has been used for estimation too. This may lead to biased estimates. Fortunately, this bias is not severe in most human surveys. By contrast, old frames can lead to dramatic biases in business surveys should these concern large business organizations.

Bias

A bias is a systematic error. It is not random like a sampling error. A biased estimate is thus systematically inaccurate. There can be several reasons behind it, due either to an incorrect estimator or more likely to problems in the data.

Finally, we will have the fifth population when we also know how much the fieldwork has succeeded.

5. Survey population or study population. It is ideal if this fifth population corresponds to the target population or even the population of interest. If not, however, the estimates are somewhat biased.

If there are clear gaps in the final data, this should be made known to the users (i.e., how much the survey population differs from the target population). This might be problematic to know exactly, but the main problems should not be difficult to identify.

2.3   The Purpose of Populations

Before continuing with survey terms, it is useful to discuss the purpose of these populations. Naturally, the first point is to approach to the targets of the survey as well as possible, so it is necessary to know all the steps and possible gaps passed or hopefully solved.

The final target is to estimate the desired estimates, such as *averages, standard deviations, medians, distributions, ratios, and statistical model parameters*. This can be done by just calculating in of any kind of way, but such figures cannot be generalized at any population level without using the survey instruments that are explained in this book. If all coverage and related problems are solved, the results can be *generalized at the target population level*. These results are called *point estimates*. This means that they are not 'true values' as in the case of the entire target population without sampling or missingness gaps.

To better understand the quality of these estimates, it is necessary to estimate their uncertainty as well. Indicators for uncertainty are standard errors, confidence intervals (margins of error), and p-values, among others. Standard software programs give such figures but it cannot be guaranteed that they are correct unless survey instruments are applied (see Chap. 14).

If this population cannot be achieved satisfactorily, it is best to talk about generalization at *the survey population level*. It is not common to report the surveys in this way, although the reality is that certain groups are not really represented among the respondents. For example, homeless, disabled, and other marginalized people who do not understand the language used in the survey are not well represented in most surveys. It is possible to attempt a generalization in another way, for example using modelling, but this issue is special and cannot be considered in this book. This generalization mainly is concerned with certain connections or explanations found in the data. Thus, it is possible to try to generalize such 'estimates' or other outcomes in some way.

The units of the target population are equal to those of the survey population, but the units of the frame population(s) can be essentially different, except in element-based sampling. The ESS survey designs vary a lot from one country to the next. There are countries where all the units are equal to individuals age 15 and older (i.e., in register countries such as Sweden and Denmark) but many countries have several units (e.g., small areas, addresses, dwellings, individuals 15+ years old).

PISA and other student surveys typically use two units: (1) 'PISA' schools (or school classes) and (2) students themselves who are needed from those classes sampled.

2.4   Cross-Sectional Survey Micro Data

We next present three schemes to illustrate the nature of the cross-sectional survey data. The first scheme is the simplest and is never found in practice (Scheme 2.1). Nevertheless, it is good to consider because it starts by presenting the concepts and symbols used in this book.

If the whole target population has been examined and no missingness's occur, there are four groups of concepts:

1. Statistical units that are often identifiers in surveys. Our general symbol of the statistical unit is k. The identifiers are of two types:
   • Ones known to be needed in survey institutions for several purposes.
   • Anonymous ones that are given for outsiders in order to protect the individuals
2. Frame variables X or x that are used in collecting the data.
3. Outcome or survey variables Y or y that are obtained by the fieldwork.
4. The sampling weights that are all equal to one because all are included in the survey and all are replied to. Such weights are not needed in the analysis.

The simplest scheme is thus never found in real life but is a micro-survey file based on a sample. This means that only a certain proportion of the frame population and of the target population is fully achieved. On the other hand, missingness because of unit non-response occurs. Other gaps are appearing as well and new concepts are needed. The following scheme illustrates these and are explained, respectively. See also Scheme 2.3.

The measures of this scheme are not the same as in real life because the sample fraction is not as big as it is here but may be 1–5% of the target population size N. (Note that the symbol U is used as the reference population of N.) The sample size, respectively, is symbolized by n, and the number of the respondents by r. The symbol for overcoverage units or ineligibles is D in the frame and d in the sample. These two concepts are helpful to distinguish because the sample ineligibles are often known if they are contacted; however, the entire D population is not necessarily well known. This may cause biases in estimates.

Scheme 2.2 includes three groups of auxiliary variables. All their symbols are X, but we now have more such variables. The auxiliary group $X1$ corresponds to the

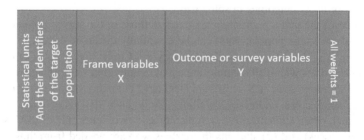

Scheme 2.1   Micro data for the entire target population

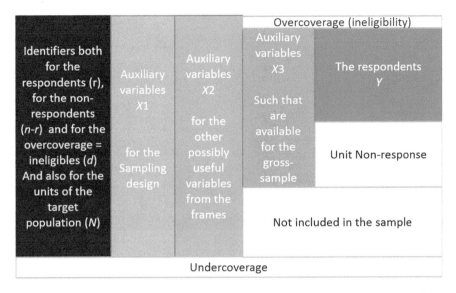

Scheme 2.2 General structure of a micro-level cross-sectional survey data file (The weights variables are not given here)

frame variables, X, in Scheme 2.1. These are used in sampling and should be available for the entire population. They are considered in more detail in the chapters on sampling—Chaps. 4, 5, and 6.

The frame is not usually complete, one reason being *undercoverage.* There can be other types of auxiliary variables than those for sampling. Variables $X2$ often are available from the same source as sampling frame variables, but also from other registers if a general register is available. Some auxiliary variables can be obtained for the gross sample. We go into detail with examples of auxiliary variables in Chap. 6, in particular. The following explains what is behind the other concepts of the Scheme 2.2.

2.4.1   Specific Examples of Problems in the Data File

- *Unit non-response:* not contacted, unable to participate, refusals (hard and soft), fieldwork mistakes.
- *Item non-response:* These are missing values for survey variables. There can be many reasons for this, such as 'do not know', 'too confidential to answer', 'refusal to answer', 'not applicable'. These are considered further in other chapters and, in particular, in empirical examples.
- *Overcoverage (ineligible):* Examples—died, emigrants, living outside the target population, errors in the frame. Some of these can be observed during the fieldwork, although not all. This is a worsening problem nowadays because, if the unit (person) is not contacted, it is difficult to know whether a unit is ineligible or a unit non-respondent.

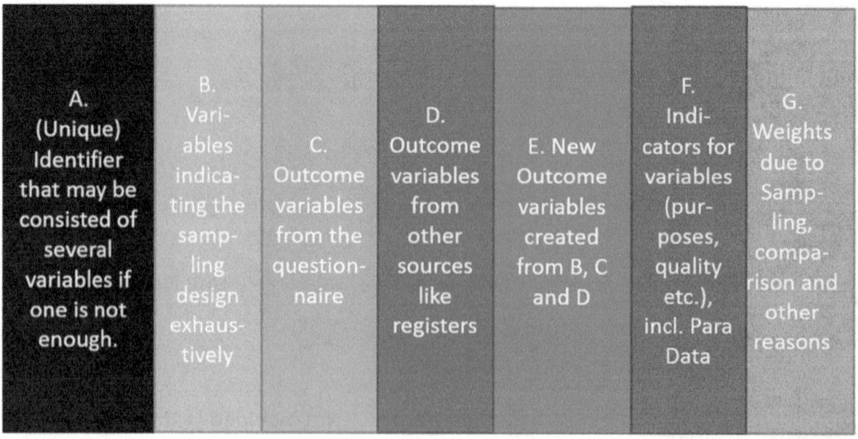

A. (Unique) Identifier that may be consisted of several variables if one is not enough.	B. Variables indicating the sampling design exhaustively	C. Outcome variables from the questionnaire	D. Outcome variables from other sources like registers	E. New Outcome variables created from B, C and D	F. Indicators for variables (purposes, quality etc.), incl. Para Data	G. Weights due to Sampling, comparison and other reasons

Scheme 2.3 General structure of a micro-level cross-sectional survey data file that consists of *r* respondents (That is, rows in a matrix)

- *Undercoverage:* Examples—new-born, new immigrants, illegally living in a country, errors in the frame. The updated frame helps to discover them. If it is not available, an effort should be made to assess its importance using external statistical sources.

A *real survey file* is not the same as the scheme in Scheme 2.2, except in some special cases such as methodological experiments using simulations. There are two real files:

- A sampling design (data) file that covers the gross sample units and auxiliary variables. This file is considered in detail in Chap. 6. From this file we usually create the sampling weights and other sampling design variables and merge these into the following.
- The file of the respondents, which is used in the analysis shown in Chap. 14, in particular. The scheme of this file is given next (Scheme 2.3).

It is possible that there are other data outside this scheme; for example, para data and content data. Good meta data should be available for all variables. If the file is released to outsiders, the identifiers should be anonymous. Initial variables rarely can be used as such in analysis.

We present examples in subsequent chapters of how either the new variables can be created from each initial variable using a different scaling or another transformation, or a new variable can be combined from several initial variables. Two larger examples of such transformations are given at the end of this chapter, thus this relates to the *E* variables.

Sampling weights are of two types:

- Their *average* for each target population = one (1) and therefore their sum = the number of the respondents. They are called *analysis weights*. Thus, they are relative weights and are good to use in comparing the weights of different surveys.
- Their *sum* = the number of the target population units (e.g., households or individuals), and each weight indicates how many units one unit represents in the target population; thus, these weights are for generalizing (estimating) the results.

▶ **Comment on Variables**

  - As noted earlier, there are X and Y variables, and they have a special role. Yet, a certain X variable also can be used as a Y variable in the analysis; however, in this case their values are only for the respondents. If a variable, such as age, is used in the sampling and is thus being an X variable, and is also included in the survey questionnaire, it cannot be guaranteed that their values will be equal.
  - There also can be aggregated information (e.g., from characteristics of a living area—village, block, municipality, locality). Their value is equal for all those living in that area.

This book does not focus on panels and longitudinal studies; nonetheless, the authors briefly illustrate such survey data in Scheme 2.4. It also mentions non-response to items, but the main missingness is because of unit non-response. It is usually highest in the first *wave* (e.g., a round in cross-sectional studies) of the panel, but still occurs in consecutive waves as in the waves $t + 1$ and $t + 2$ here.

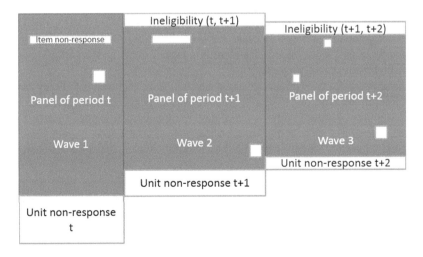

Scheme 2.4 General structure of cohort type of panel or longitudinal data

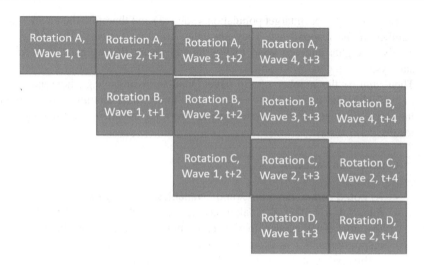

Scheme 2.5 Example of a rotating panel of the four waves

Naturally, some ineligibility occurs at the same time. The cohort panel therefore decreases over time. Consequently, various types of rotating panels are created. Their purpose is to update the data with new panels to estimate both cross-sectional and change estimates as well as those that are possible. Scheme 2.5 illustrates a rotating panel that has been used in several countries for the Eurostat EU Living and Income Survey (EU SILC).

The best cross-sectional estimates of Scheme 2.5 can be obtained from four files of the same year, thus for *t + 3* in this scheme. Each wave gives an opportunity to estimate some cross-sectional figures, but the number of valid respondents is not as large in most cases. Each rotation group, such as *A* and *B* here, can be used for change estimations of individuals or households if the unit is the household. These are therefore cohort surveys. Because each rotation group is decreasing, estimates may be more and more biased. They are less biased if changes between only two consecutive years are estimated.

The cross-sectional estimates can be calculated from each wave, but they are not very accurate because of the small number of respondents. It is beneficial to cover more data files in order to improve accuracy. For example, it is possible to get four datasets for time *t + 3*. If the sampling weights are calculated correctly for this reference time, the estimates are the best possible. We do not give any concrete example of such a case in this book.

One problem when calculating the appropriate weights is that there are more problems in long panels with updating the missingness of older waves, because it is possible that the non-respondents of one wave do not remain as the non-respondents, but change to ineligibility groups, for example. The opposite movement also is possible. Getting complete missingness information is difficult in such cases.

2.5   *X* Variables—Auxiliary Variables in More Detail

These variables can be found, collected, and/or downloaded from different sources, as follows:

- Population register (e.g., age, gender, members living at the same address, house type and size, kitchen type) there are many regional or areal options are available as well, including grids.
- Other registers, such as a tax register or a job seekers' register, formal education register (e.g., taxable income, unemployed, education level).
- Other administrative sources, often at an aggregate level (e.g., percentage of owners' occupations, percentage of social renting, percentage of detached housing, percentage of people divorced, percentage of undercrowding, percentage who own two or more cars and/or one or more cars, percentage of owners' occupation, percentage of those unemployed, percentage of long-term unemployed individuals, percentage of those who are highly educated); the aggregate here may vary as a result of municipality, postal area code, grid square, block, and/or village.
- In panels and longitudinal analysis, the variables of preceding points in time can be used as auxiliary variables if their values are believed to remain correct.

It is possible to use interviewer observations of the immediate vicinity of the houses in the sample units about visible signs of neighbourhood disorder. Such observations of disorder or decay can be linked to the 'broken windows' hypothesis. The neighbourhood has been classified into one or more variables by an interviewer using harmonised rules. This type of *X* variable is becoming more common, but it is difficult to get, regularly in particular.

X variables have several roles that will be discussed in more detail later in this book; nevertheless, we mention the following important things as an introduction:

- Quality analysis of the survey data themselves
- Quality analysis of the data-collection process
- Identify reasons for non-response and ineligibility
- Compute ineligibility rates = number of ineligibles/gross sample size
- Compute response rates = number of respondents (gross sample size − ineligibles)
- Compute items' non-response rates and other characteristics of them
- Use the data for weighting and reweighting
- Use the data for checking and other editing
- Use the data for imputations

Meta data means information about the data. This information is available in diverse formats, including:

- The questionnaire is the most important concerning survey variables
- The survey methodology documentation is as important, including sampling, fieldwork, and IT tools.

Meta data of a survey's micro file currently readily are available in SPSS, SAS, and other general software packages, including:

- The variable label meta data that usually gives a short description of the corresponding questionnaire text.
- In the case of a categorical variable, their labels, respectively.
- Possibilities to include the information about missingness and the range of the values; this information can be called *para data*. If the specific values, such as 9, 99 or 999, are marked as missing, they are not included in the ordinary analysis. If one wants to use them in the analysis, it is possible to change this option or to create a new variable of a different kind.

Table 2.1 is a piece of meta data from the European Social Survey. The column 'Name' is the variable name and is used in all further operations. The column 'Label' is the meta data of this variable. The column 'Values' includes both proper values and their meta data as the text. The same applies to the column 'Missing', which is an example of para data at the same time, indicating the missingness codes. These can be fairly automatically excluded from the analysis but can be included as well.

Para data may be of many other things, giving information about the survey process, its problems and successes. Such data can be like ordinary data; however, it is often supplementary data and is thus described separately. For example:

- Reasons for non-response and ineligibility
- The date and time when the interviewing/replying began and ended, and its length
- Opinion of interviewers about the quality of an answer from the respondent
- Data of a survey for interviewers after the fieldwork
- Number of attempts to contact an interviewee
- Interviewer code
- Incentives given to interviewees and interviewers
- Mode of the survey

In addition to the preceding data, it is beneficial to collect separate data about the following:

- Survey climate and the variables tried for use in this measurement.
- Contextual data that describe the environment in which individuals reside and behave.

Table 2.1 A small extract from the SPSS micro data variables of the European Social Survey with meta data

Name	Type	...	...	Label	Values	Missing
cntry	String	6	0	Country	{AT, Austria}...	None
ppltrst	Numeric	2	0	Most people can be trusted, or you cannot be too careful	{0, You cannot be too careful}...	77, 88, 99
pplfair	Numeric	2	0	Most people try to take advantage of you or try to be fair	{0, Most people try to take advantage of me}...	77, 88, 99
trstlgl	Numeric	2	0	Trust in the legal system	{0, No trust at all}...	77, 88, 99
trstplt	Numeric	2	0	Trust in politicians	{0, No trust at all}...	77, 88, 99
vote	Numeric	1	0	Voted last national election	{1, Yes}...	7, 8, 9
imsmetn	Numeric	1	0	Allow many/few immigrants of same race/ ethnic group as majority	{1, Allow many to come and live here}...	7, 8, 9
imbgeco	Numeric	2	0	Immigration bad or good for country's economy	{0, Bad for the economy}...	77, 88, 99
happy	Numeric	2	0	How happy are you?	{0, Extremely unhappy}...	77, 88, 99
health	Numeric	1	0	Subjective general health	{1, Very good}...	7, 8, 9
ctzcntr	Numeric	1	0	Citizen of country	{1, Yes}	7, 8, 9
almuslv	Numeric	1	0	Allow many or few Muslims to come and live in country	{1, Allow many to come and live here}...	7, 8, 9
cgtsday	Numeric	3	0	How many cigarettes smoked on typical day?	{666, Not applicable}...	666–999
alcfreq	Numeric	2	0	How often drink alcohol?	{1, Every day}...	77, 88, 99
height	Numeric	3	0	Height of respondent (cm)	{777, Refusal}...	777, 888, 999
weight	Numeric	4	1	Weight of respondent (kg)	{777,0, Refusal}...	777,0, 888,0, 999,0
hhmmb	Numeric	2	0	Number of people living regularly as member of household	{77, Refusal}...	77, 88, 99
gndr	Numeric	1	0	Gender	{1, Male}...	9
gndr2	Numeric	1	0	Gender of second person in household	{1, Male}...	6, 7, 9
agea	Numeric	4	0	Age of respondent, calculated	{999, Not available}...	999

(continued)

Table 2.1 (continued)

Name	Type	...	...	Label	Values	Missing
yrbrn	Numeric	4	0	Year of birth	{7777, Refusal}...	7777, 8888, 9999
yrbrn2	Numeric	4	0	Year of birth of second person in household	{6666, Not applicable}...	6666– 9999

2.6   Summary of the Terms and the Symbols in Chap. 2

- U = target population (universe)
- D = overcoverage or ineligibles at the frame level
- N = size of the target population (undercoverage may be a problem)
- d = number of ineligibles in the gross sample
- r = number of (unit) respondents = net sample size
- n = number of units of the target population in the gross sample
- $n + d$ = gross sample size
- k = statistical unit—for example, for the respondents, $k = 1, \ldots, r$ or $k=1, \ldots, n$ for the gross sample
- $r(y)$ = number of responses to the variable y

2.7   Transformations

This section deals with transformations, thus concerns variables E of Scheme 2.3. Each single variable can be transformed into another scale or into categories different from the initial ones. The simplest transformation is linear and only changes the scaling, even though the results are similar. The purpose of this linear transformation is to make the results easier to interpret. The following are examples of other typical transformations that lead to a new (and hopefully better) interpretations, or that satisfy the model conditions:

- Logarithmic for ratio–scale variables, such as income and wage, in which case the outcomes are relative (log-percentages)
- Exponential, which is most often used to return from the logarithmic to the initial, but this transformation, in a few cases, can be possible, such as if the distribution is 'peculiar'
- Categorization into two or more categories, the most common being a binary (dichotomous) variable

We will come back to these cases in examples later in this book.

The two most commonly used transformations for several initial variables are given at the end of this chapter. The outcome of such transformations is called the 'summary variable' or 'compound variable'. The two most common techniques for constructing this variable are:

- Linear transformations of each initial variable into an equal scale, and then taking the average of them; see Example 2.1 that follows.
- Exploratory factor analysis of the variables with the same phenomenon that leads to a smaller number of variables (e.g., Fabriger & Wegener, 2012); see Example 2.2 that follows.

The two examples of these summary variables are given next. The data are from Round 7 of the European Social Survey.

Example 2.1 Summary Variable with Linear Transformations
The core questionnaire of the European Social Survey includes six variables on the attitudes towards foreign-based people living in the country. These variables have two scales:

1. The three variables IMPCNTR, IMSMETN, and IMDFETN have four categories, and three missingness categories, similar to the variable IMPCNTR.

   Question B 31
   How about people from the poorer countries outside Europe?
   Variable name and label: IMPCNTR
   Allow many/few immigrants from poorer countries outside Europe.
   Values and categories

- Allow many to come and live here
- Allow some
- Allow a few
- Allow none
- Refusal
- Don't know
- No answer

   The variables IMSMETN and IMDFETN, respectively, concern either the same or different ethnic groups. The three other variables IMBGECO, IMUECLT, and IMWBCNT include 11 response categories in addition to the missingness categories.

(continued)

Example 2.1 (continued)
   Question B 32

2. Would you say it is generally bad or good for [country]'s economy that
   people come to live here from other countries?

   Variable name and label: IMBGECO
   Immigration bad or good for country's economy
   Values and categories

- 00 Bad for the economy
- 01 1
- 02 2
- 03 3
- 04 4
- 05 5
- 06 6
- 07 7
- 08 8
- 09 9
- 10 Good for the economy
- 77 Refusal
- 88 Don't know
- 99 No answer

The variables IMUECLT and IMWBCNT, respectively, concern either
cultural enrichment versus undermining or better versus worse living
conditions.

We can see that the meaning of the first variable group is different from that
of the second. This should be considered first. The authors decided to consider
the phenomenon from the perspective of positiveness, therefore we call the
new summary variable 'Foreigner_Positiveness'. On the other hand, the direction of these scales is different. This requires one to make linear
transformations so that the re-scales are equal. Because the scale [0, 100]
often is easiest to interpret, this scale is used. The final question concerns
missingness codes. Without imputation, the only rational strategy is to exclude
these values when making the linear transformation for each individual
variable.

This transformation for the first group is obtained with the function
$(100/3) \times (4\text{-IMBGECO})$ and then analogously for the two other variables,
while multiplying with ten for the second group.

(continued)

Example 2.1 (continued)

Finally, *the average of all these linearly transformed variables is our new summary variable*. Because there are slightly different amounts of missingness, the authors' recommended strategy is to average over valid values. We therefore lose only those respondents who did not reply to any of these six questions. Fortunately, the item non-response rates are relatively low for these variables (around 1–2%).

Figure 2.1 shows the results that indicate fairly big differences between countries, even though the average of seven countries (i.e., Lithuania, Belgium, Slovenia, United Kingdom, Estonia, France, and Portugal) does not differ from the 'neutral score' of 50. We leave further interpretation to the readers.

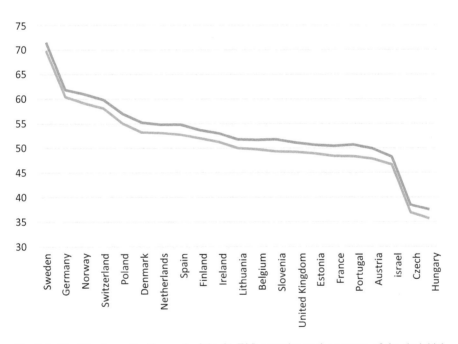

Fig. 2.1 The 'Foreigner_Positiveness' of the 21 ESS countries as the average of the six initial variables; confidence intervals of 95% are included

Example 2.2 Summary/Compound Variable Using Exploratory Factor Analysis and Factor Scores

It is common for the survey/study to include many questions/variables that can, of course, be analysed individually, but to do so does not always make sense. Therefore, it is appropriate to find the 'dimensions', or summary variables, that can be used for further analysis.

This strategy is used even in school assessment studies such as the PISA. There is a special reason in the PISA as well: the examination questions and some real survey questions are not exactly equal for all students, but the final scores needed to have the same scales. For this reason, the PISA uses basically a similar solution to the one we present here for the ESS—that is, the 'variable aggregation' based on factor scores. The factor scores can be linearly transformed further as in the PISA student assessments, in which their average of the OECD countries is equal to 500 and the standard deviation, respectively, is 100. The exploratory factor analysis presented here in its ordinary way so that the factor scores are normally distributed with the zero average and one standard deviation. These can be linearly transformed further into another interval if that is considered more illustrative, as in the PISA.

The initial factorised variables are Shalom Schwartz's Human Values of the ESS, of which there are 21 altogether (Schwartz, 2012). There are six alternatives in the questionnaire to answer, so there can be no completely neutral category (see also Chap. 3). Thus, we want to find a much smaller number of dimensions of human values by exploratory factor analysis. The step here is to omit values with missingness codes. Fortunately, their number is quite small (around 0.5–2.0%).

Table 2.2 shows the VARIMAX rotated factor pattern of all 21 questions for the four factors. This same number has been obtained in each round, but the order of the factors varies to some extent. The table also includes the factor loadings that help in the interpretation of these four dimensions. The highest loadings are marked.

The factors of the factor analysis are sorted by their significance. Thus, the first factor is the most significant and then the others, respectively. All four factors explain 49% of the variation. The respective percentages by each factor are 13.4, 13.0, 11.5, and 11.1—that is, their importance does not differ substantially.

The *second step* is to interpret the factors. It is useful to try to find as simple a variable name as possible, even if it does not describe all the characteristics of each dimension extremely well. When using these factors later, it is important to

Table 2.2 Rotated factor pattern of the human values of Schwartz. Derived from data from 21 countries in the ESS Round 7

		Factor 1	Factor 2	Factor 3	Factor 4
ipcrtiv	Important to think new ideas and being creative	**0.50039**	−0.19926	0.36534	0.19092
imprich	Important to be rich, have money and expensive things	−0.19119	0.05636	**0.67597**	0.20425
ipeqopt	Important that people are treated equally and have equal opportunities	**0.68608**	0.03273	0.04745	−0.06398
ipshabt	Important to show abilities and to be admired	0.16097	0.10197	**0.72829**	0.17537
impsafe	Important to live in secure and safe surroundings	0.19957	**0.57004**	0.27976	−0.17525
impdiff	Important to try new and different things in life	0.32647	−0.05826	0.26154	**0.57487**
ipfrule	Important to do what is told and follow rules	−0.01832	**0.63355**	0.09810	0.03434
ipudrst	Important to understand different people	**0.65828**	0.12926	−0.08800	0.16965
ipmodst	Important to be humble and modest, not draw attention	0.28233	0.49916	−0.26870	0.02342
ipgdtim	Important to have a good time	0.14466	0.04653	0.16798	**0.71054**
impfree	Important to make own decisions and be free	0.47514	−0.01510	0.25188	0.21841
iphlppl	Important to help people and care for others' well-being	**0.62314**	0.27703	−0.04811	0.17742
ipsuces	Important to be successful and that people recognise achievements	0.10018	0.17724	**0.70252**	0.27157
ipstrgv	Important that government is strong and ensures safety	0.24328	0.54689	0.21960	−0.05419
ipadvnt	Important to seek adventures and have an exciting life	0.05952	−0.16632	0.31919	**0.67231**
ipbhprp	Important to behave properly	0.14602	**0.70628**	0.06306	−0.01267
iprspot	Important to get respect from others	−0.00533	0.42353	0.53092	0.14803
iplylfr	Important to be loyal to friends and devoted to people close	**0.56952**	0.27867	−0.05466	0.24730
impenv	Important to care for nature and environment	**0.57448**	0.26809	0.00743	−0.01528
imptrad	Important to follow traditions and customs	0.04373	**0.64219**	0.02138	0.04902
impfun	Important to seek fun and things that give pleasure	0.09437	0.08629	0.10504	**0.79910**

Table 2.3 An interpretation of the four factors on Schwartz's Human Values Scale

Factor name	Interpretation: It is important that
Factor1 = (**Equality**)	People are treated equally, understand different people, help people
Factor2 = (**Tradition**)	Behave properly, follow traditions and rules
Factor3 = (**Success**)	Show abilities and be admired, be successful and rich
Factor4 = (**Enjoy**)	Seek fun and things that give pleasure, have a good time

Table 2.4 The final factor score variables

Equality = − Factor1
Tradition = − Factor2
Success = − Factor3
Enjoy = − Factor4

understand the meaning of each factor more broadly than in its wording. The list in Table 2.3 helps in this interpretation; however, everyone can do his or her own naming and interpretation.

We thus give the variable name for each factor. The *final step* is to compute the factor scores of each factor variable. This can be done easily with standard software so that the average of each score is zero and the standard deviation is equal to one. This is not enough. It also should be ensured that the score values match with the factor names. For example, if we use the name 'Equality', it is expected that a higher score means that that respondent thinks that the Equality is for him or her is more important than for another person whose score is lower. Consequently, it is necessary to check the question itself. We see that the highest score for the question is equal to one if this value is the most important, whereas the higher value of the question means it's the least important. Thus, the final step is consequently to change the sign, as shown in Table 2.4.

Now it is possible to use these new variables in all analyses of the micro data. We do not illustrate everything but give two examples. Figure 2.2 is from the two most important factors, 'Equality' versus 'Tradition'. The average equality for Lithuania (LT) and the Czech Republic (CZ) differs greatly from the other countries, meaning that it is not considered so important that people are treated equally, or it is not very important to understand different people and help other people in these two countries. On the other hand, the respondents from these countries do not differ much from the others in the variable 'Tradition'. Nevertheless, such things are relatively important in Slovenia (SI), Poland (PL), and Israel (IL), while less important in Sweden (SE), France (FR), and the Netherlands (NL).

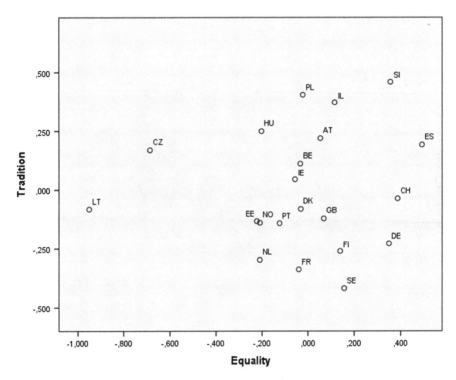

Fig. 2.2 The scatter plot of 21 ESS countries between the two first factors of Schwartz's Human Values Scale, Round 7, with the two-digit country codes

Figure 2.3 uses the aggregates of both datasets of this section, thus both 'Foreigner_Positiveness' and the third important human values factor, 'Success'. Sweden is an outlier on both variables.

People in France (FR) and Finland (FI) do not regard either richness or success as very important in their lives, whereas Lithuanians do. The aggregate correlation is negative, but it cannot be interpreted in a straightforward way.

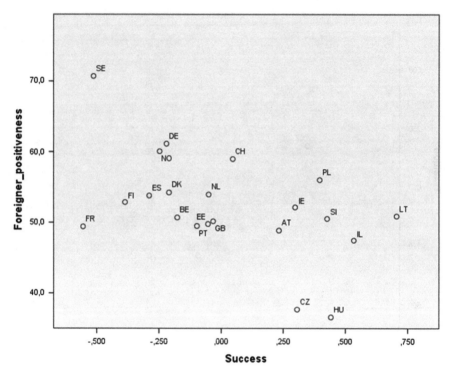

Fig. 2.3 The scatter plot of 21 ESS countries between the 'Success' factor of Schwartz's Human Values Scale and 'Foreigner_Positiveness', Round 7, with the two-digit country codes

---

References

Fabriger, L. R., & Wegener, D. T. (2012). *Exploratory factor analysis*. New York: Oxford University Press.

Laaksonen, S. (2012). Chapter "Surveys". In: M. Gellman, & J. R. Turner (Eds.), *Encyclopedia of behavioral medicine*. Accessed May 2016, from http://www.springer.com/medicine/book/978-1-4419-1004-2

Schwartz, S. F. (2012). An overview of the Schwartz theory of basic values. *Online Readings in Psychology and Culture, 2*(1). https://doi.org/10.9707/2307-0919.1116.

Designing a Questionnaire and Survey Modes

3

Europos Parkos, Lithuania

We start from the cornerstones of survey research that give a general understanding of this chapter (Scheme 3.1) based on Salant and Dillman (1994) and De Leeuw, Hox, and Dillman (2008b). This chapter concentrates on measurement in surveys, the target being specifically to avoid measurement error or to evaluate its impact on estimates.

The best results are achieved only if the questionnaire and its validity are optimal and well connected to the survey mode used. This is the major part of *data collection*, but the three other cornerstones are considered in more detail in following, although:

© Springer International Publishing AG, part of Springer Nature 2018   27
S. Laaksonen, *Survey Methodology and Missing Data*,
https://doi.org/10.1007/978-3-319-79011-4_3

Scheme 3.1 The cornerstones of survey research

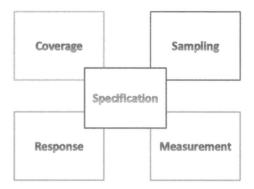

- Non-response may be because of a bad measurement if a potential respondent is not sufficiently motivated to participate, the survey mode used is inappropriate, or he or she does not like the questions in a questionnaire or considers them incorrect or invalid.
- Coverage cannot be equally achieved with all types of survey data-collection modes. For example, phone numbers are not available for all people, while the web is not used by all as some have no available device or are unable to use it correctly.
- Using interviewers or not—that is, using self-administered answering—there can be an influence both for non-response and measurement, and even for coverage.

▶ **Remark** The topic of this chapter is so broad that the author only can consider basic things that are necessary from the point of view of the other chapters. The hope is that you will read other books and articles, not only those that are in the reference list at the end of the chapter, including those by de Leeuw et al. (2008a), Schaeffer and Dykema (2011a, b), Schaeffer et al. (2013), Couper and Zhang (2016). Look also at the references in what you read.

3.1   What Is Questionnaire Design?

Questionnaire design is a big part of the whole process of data collection and should be implemented completely before the fieldwork begins. At the same time, the potential respondents should be selected by sampling and a more or less complete list of them should be available. This is not always the case, as in ad hoc surveys. These issues are not considered to a great extent in this chapter, where *first* we discuss survey modes. *Then*, we try to give a summary on designing the questions themselves for the survey. The final section focusses on *examples* of various survey types, but mainly on the European Social Survey (ESS); it is useful to look at the ESS methodology from its website, for example concerning data collection, at http://www.europeansocialsurvey.org/methodology/ess_methodology/data_collection.html

Survey Modes

There are several modes or platforms to be used in survey data collection—that is, in the survey fieldwork. We present here a summary that includes their acronyms.

Face-to-face (f2f) interviewing was used first in surveys because it does not require that an interviewee is able to read and write, but that the individual understands the questions with the help of an interviewer. The questionnaires and the response files were in a paper format. Thus, this mode is known as a '*Paper and Pencil Interview*' (PAPI).

The PAPI is still used in countries where computer-assisted systems are not developed well enough, as in many developing countries, and it can be the best method for certain specific surveys. If the interviewees cannot read and write well enough, it may necessarily be the only valid mode.

Nevertheless, a *postal* or *mail survey* with the paper questionnaire is appropriate and relatively inexpensive in population groups who can read and understand the questions and write/mark their answers. The answers to a mail survey can also be saved into an electronic file and then submitted to the survey institute.

Nowadays, face-to-face interviewing is applied using computer-assisted equipment, thus the term *Computer-Assisted Personal Interview* (CAPI) is its most common tool. This term applies also if telephone (phone) or SKYPE is the technical equipment used; however, the term *Computer-Assisted Telephone Interview* (CATI) is then the usual term. Such data collection is done in so-called CATI centres, where sophisticated IT technologies are applied for selecting and contacting interviewees.

Computer-assisted technologies are naturally the only workable tools in *web* or *Internet* surveys. These technologies have being developed since the 1990s, when the mode was first implemented in some countries. The best technologies are those that are more or less as user-friendly as personal interviews. This means that all the required information is easily available in the computer system (including pop-ups for delivering information).

On the other hand, the questionnaire needs to be able to motivate respondents to participate and to reply. An obstacle to the success of web surveys is *smartphone* technology, which is being used more and more as a web tool. Unfortunately, the electronic questionnaire cannot be easily adjusted in smartphones to make responding user-friendly. The main reason is its small screen. If the questionnaire is short and the response categories are limited, smartphones work better; however, this is not the case in most ordinary surveys.

A general term for self-administered interviewing is *Computer-Assisted Self-Interview* (CASI). Web surveys are included in this group, but it is also common in CAPI face-to-face surveys that include sensitive questions. In this case, the interviewer gives a computer, laptop, or tablet to the interviewee to reply anonymously, similar to ordinary web surveys. This strategy with two modes was used in the Finnish Security Survey, for instance, and helped to get more reliable results (Laaksonen & Heiskanen, 2014) for sensitive questions.

The Frame for Web Surveys

If the correct email addresses are available, a web survey can be conducted more easily than without them. Still, the same frame as in f2f or mail surveys can be attempted for web surveys as well. In such a case, the invitation letter should include the necessary information for replying via the web. Naturally, the respective website should be given to the individual too. This was the procedure used in Laaksonen and Heiskanen (2014) and Laaksonen et al. (2015).

Contact via email is possible whenever the address is known, which is common within a workplace, a student group, or clients. Yet, this is rarely possible for general surveys covering the whole country, for example. There are, however, fairly complete email address lists in some register countries that have been collected using contacts made for taxation, allowances, or other public purposes by such administrations. Such email registers cannot be easily used by all for confidentiality reasons.

Addresses from the population register commonly used for surveys maybe excluding a few security or other special persons. Telephone numbers can be obtained from telephone companies to some extent, depending on the country. Thus, email addresses are obviously becoming more commonly used but only in a few countries.

3.2 One or More Modes in One Survey?

Using a *single mode* has traditionally been the most common strategy for surveys of persons or households—that is, when only mail, f2f, phone, or web has been used. Business surveys often use multiple modes (*multimode* surveys) so that large businesses participate with electronic modes since this is easy for them; respectively, small businesses might participate with more manual modes because they cannot invest in high-level technologies. It is also feasible for the interviewer to call these small businesses and get reasonable answers. The multimode methodology thus means that a different mode is applied for diverse target population groups. It is possible in social surveys as well if several frames are required to reach the entire target population.

This book does not go into detail about multimode surveys. On the other hand, we pay more attention to *mixed-mode* strategies. A survey is mixed-mode if the use of two or more modes has been attempted to approach a target population. This may mean that we have one gross sample that has been approached such that the potential respondent can choose whether to reply, for instance, by web or PAPI, f2f, or phone, or even using several alternatives.

The big question in mixed-mode surveys is how to approach gross sample units and how to motivate them. The most common strategy is to send an invitation by mail and motivate individuals to participate preferably in one mode such as via the web, because this helps to get the first data file easily. If the preferred mode is not chosen, the second mode is the only other option. If this mode is a paper questionnaire, it should already be enclosed with the invitation letter; however, if it is a phone questionnaire, it is enough to advise that the interviewer will make contact soon.

The mixed-mode strategy is rational in longitudinal surveys wherever the first interview is made by f2f but the second one is by phone or web. Thus, this means that the interviewer will outline this strategy in the first interview and motivate the individual to participate later by another mode.

Examples of Mixed-Mode Surveys

The following are examples of mixed-mode surveys:

– The European Social Survey is mainly a face-to-face (f2f) survey, but it includes a supplementary questionnaire as well. At the end of the interview, the interviewer gives this second part to the respondent and invites the individual to fill in this paper questionnaire and submit it later. The supplementary part includes the pattern of Shalom Schwarz's Human Value Scale questions and those being tested. The item non-response rates are relatively low in this part.

– The budget is often small for academic surveys. Consequently, the face-to-face mode has fallen out of favour as it is the most expensive, although the quality is often the best. The second most expensive mode, phone, has been rejected for the same reason, but also because of the problems in frame coverage. The pure web survey is problematic in general social surveys as well, but if this mode is combined with the traditional paper questionnaire using the mail invitation, the results can be satisfactory. The good point is that the frame can be complete, but high response rates are not ensured. This mixed-mode is less expensive than a pure mail survey because the data entry is done by the interviewee for the web part. The biggest issue is how to motivate people to participate as much as possible for this web part.

– The response rate is expected to be higher than in the pure mail survey because certain people are more willing to participate electronically than manually. This was the case in the Southern Finland Grid-based Survey (Laaksonen et al., 2015). Nevertheless, the response rate was not high, but this was anticipated, and the gross sample size was adjusted accordingly.

Estonian Pilot Mixed-Mode Survey 2012 for the ESS

The Estonian mixed-mode experiment (Ainsaar, Lilleoja, Lumiste & Roots, 2012) consisted of a sequential online mode followed by a f2f mode. They compared the results of the mixed-mode survey to the main ESS in terms of cost, response rates, response distributions, mode effects, and data quality.

The survey staff concluded that, despite the overall expectations that an online survey would be less expensive, the total cost related to the mixed-mode survey were effectively equal to the financial benefits. Some of the expenses of the mixed-mode survey were related to the novelty of the online survey design and technical difficulties. The central distribution of an online survey programme can essentially reduce these costs. Another source of additional expenses is the heavy workload related to the preparation of two

(continued)

data-collection modes in diverse languages. These costs increase exponentially with the number of languages in a country.

Mixed-mode surveys can become less expensive if the wording and structure of the questionnaire in both survey modes can be kept as similar as possible. The total benefits of surveys, which combine online and other modes, depend on the Internet and computer access in a country, but in the extended perspective, the effectiveness of online surveys may increase thanks to the spread of Internet access and related skills.

The experiment proved that the online mode does indeed capture the younger and educated urban population better. This population is difficult to reach with the traditional face-to-face mode. Several data quality indicators proved the benefits of the online mode as well. Nevertheless, preliminary analyses also detected mode effects, which could make it challenging to combine the data of the two modes.

The success of the Estonian mixed-mode experiment stemmed from active data collection via the Internet. Mixed-mode surveys are rare in Estonia, but all Estonians are informed about this approach because the latest Population Census in 2011 used the same principle (mixing web and f2f modes). Sixty percent of Estonians filled out the Population Census survey online. The impressive work of the census team, who advocated the use of the web-based survey environment, might have had an impact on the ESS experiment as well because it could take advantage of the frame of the census. Several ESS interviewers indicated that people do not know the differences between the various international surveys and ESS might have benefitted partially from the image and trust created by the Population Census a year earlier.

Mode Effects in Estimates

It has been realized that estimates can vary by mode. A big factor here is how confidentially an interviewee can give her or his answer. In CATI surveys, it is not possible, but the results can be satisfactory if the interviewee trusts the interviewer. CAPI face-to-face with CASI for sensitive questions has been found to be reliable. For example, Laaksonen and Heiskanen (2014) received very similar results with this mode using the web, which is completely anonymous. CATI gave estimates that were downward-biased for sensitive victims of crimes. The researchers could not test any mixed-mode strategy, but they think that this confidential survey could work with a mixed-mode that exploits both the web, CAPI, and CASI.

(continued)

It has been found in several surveys that the web often leads to slightly less conventional estimates than CATI or CAPI, without CASI, does. In crime victimization surveys, this means lower crime rates, while in opinion polls extreme opinions are rare. The big question is which ones are correct? Why is the answer in an extreme category not correct? This is often a reason not to adopt a mixed-mode survey because the estimates of the web part are less desirable, as is the whole estimate as well. Of course, the result itself should be a reason to change, not the mode, but the quality of the survey. In some cases, this is difficult to know.

3.3 Questionnaire and Questioning

This section summarises and extends the preceding discussion about the questions that need to be considered by the fieldwork team. Basically, questions 1, 2, 3, and 4 should be answered:

1. **How to contact/approach a potential respondent?**

Alternatives:

- Invitation letter by mail
- Direct contact at home (door) or another location
- Phone, SMS, e-mail
- General invitation in media, web, social media, poster
- Automatic invitation on a website to those who are join the site
- A respondent who has been contacted in the street, at a shop, sports event, cultural event, training course, outside the voting location—as in exit polls
- After using a service, customers often are asked to answer a few questions about the service quality
- A respondent has been contacted when outside (e.g., driving, walking, or standing at a certain area); the individual does not necessarily know that she or he has been picked for survey data. This may lead to confidentiality problems if entering sensitive information in the data but counts or other aggregates are not so sensitive (e.g., how many students, teachers, and others entered the building today?).
- Shops and other commercial companies or their groups contact their clients and offer bonuses or bonus cards, which gives them an opportunity to collect data on the clients or potential clients; a client cannot know exactly which data company is collecting and how the data are to be used; in this case, points 2, 3, and 4 in the following are done easily.

Advance Letter and Invitation Letter

If the gross sample has been selected, and the survey format is known, it should have been carefully considered as to how to get access to potential respondents. If the contact address (i.e., postal address, phone, email) is not correct, making contact is more difficult, but everything should be attempted. We assume that the address is correct, and that the survey principles have been decided. Now, there are two options; in both cases, it is good to indicate in some way that the respondent is lucky to have the opportunity to participate in the survey:

1. Contact so that the survey begins as soon as possible
2. Contact preliminarily to inform about the survey and how important it is, and when it is expected that the individual will be contacted again, and when the survey will start.

This latter case is called an 'advance letter'. It is useful in tending to increase the response rate.

Note that if any incentives are to be given to the respondents, this should be mentioned in both letters. The incentives can be unconditional—that is, even to those who do not answer—or conditional, which is much more common.

2. **How is the information saved/uploaded into the file?**

Alternatives:

– An interviewer asks and saves the answers into a paper or other manual file
– An interviewer asks and saves the answers into an electronic file
– A respondent reads, looks at, and/or listens to the questions and saves the answers into an electronic file (self-administered survey)
– A respondent reads, looks at, and/or listens to the questions and the interviewer saves the answers into a file
– An IT system submits the questions to a respondent and she or he answers by email or by web questionnaire
– An IT system collects the data automatically from the database of the respondents (this should be accepted by the respondent or his or her representative); this is typical for business surveys and employer–employee surveys.

3. **What kind of formats do the questionnaires use?**

Note that the format can be converted into a new format after initial data collection.

– A paper questionnaire that can be filled in manually or printed from an electronic file
– An electronic local format such as a memory stick
– SMS, email, attachment to the email
– Specific driver on the web, open or closed

▶   **Comments on Web Driver** The *Closed* driver is the only acceptable
        solution for proper surveys. The address of this driver should be given

to each respondent, and access to the questionnaire should require a password that is unique for each. It is not possible for anyone to respond without this password. It is, of course, possible that an outsider can reply even if the unique password is used, but this is illegal.

There are surveys that have an *Open* driver. This means that everyone can participate and as many times as the individual desires, unless any restriction is used (e.g., allowing only one answer from each computer). This technology is easily possible but not always used. A survey with open access is called a *self-selection* survey. In a few special cases it may be the only strategy to get reasonable results, but it gives the opportunity to manipulate surveys as well, as Bethlehem (2015) illustrates for the Netherlands.

4. **How to submit the data?**

Alternatives:

- If the data are already uploaded into an electronic file, it is ready.
- The paper responses can be submitted by mail or after scanning by email, for instance.
- Electronic files also can be submitted, forwarded by mail or email, or uploaded to an appropriate location.
- It is possible in small-scale surveys to submit the answers by phone; this means that they are then saved electronically.

3.4 Designing Questions for the Questionnaire

This is, of course, a very big area within the whole survey process. The questions are implementations of the measurement that it is desired to study—that is, they should be valid. At the same time, the measurement instruments should be reliable. How to succeed satisfactorily in measurement? The following are some practical strategies:

1. Try to find appropriate questions from earlier studies. This is often possible unless your field is very new and/or never tested or validated. Still, it is good to search for good questions, question models, or question banks. Go and look at the surveys done in your interest area. There are, of course, many websites, and do not forget the questionnaires of the European Social Survey (http://www. europeansocialsurvey.org/methodology/questionnaire/) or the PISA (https:// nces.ed.gov/surveys/pisa/pdf/MS12_StQ_FormA_ENG_USA_final.pdf).
2. If you have a new type of target, it is still good to utilize general models, but then try to develop your own strategy by reusing questionnaire bank questions, for example; however, not alone but in the team. Next, test it in your neighbourhood first, and after that *pilot* the whole questionnaire with appropriate people. This is

called a *pretest*. There are two main strategies for selecting the 'sample' for this pretest:

- If the purpose is to get preliminary estimates of the survey field, the sample should be as good as in the ordinary survey, even though somewhat smaller, leading to more uncertain estimates. Some questions can be revised before the final survey is done if they do not work well enough.
- Usually, the representativeness of the pretest survey is not important, but it might be when testing the questions among diverse types of potential respondents. Thus, it is often good to find respondents who are not 'ordinary' but important from the point of view of the survey. For instance, it is advantageous to include respondents who have problems in answering in this 'sample,' and to exploit this survey in order to improve the questions and the questionnaire. For tips for testing questionnaires, see for example, Radhakrishna (2007).

3.5   Developing Questions for the Survey

It is beneficial to answer at least the following seven questions:

1. How well does the question address your research target, and how well formulated is it in this direction (validity)?
2. Is the question definitely useful? The question should add some value for your analysis.
3. Are you sure that the respondents understand the target of the question?
4. Does the respondent have reasonable information to answer the question correctly (i.e., can the terminology be understood—tools such as pop-ups might help)?
5. Are the respondents willing to answer the question?
6. Should the question be presented to all or just a certain group of the sample?
7. Can you find other information in order to analyze the answers given, and how **reliable** are they?

As soon as your team can answer 'Yes' to the first five questions, the questionnaire is satisfactory. Question 6 should be considered carefully, and a 'Yes' answer should be possible (see the following section on 'Screening'). The author thinks that you can find some positive answers to Question 7.

Size of the Questionnaire
The size of the questionnaire is a big issue. It should not be too long, but neither should it be too short to avoid losing useful information. How do we select the optimal size?

1. First, it does not matter much whether you initially have all possible questions in the list, but later it will be necessary to choose the best combination so as to avoid overlapping, for example.

2. Finally, your team will make the first selection, which should be piloted with 'real respondents'.
3. Always check that the question is valid and that the estimates you intend to compute using it are applicable.
4. It is possible that some subjects cannot be measured with one question but need a pattern of questions using the same formulation. Do not avoid this because a good pattern may help in getting reliable data for your measurement. Later, you may be able to create some factors from this pattern and to interpret and use these correctly.
5. Estimate the time needed to fill in the questionnaire; also take into account the response burden of the average interviewer.

It is good to *remember* that there are useful validated patterns for several fields such as Shalom Schwarz's Human Values Scale in the ESS. His pattern consists of 21 questions that were discussed at the end of this book's Chap. 2. When analyzing this pattern with exploratory factor analysis, we found four factors: *Equality, Enjoy, Tradition,* and *Success.*

It is best to use validated patterns rather than trying to create a new pattern that needs much work and a new validation. Shalom Schwartz's pattern seems to work well, so why not use it or others that have been validated? Still, in each case it is good to think about which pattern corresponds best to your study target. If you do not trust any of them, create your own pattern. It may take several years to become completely validated.

Order of Questions
The order of questions is also essential, but we cannot recommend any single optimal order. Consider at least these points.

1. The first real question is important. It is good if it already concerns one big issue of the survey, but it should not be too difficult to answer. Naturally, this question should be for all respondents, not for just some.
2. Where should you put so-called background questions (i.e., gender, age, education, occupation, marital status)? Some prefer to put all these at the end, but others include them at a quite early stage as far as nonconfidential questions are concerned, although confidential questions (i.e., salary, income) it is better to place them at the very end. Note that if you already know the preceding variables from registers, for example, do not ask them again, except for testing purposes.
3. Each survey should have certain specific key areas/subjects and attention should be concentrated on these. Thus, it is good to design the questionnaire carefully so that such key questions are in an optimal position, not at the very end. It does not matter where 'side' questions are, if such are needed, but they mainly should be in the last part of the questionnaire.

Two Types of Question
Fortunately, there are only two types of possible questions. They concern either (1) facts (i.e., age, gender, area of residence, industry class, occupation, salary,

income, partnership status, education) or (2) subjective features (i.e., attitudes, opinions, assessments, purposes, arguments).

Naturally, the questionnaire layout often is essentially different with regard to these two questions. Basically, the first ones are easier to formulate, and their scaling is often initially clear. Of course, different groupings can be used for categorical variables such as for partnerships, occupations, or education. Constant variables either can be asked as continuous, or they can be categorised, even age or salary. Logically, using them as continuous gives more options to categorise them later, but how satisfactorily it is possible to get correct answers is another point.

As far as *attitudes, opinions, assessments, purposes,* and *arguments* are concerned, there are various standards in the literature—for example, concerning scales. The earlier ordinal scales seem to be shorter than currently in the ESS, for instance. The ESS scales often have 11 categories (0 = minimum and 10 = maximum), whereas just five categories (1 = minimum, 5 = maximum) were used earlier (see Example 3.5). Nevertheless, the scale remained the same in such questions when it was difficult to change the scale without violating the time series (see Example 3.1).

Example 3.1 Instance in Which the Scale Was Kept Similar to Earlier Social Surveys

The following question has been used in many other surveys, including Earlier Social Surveys (ESS). This seems to be rather easy to answer. A question with more alternatives would be difficult to formulate.

How safe do you—or would you—feel walking alone in this area after dark?

Variable name and label: AESFDRK

Feeling of safety of walking alone in local area after dark

Values and categories

1. Very safe
2. Safe
3. Unsafe
4. Very unsafe?

Show Cards

Show cards are cards that facilitate a respondent's understanding of the scale of the survey question. Basically, such a card is present automatically in a paper questionnaire and a web questionnaire, but not at all in telephone 'questionnaires'. Their use is not necessary in f2f surveys, but it is useful and used regularly in the ESS, for instance. The respondent does not even need to say his or her answer, but only to show which category is correct. Two ESS examples of show cards are shown in Figs. 3.1 and 3.2.

You can't be too careful										Most people can be trusted
0	1	2	3	4	5	6	7	8	9	10

Fig. 3.1 A typical ESS scale with 11 categories

No time at all

Less than ½ hour

½ hour to 1 hour

More than 1 hour, up to 1 ½ hours

More than 1 ½ hours, up to 2 hours

More than 2 hours, up to 2 ½ hours

More than 2 ½ hours, up to 3 hours

More than 3 hours

Fig. 3.2 The ESS scale about spending time watching television

Screening

It is better to ask certain questions, often about facts, in the following way:

The first question concerns whether you have been involved in or experienced or met a phenomenon. There are two possible categories here: 1. Yes, 2. No. This also is called the 'filter' question.

The second question is only addressed to those who answered 'Yes' to the first question.

Unfortunately, this strategy is not always applied, but a respondent may be asked, for example, for an opinion about a public service even though he or she has never used it or not used it recently. Thus, the opinion is not based on the experience of this service at all but on a general feeling. Such results can therefore be very biased.

Fortunately, screening is used in effective surveys such as the Finnish Security Survey, which was the pilot survey of the European Union (EU). Its experiences will be used in forthcoming EU surveys. The example that follows is from this survey.

Example 3.2 Screening Example of the Finnish Security Survey
The information here is from Laaksonen and Heiskanen (2014), Appendix 1.

A12 – Over the last year, has anyone in your household had a car, van, or truck for private use? [Yes; No]

(continued)

Example 3.2 (continued)

A13 – If A12 = Yes, How many cars has your household had use of for most
of the time? Number of Cars: [1–5]

C1 – If A12 = Yes: During the last 12 months have you or anyone else in your
household had a car or a van stolen or driven away without permission?
[Yes; No] (Company Cars Included)

C2 – If C1 = Yes: How many times did this happen? [1–9]

C3 – If A12 = Yes (apart from this): During the last 12 months have you or
anyone else in your household had anything stolen from (your/their)
vehicle or out of it (parts of the vehicle, personal possessions or other
things)? [Yes; No]

C4 – If C3 = Yes: How many times did this happen? [1–9]

How to Put the Answers in the Questionnaire

It is not possible to give any sufficient answer to this question, but the following
notes are relevant:

If a continuous variable is used as continuous: There should be a maximum number
of digits, not more; if the decimal is needed, this already should be there. In the
computerized questionnaire, it is possible to include some edit rules so that the
accepted answer may vary by respondents, but this is often difficult to do well. If
this variable is in the paper questionnaire or in the respective web one, a value box
also can be used. This enables the respondent to answer correctly.

A categorical variable in the electronic questionnaire should be organized so that the
answer can only be marked in a correct category. If several categories are
accepted, it may work, but it is better to request an answer in each category
with either 'Yes' or 'No'.

3.6   Satisficing

The response burden is a big problem to some extent, even in short questionnaires.
The expected time is always indicated in advance to the respondent, and in the web
survey there should be a measurement indicator that tells the user how far the survey
has proceeded.

An interesting side effect relating to the response burden is known as *satisficing*.
Some types of this are described here:

Since I have started to reply but it seems to take a longer time than expected or the
questions are too boring, I will continue to answer even though I am too tired to
really think about my answers.

OK, I will answer, although too many questions are not smart; my solution is that I will reply with 'I don't know' or 'I don't wish to state my opinion', or I just put in an average score.

Satisficing has not been examined widely, and it is not easy either. Typical cases can be found under the themes 'No Answer' and 'Straightlining'.

No Answer
There are various options for getting 'no answer', including the folloiwng:

Doesn't know
Isn't willing to answer (refusal)
Question does not concern the respondent
Unable to answer correctly
No time to answer correctly
Lost answer
Other reason

Naturally, it is desirable to avoid 'No Answer' answers and formulate the questionnaire so that the number of such answers is as low as possible except in the third case, which in some cases can often be a key indicator (e.g., if this is a second question relating to details of crimes that occurred, when the first question already gives information that some crime occurred). Thus, if the relative number of 'No Answer' answers is high, the questionnaire or interviewing is not working well, and any estimates should not be published.

Filtering 'Don't Know'
There are three ways of dealing with 'Don't know'.

Standard format: The 'Don't know' option is not presented to the respondent, but is recorded if the respondent volunteers it.
Quasi filter: The 'Don't know' option is included among the possible responses.
Full filter: First the respondent is asked whether they have an opinion. Then, if 'Yes', the question is asked.

Basically, similar filtering can be applied for the 'Isn't willing to answer' alternative. Some questionnaires do not give an opportunity to choose any of these alternatives at all. It has even been known for someone to stop filling in such a questionnaire and to try to write an opinion somewhere For example, 'I cannot give my opinion, since your questionnaire is catastrophic. Do not publish anything based on such violated data!'

3.7 Straightlining

Straightlining seems to be a general problem when using a pattern of questions with the same scales. It is common in paper questionnaires where there is a pattern of the 21 questions on the basic values in Shalom Schwartz (2012) and also when using the web; however, it is easy to avoid this format in the web by showing only one question on the screen at a time. This problem is illustrated with the first six questions in Schwartz's European Social Survey (Tables 3.1 and 3.2). Answering

Table 3.1 Possibly Correct Replies to Some Human Values Questions from Schwartz

Now I will briefly describe some people. Please listen to each description and tell me how much each person is or is not like you. Use this card for your answer.

	Very much like me	Like me	Some -what like me	A little like me	Not like me	Not like me at all	(Don't know)
Thinking up new ideas1 and being creative is important to him/her. He likes to do things in his own original way.	x						
It is important to him/her to be rich. He wants to have a lot of money and expensive things.					x		
He/she thinks it is important that every person in the world should be treated equally. He believes everyone should have equal opportunities in life.	x						
It's important to him to show his/her abilities. He/she wants people to admire what he does.						x	
It is important to him to live in secure surroundings. He/she avoids anything that might endanger his safety.				x			
He/she likes surprises and is always looking for new things to do. He/she thinks it is important to do lots of different things in life.		x					

Table 3.2 Possibly Incorrect Replies to Some Human Values Questions from Schwartz

Now I will briefly describe some people. Please listen to each description and tell me how much each person is or is not like you. Use this card for your answer.

	Very much like me	Like me	Some -what like me	A little like me	Not like me	Not like me at all	(Don't know)
Thinking up new ideas1 and being creative is important to him/her. He likes to do things in his own original way.				x			
It is important to him/her to be rich. He wants to have a lot of money and expensive things.				x			
He/she thinks it is important that every person in the world should be treated equally. He believes everyone should have equal opportunities in life.				x			
It's important to him to show his/her abilities. He/she wants people to admire what he does.				x			
It is important to him to live in secure surroundings. He/she avoids anything that might endanger his safety.				x			
He/she likes surprises and is always looking for new things to do. He/she thinks it is important to do lots of different things in life.				x			

the questions in Table 3.1 might be possible if the respondent really thinks enough before responding.

If the respondent just wants to fill in the quis not really thinking about the questions, it is possible to get the answers shown in Table 3.2. This is a case of straightlining.

Example 3.3 Textual Versus Coded Categories

The ESS tests new questions as well as those used already, in which case a different scaling may be applied. This example concerns exactly the same scaling but in two formats: (1) completely textual categories ('Text' in graph), and (2) the same 11 categories but where only the extreme categories are given in the textual format and similarly to case (1)—that is, 0 = Extremely Unimportant, ..., 10 = Extremely Important ('Codes' in graph).

Figure 3.3 shows that the distributions are quite different when the question is *'whether it should be required that immigrants can speak a language of the country'*. The average in case (1) = 5.98 and in case (2) = 6.08, respectively. Thus, it does matter how the categories are coded as far as the average is concerned; nonetheless, there are clear differences in categories. The completely textual format is not used in the ESS if the number of categories

(continued)

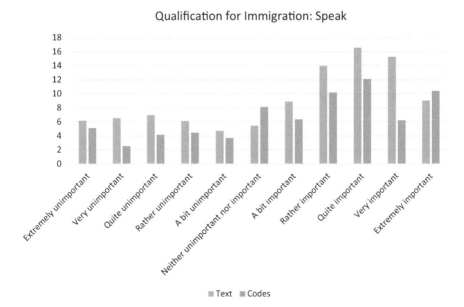

Fig. 3.3 Should immigrants who can speak a language of the country—textual versus coded alternative

Example 3.3 (continued)

is large. It also could be more difficult for the interviewer to explain even when show cards are used. The author recommends using the current scales and codes.

3.8   Examples of Questions and Scales

The remaining part of this chapter consists of two larger examples that illustrate the questions and scales. They are based on real survey data—the first on the ESS and the second on both the ESS and the World Values Survey (WVS).

Example 3.4 Two Alternative Lengths of Scales

This is from the European Social Survey test questionnaire, when the two different scales are used for the same question: 'How easy is to take part in politics?' The alternative (1) gives the opportunity to answer in 11 categories: $0 = $ Extremely difficult, 1, . . ., 9 without text, and $10 = $ Extremely easy. Respectively, alternative (2) includes five textual categories: Not at all easy, A little easy, Quite easy, Very easy, and Extremely easy.

It is not clear how to compare these results because only one category is exactly the same (i.e., 'Extremely easy'). The results of this category are about equal as well. Still, we wish to compare the frequencies in all categories, which is not easy. We decide that 'Extremely difficult' corresponds to 'Not at all easy', and the categories in between are merged together as linearly as possible.

The categories of Fig. 3.4 are from case (1) in which the first category 'Not at all easy' is much more common than in the first case with several categories

(continued)

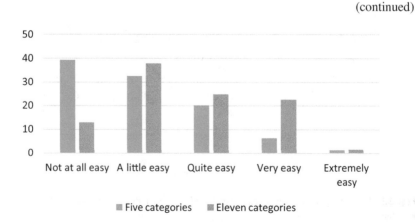

Fig. 3.4 Easiness of taking part in politics with the two different scales, from the ESS

Example 3.4 (continued)

in this part. This suggests using many categories rather than a few. When the categories are rescaled within [0, 100] so that the easiness increases, then the averages are very different: 24.6 with 5 categories and 40.5 with 11 categories.

The author's interpretation is that the form of the regular survey with 11 categories is better.

Example 3.5 Different Scales for 'Happiness' in the Two Questionnaires

Happiness and life satisfaction have been examined in several surveys but not always in the same way. Here, the two multinational surveys are compared: the World Values Survey (WVS) and the European Social Survey (ESS). The history of the WVS is much lengthier than that of the ESS. The first results from the website (http://www.worldvaluessurvey.org/WVSDocumentationWV1.jsp) are from 1981, whereas the first ESS files (http://www.europeansocialsurvey.org/data/) are from 2002.

There are differences concerning various points in these surveys. We compare two variables that are inquired about broadly in a similar way by the questionnaires' text, but with scales that differ. The scales both for 'happiness' and 'life satisfaction' are from 0–10 (11 categories) in the ESS; however, the WVS has different scales for both variables: 0 = 'Extremely dissatisfied/Unhappy', ..., 10 = 'Extremely satisfied/Happy'. The WVS categories for 'happiness' are: 1 = 'Very happy', 2 = 'Rather happy', 3 = 'Not very happy', 4 = 'Not at all happy'. Respectively, there are ten categories for life satisfaction: 1 = 'Completely dissatisfied', 2 = '2', ..., 10 = 'Completely satisfied'.

When comparing the results of the two surveys, the scales should be equal. We use a linear transformation so that the WVS scales are transformed to be equal to the ESS scales. The linear function for 'happiness' is thus 'ESS_Happiness' = (**4**−WVS_Happiness) × (**10/3**); and for 'life satisfaction' is 'ESS_Lifesatisfaction' = (WVS_Lifesatisfaction−**1**) × (**10/9**). As we can see, the latter scale of the WVS is not satisfactory because a respondent cannot give a neutral answer, which would be 5.5; instead, the individual more often chooses alternative 5 rather than alternative 6.

The ESS scaling is in this respect good because the neutral alternative 5 can be chosen. We do not think that this small problem has much influence on the results, even though the linear transformation slightly reduces the 'Life satisfaction' scores. The difference in the case of 'happiness' is more influential because the selection of the four categories in the WVS might be more difficult than the 11 alternatives in the ESS. This can be seen from the fact that the

(continued)

Example 3.5 (continued)

alternative 'Rather happy' is selected relatively more often, whereas the ESS respondents seem to choose one of the alternatives—6, 7, or 8.

We compare the results for four countries that participated in both the 2012–2013 ESS and the closest WVS—that is, 2011–2012 (Tables 3.3 and 3.4). We do not present medians or other distribution figures that are automatically different because the ESS medians, for instance, are integers (e.g., for the Netherlands both are = 8.0), while the WVS medians include decimals (e.g., for the Netherlands 6.666 and 7.777).

The averages do not differ substantially, but the ranking of the countries is also interesting. The ranking of the countries shown in Tables 3.3 and 3.4 is based on the ESS. As far as 'happiness' is concerned, the order is not the same as that seen in the WVS. The 'happiness' average is thus higher in Poland than in Germany, which is not the case for any other estimate. The scale of the four alternatives only is one reason for this result, which also can be seen from a low variation based on the coefficient of variation because 71% of the Polish respondents answered 'Very happy', while only 63% give the same answer in Germany.

The Netherlands seems to differ from the other countries so that ESS means are higher than those of the WVS. On the contrary, the difference is opposite in Russia and Poland. The German estimates of both surveys are relatively close to each other. These differences obviously are not only because of the scaling but the survey format including sampling as well. We do not try to solve the question further, although the author's opinion is clear: *The ESS scales are better.*

Table 3.3 'Happiness' results both from the WVS and the ESS for four countries

WVS 2011 or 2012			ESS 2012–2013	
Country	Mean	Coeff. of variation	Mean	Coeff. of variation
Russia	6.34	34.7	6.20	35.5
Poland	7.20	24.3	6.95	31.0
Germany	6.90	31.4	7.03	26.9
Netherlands	7.50	26.2	7.84	16.8

Table 3.4 'Life satisfaction' results from both the WVS and the ESS for four countries

WVS 2011 or 2012			ESS 2012–2013	
Country	Mean	Coeff. of variation	Mean	Coeff. of variation
Russia	5.75	42.2	5.58	44.1
Poland	6.76	32.3	6.59	37.2
Germany	7.07	30.9	7.03	31.7
Netherlands	7.21	20.9	7.71	19.6

References

Ainsaar, M., Lilleoja, L., Lumiste, K., & Roots, A. (2012). *ESS mixed mode results in Estonia*. Institute of Sociology and Social Policy, University of Tartu, Estonia. Accessed September 2017, from http://www.yti.ut.ee/sites/default/files/ssi/ess_dace_mixed_mode_ee_report.pdf

Bethlehem, J. (2015). Essay. Sunday shopping—The case of three surveys. *Survey Research Methods 9*, 221–230. European Survey Research Association. Accessed May 2017, from http://www.surveymethods.org. https://doi.org/10.18148/srm/2015.v9i3.6202.

Couper, M. P., & Zhang, C. (2016). Helping respondents provide good answers in web surveys. *Survey Research Methods, 10*(1), 49–64. https://doi.org/10.18148/srm/2016.v10i1.6273. European Survey Research Association. Accessed August 2017, from http://www.surveymethods.org

De Leeuw, E., Hox, J., & Dillman, D. (2008a). *International handbook of survey methodology*. 549 pp. Accessed May 2017, from http://joophox.net/papers/SurveyHandbookCRC.pdf

De Leeuw, E., Hox, J., & Dillman, D. (2008b). The cornerstones of survey research. In E. D. de Leeuw, J. J. Hox, D. A. Dillman (Eds.), *International handbook of survey methodology* (pp. 299–316). New York: Taylor & Francis Group.

European Social Surve y methodology: Data Collection. Accessed August 2017, from http://www.europeansocialsurvey.org/methodology/ess_methodology/data_collection.html

Laaksonen, S., & Heiskanen, M. (2014). Comparison of three modes for a crime victimization survey. *Journal of Survey Statistics and Methodology, 2*(4), 459–483. https://doi.org/10.1093/jssam/smu018.

Laaksonen, S., Kemppainen, T., Kortteinen, M., Vaattovaara, M., Stjernberg, M., & Lönnqvist, H. (2015). Tackling city-regional dynamics in a survey using grid sampling. *Survey Research Methods, 9*(1), 45–55, European Survey Research Association. Accessed June 2017, from http://www.surveymethods.org

Radhakrishna, R. B. (2007). Tips for developing and testing questionnaires/instruments. *Journal of Extension, 45*(1). Accessed September 2017, from https://www.joe.org/joe/2007february/tt2.php

Salant, P., & Dillman, D. A. (1994). *How to conduct your own survey* (p. 256). New York: Wiley.

Schaeffer, N. C., & Dykema, J. (2011a). Questions for surveys: Current trends and future directions. *Public Opinion Quarterly, 75*(5), 909–961.

Schaeffer, N. C., & Dykema, J. (2011b). Coding the behavior of interviewers and respondents to evaluate survey questions: A response. In J. Madans, K. Miller, A. Maitland, & G. Willis (Eds.), *Question evaluation methods: Contributing to the science of date quality*. New York: Wiley.

Schaeffer, N. C., Garbarski, D., Freese, J., & Maynard, D. W. (2013). An interactional model of the call for survey participation: Actions and reactions in the survey recruitment call. *Public Opinion Quarterly, 77*((1), Spring), 323–351.

Schwartz, S. F. (2012). An overview of the Schwartz theory of basic values. *Online Readings in Psychology and Culture, 2*(1). https://doi.org/10.9707/2307-0919.1116.

World Values Survey (WVS). Accessed February 2017, from http://www.worldvaluessurvey.org/WVSDocumentationWV1.jsp

Sampling Principles, Missingness Mechanisms, and Design Weighting

4

Various sample units

The schemes of Chap. 2 showed that sample survey data can have some missingness, both intentional missingness and inevitable missingness. Intentional missingness is mostly because of sampling, while inevitable missingness arises from non-responses, ineligibility, undercoverage, and measurement errors. Intentional missingness is, or should be, mostly random, but inevitable missingness is virtually systematic or selective.

This chapter focusses on sampling, which is used for several reasons. The most important being that the target population is large, whereas resources are limited so that a 100% sample is rarely achievable. On the other hand, it is possible to get more precise estimates by sampling because the most moderate workload gives the opportunity to collect data more carefully. The third key point is that sampling in its efficient form gives an opportunity to obtain the desired estimates sufficiently

© Springer International Publishing AG, part of Springer Nature 2018
S. Laaksonen, *Survey Methodology and Missing Data*,
https://doi.org/10.1007/978-3-319-79011-4_4

fast. Here, we include some missingness questions in the sampling because this is the reality in all surveys.

We present a compact framework for sampling here. This is called *sampling design*. Often a narrower framework is given. The framework is for *probability sampling*, not for quota or other *nonprobability sampling*. Nowadays, voluntary sampling is becoming too common, especially when using web arsenals. Such methods are often nonprobability methods from a sampling point of view. Before looking at the details of probability sampling, we present some views about nonprobability sampling, focussing on principles that do not work too improperly, or that may be the only alternatives for certain inquiries. In general, it is effective to try to be *as close as possible* to probability-based sampling even when using nonprobability approaches. This means, specifically, that the selection of the sample units should be as randomized as possible.

This chapter also covers the principles of design-based weighting. Such weights can be calculated in a fairly straightforward way as the inverses of the inclusion probabilities, thus not taking advantage of the proper auxiliary variables; those weights are considered in Chap. 8. This term, 'design weight', definitely is correct if all the inclusion probabilities exist. Unfortunately, this is not always the case, which leads to the problems that are discussed later in this chapter. Nevertheless, we still use this same term, even for the sampling weights of the respondents, in which case selective missingness occurs. One example of this is the European Social Survey (ESS).

The reason for using this somewhat incorrect term is obviously that the simpler term '*design weight*' is more easily understood by many users. We use the term for the respondents, and for this we assume that the missingness is ignorable. Valliant, Dever, and Kreuter (2013) use a very similar label, 'base weight', but mention 'design weight' in parentheses.

4.1　Basic Concepts for Both Probability and Nonprobability Sampling

The following are examples of probability and nonprobability sampling concepts:

Sampling stage: Sampling can be done in one or several stages, and it is then called single-stage, two-stage, three-stage, or multistage sampling. The sampling method can be different in each stage.

Sampling phase: It may be enough to take one sample only, or it may be necessary to continue so that a new sample is drawn from the first sample. This rarely is done several times, but two phases might be possible. Usually, there is one phase only.

Sample/sampling unit: This is a unit that is drawn at a certain stage and then included in the gross sample.

Primary sampling unit (PSU): This is a sample unit that has been included in the sample at the first step or stage. The PSU may be a final sample unit (if there is single-stage sampling) or a cluster (if there is multistage sampling).

Secondary sampling unit (SSU): This is a unit that has been selected at the second stage within a particular PSU. SSUs are skipped in single-stage sampling.

Cluster: This is a group of 'individuals' who are close enough to each other. The following are examples in surveys:

- A small area, where residents, birds, or businesses are the individuals
- An enumeration area or census district, where people or businesses are the individuals
- A grid square (e.g., 250 m × 250 m), where people or businesses are the individuals
- A school, where the students or teachers are the individuals
- A household, where its members are the individuals
- An address, where the residents or employees are the individuals
- An enterprise, where the employees are the individuals

Stratum: This is the group or subpopulation, or quota, that will definitely be included in the sample. Each stratum is independent of the others. This means that a different sampling method can be used in each stratum. Even if the method is the same, the rules may vary by strata.

Selection probability: This is the probability that one sample unit will be included in each stage, as follows:

- *(Single) Inclusion probability*: This is the probability that a PSU or an SSU, and so on, will be included in the gross sample of this stage or phase. In probability sampling, the probability must be greater than zero (the maximum of one is naturally true) because otherwise some units cannot be drawn in the sample, leading automatically to undercoverage. If this is intentional, it should not be allowed, but to some extent it might be accepted if data are absent.
- *Final inclusion probability*: An inclusion probability is first determined for each stage, stratum, phase, or quota, and then, using these probabilities, the final inclusion probability is found at the entire gross sample level. In the simplest case, only one stage/level is needed, and this inclusion probability is the final one; however, in the case of a more complex design, a new calculation is needed. If the sampling at each stage is independent, the *final* inclusion probability is the product of all the single inclusion probabilities. This is so even though a general problem is that all the single inclusion probabilities are not known for all the units. It is possible that these probabilities are not independent, but here we do not consider such cases in detail (see, e.g., Laaksonen et al., 2015). The final inclusion probability basically relates to a phase, but it may be more complex. The *stratum* and the *quota* are like subtarget populations, and therefore their own rules apply within them.
- *Sampling fraction*: This is the number of gross sample units divided by the number of the target population. This fraction can be the same in each stratum, or it may vary depending on the precise targets of the survey.

- *Design weight or basic sampling weight*: This is the *inverse* of the final inclusion probability (design weight) or its conversion for the respondents (basic weight), assuming that missingness can be ignored. These mechanisms are explained in Sect. 4.2.

Second-order inclusion probability: This is the probability that two sample units belong to the target population. This is not considered in detail in this book. Nevertheless, it is good to know that this probability is particularly needed for calculating the variance estimate and its square root (i.e., the standard error and the confidence interval, respectively). Fortunately, the estimates of these in ordinary cases can be found with good software that can be used without knowing the detailed techniques. Readers who are interested in learning about these should read relevant books and articles from the reference list at the end of this chapter and the list at the end of the book.

▶   **Remark** The literature is not clear as far as selection probability is concerned. Some earlier authors do not use the term 'inclusion probability' at all—that is, the selection probability is the same as the inclusion probability. This is not ideal because the inclusion probability requires a decision to be made about the gross sample size even though the selection method is the same. This decision about the sample size thus is crucial in calculating the inclusion probability.

4.2   Missingness Mechanisms

In this introduction to sampling, it is beneficial to discuss missingness as well. As we said earlier, some missingness always occurs, particularly as a result of non-responses and ineligibility. Undercoverage or measurement errors cannot easily be included during the sampling process.

The terms 'missingness mechanism' and 'response mechanism' are practical terms that we use here. The terms that follow are commonly used in ordinary literature, but we have extended the list slightly.

MN (Missing Not in the entire population): This is a survey with a 100% sample, and without missingness, and is not encountered in real life.

MIG (Missing Ignorable in the entire population): The sampling fraction is 100% but some missingness occurs. Nevertheless, missingness is not considered, and all calculations are done on the assumption of a full response. This is not ideal, but the method is used and leads to some bias in the estimates.

MCAR (Missing Completely At Random): If this was true, it would be quite easy to handle the data. The assumption of MCAR is used often even though it does not hold true. It could be accepted if some auxiliary variables do not exist, or if they are useless. On the other hand, it means that the survey has not been done carefully.

MARS (*Missing at Random Conditional to Sampling Design*): This means that the missingness only depends on the sampling design. This is used often with the assumption that MCAR holds true within strata or quotas, but not between them. These strata are therefore auxiliary variables. The first sampling weights, the basic weights, usually follow the MARS assumption.

MAR (*Missing at Random Conditionally*): In this case the missingness depends on both the sampling design variables and all the other possible auxiliary variables. If many good auxiliary variables exist, it is possible to obtain a substantial reduction in the bias in the estimates by, for example, creating new weights (see Chap. 8); however, if such variables are missing, we can only assume that the mechanism is either MCAR or MARS.

MNAR (*Missing Not at Random*): Unfortunately, this is, to some extent, the most common situation in real life. This means that when all the auxiliary variables have been exploited, the quality of the estimates has been improved; nonetheless, it is still quite clear that the estimates are not ideal. It is possible to know something about the problems and the direction of the bias, and one should try to describe this in the report. In the case of MNAR, the missingness depends on the survey variables, Y. It is hoped that this correlation is as small as possible.

4.3 Nonprobability Sampling Cases

A good article on nonprobability sampling is the one by Baker et al. (2013). They say in their introduction:

> A wide range of nonprobability designs exist and are being used in various settings, including case control studies, clinical trials, evaluation research designs, intercept surveys, and opt-in panels. Generally speaking, these designs have not been explored in detail by survey researchers even though they are frequently used in other applied research fields.
>
> Because of their limited use in surveys, the assumptions required to make valid inferences from nonprobability samples are not thoroughly understood by survey researchers.

Baker and colleagues discuss 'statistical inference' in detail because this phrase has many meanings and implications. They define it as a set of procedures that produces estimates about the characteristics of the target population and provides some measure of the reliability of those estimates. A key feature of statistical inference is that it requires some theoretical basis and an explicit set of assumptions to make the estimates and judge the accuracy of them. The Baker et al. authors consider that methods for collecting data and producing estimates without a theoretical basis are not appropriate for making statistical inferences.

This section next presents several concrete cases that follow nonprobability principles.

Cases When There Is a Desire to Generalise to a Target Population Afterward
A survey that does not have a proper sampling design when survey data are collected
is not unusual. For instance, a subject matter researcher may create a questionnaire
that she first uses for her own clients in social services. Given that the results look
interesting, but no reference group exists for comparison, she invites the clients of
other institutions to participate as well. Now the number of respondents is growing,
and the results look more interesting; nevertheless, when she wishes to publish them,
this is not automatically possible without making a generalisation to a target
population.

What should she do? The first step is to determine the target population and to
obtain the statistics for it. The second step is to decide on the sampling design. It is
not possible to do this well, of course, but if the selection of the respondents is
random within each subgroup (stratum), weights can be created. If the selection is
not random, this leads to bias, and the results should not be accepted in any
respectable forum; maybe this could be used as a pilot study instead. Still,
generalisation is possible if the assumption (MARS) holds true or has at least been
assumed to hold true.

Opinion polls **by market research institutes** are often based on CATI surveys.
The institute may create strata or quota before calling. The quota are based on, for
example, the cross-classification of two genders, five age groups and four regions, or
$2 \times 5 \times 4 = 40$ quotas altogether. It is known from recent population statistics how
many people in the target population belong to each quota—let us say this is N_h,
where h is a quota. The client of the survey institute decides the overall number of
respondents (e.g. $r = 2000$). The survey institute calculates the proportions for each
quota, $q_h = \frac{N_h}{N}$, and the basic option is to allocate the number of the respondents
relatively equally (proportionally) to each quota, that is $r_h = rq_h$.

There is no guarantee that exactly this number will be reached during a relatively
short fieldwork period. Therefore the survey institute states at least a certain minimum and a maximum for its CATI centre. This method works well if every random
attempt to contact a person is successful and each of these contacts participates in the
survey, but usually this will not be the case. It means that, in fact, some
non-responses will be encountered. If the respondents are a random selection of
each quota target population, the MARS mechanism holds true and the survey
institute can be content with the data quality, but it is actually difficult to know
how good the quality is.

Thus, this method is partially probability-based, and the survey weights will be
calculated on the assumption that the respondents were selected at random within
each quota. This may hold true reasonably well but is not completely true for the
following reasons: (1) If a person does not answer the telephone, he or she will be

automatically out of the survey. (2) If a person refuses to participate, he or she also will be left out.

These preceding points mean that in some sense there are no non-responses at all because a non-respondent is replaced by a voluntary respondent. The market research institutes do not usually disclose how many attempts are made before there is a response. Some have argued that the actual response rate is around 10–20%.

A Quota Sample May Work Reasonably Well in a Few Cases

The response mechanism for quota sampling is unclear. It has been found that quota sampling works relatively well in voting behaviour surveys. The target population of such surveys includes those who are eligible to vote in the next election. The sampling frame of this population cannot exist, but attempts have been made to approach it with telephone calls. It has been possible to use the voting register to evaluate who does not vote in elections. These analyses have shown that people who do not vote are almost identical to people who do not respond in social surveys.

It is, of course, not clear whether the same is true for quota sampling surveys, but one would expect so. If this is the case, quota-sampling estimates of voting behaviour are relatively satisfactory. The same cannot be said of surveys that attempt to give a good estimate of figures for the ordinary population. These estimates, in most cases, are very biased because marginal groups (e.g., homeless people, people with low education levels, single males, underprivileged people, extremely rich people, and mobile people) rarely participate.

Self-Selection Sampling

Self-selection 'sampling' is being more commonly performed using web questionnaires because it is easy and basically inexpensive. The method may be acceptable for online television programmes in which a journalist invites the audience to comment on a certain topic using a simple binary question with a 'Yes' or 'No' answer. Such answers cannot be generalised to any concrete population. This is well understood by most of the audience, but it is possible that some people believe, for example, that the result represents the opinion of the population of the country. This bias is more obvious if the journalist becomes convinced that the result is reliable, saying, for instance, that a large number of answers (e.g., several thousand) were received, so the result looks fine. Nevertheless, it is not possible to say anything about the quality of such a study. All such estimates can be close to a true value only with good luck. For more information see a Dutch case study by Bethlehem (2015) in which he describes how self-selection can be used for manipulating estimates.

Self-selection sampling, in some cases, may be the only way to shed some light on a certain phenomenon. If no good sampling frame exists for approaching a target population, a preliminary estimate might be obtained using a well-managed invitation to participate in a survey. The invitation could be published in media that have been followed by those who would be expected to participate in and to respond to a survey. There is still a danger that one respondent may reply more than once. This can be avoided to some extent in web surveys, at least, by ensuring that an answer cannot be given twice from the same computer.

The quality of a self-selection survey could be thoroughly checked if a proper probability survey of the same target population could be conducted at about the same time with several of the same questions. On the other hand, it is possible to collect a good pattern of auxiliary variables for the same purpose and to use these to adjust for the weights of the self-selection survey.

Snowball Sampling and/or Respondent-Driven Sampling

Snowball sampling and/or respondent-driven sampling (RDS) methods are closely related and are used when no reasonable sampling frame exists but when, fortunately, some units are known to belong to the target population. Using these units, or the people behind them, an attempt is made to find new eligible persons—that is, to create a sampling frame step-by-step with the help of the respondents (see, e.g., Heckathorn, 2002; Lee, Suzer-Gurtekin, Wagner, & Valliant, 2017). This methodology can be applied in various circumstances, such as the following:

- If it has been found that people in the target population are living in certain villages and at least one member has been identified who is willing to recruit and interview other people in his/her village. This person may be a coresearcher for the study and also may be paid.
- If each respondent is asked whether she or he knows similar persons and can legally give their contact details. This technique is used mainly for populations of rare individuals or hard-to-reach populations such as anonymous narcotics users, participants in special hobbies for which no registration is required, or illegal or nonregistered migrants.

The main criticism about such chain-referral, or snowball sampling, is the bias toward recruiting subjects who are more cooperative and the tendency toward masking (protecting close friends or relatives by not referring them, especially if there is a strong privacy concern associated with the study's subject). In addition, it is suggested that those with extended personal networks tend to be oversampled and isolated people tend to be excluded from such studies.

Adaptive Sampling

Adaptive sampling is a technique that is implemented while the fieldwork for a survey is being performed—that is, the sampling design is modified in real time, as data collection continues, based on what has been learned from earlier completed sampling. The purpose is to improve the selection of elements during the remainder of the sampling, thereby improving the representativeness of the data generated by the entire sample.

This technique also has been used when trying to find new respondents if the lack of responses from particular subpopulations is too high after a certain period of fieldwork. It then means that more attempts are made to approach such units (i.e., persons or through certain persons). This technique, which also is called *responsive design*, is being studied and used more and more (e.g., Lundquist & Särndal, 2013). This design can, for example, take advantage of response propensities, which are thus estimated based on both the respondents and the non-respondents. Then, the first attempts at contact are made with non-respondents with low propensities. For further detail about propensities, see Chaps. 7 and 8.

Online, Internet, or Web Panels

An online panel is a *selected group* of participants who have agreed to reply over a reasonable period to survey questions on a website. What the reasonable period is depends on the survey organization, but usually it could be expected to last more than one year. Typically, incentives, which increase as participation time increases, are given.

An Internet panel is not usually a single web survey, although it can be. Recruitment to the panel can be done using a survey conducted earlier, with a respondent being asked at the end of the interview, for example, whether he would be willing to be a member of a panel in the future. Naturally, people who respond to the survey are more often asked to be on the panel than non-respondents. On the other hand, if a person has access to the Internet and is sufficiently able to use it, she or he could be a good person to recruit.

These requirements mean that the representativeness of Internet panels may not be reliable. People without Internet access or with low competence with computers are seldom on such panels. This is so even though certain statistical characteristics of the population can be satisfied so that, for example, the distributions by gender, age group, and region may be like those in the target population.

It is, of course, possible to recruit individuals to the panel so that those gaps are filled, by giving computers with Internet access to those who do not have them, and by training them to use the Internet to give their replies. If they can use the computer for their own purposes at the same time, this is a good incentive. This investment is naturally expensive and is rarely used, but one exception is the Dutch LISS panel (see https://www.lissdata.nl/lissdata/) and obviously more are coming.

The number of registered persons in online panels can be large, numbering several tens of thousands. This gives the opportunity for a special sample to be drawn for each survey, and it enables the workload for each person to be suitable.

It has been discussed as to whether a respectable online panel could replace an ordinary survey because it may ensure a reasonable response rate compared to that for an ordinary repeated survey. The problem is that the panel cannot easily be used for a single cross-sectional case, which is the most common survey type.

Some Features of the Dutch LISS Panel

The reference population for the Longitudinal Internet Studies for the Social Sciences (LISS) panel is the Dutch-speaking population permanently residing in the Netherlands who are 16 years old or older. The initial wave of the survey is very representative because Internet technology is given to those who do not already have it. Panel members complete online questionnaires every month, taking about 15–30 min in total.

Naturally, new recruits are needed all the time in order to maintain the quality. On the other hand, non-responses are still a problem, and this often gets worse as the duration of participation increases.

4.4   Probability Sampling Framework

The framework/taxonomy shown in Table 4.1 gives a comprehensive understanding of the factors that need to be considered for sampling and for implementing the sampling design. This is not always used in practice to describe which questions should be considered when planning the sampling. It is useful to point out that even though this taxonomy looks long, it is not difficult because there are not many questions to think about in each box.

Thus, an optimal alternative should be chosen and all the preceding questions/tasks (i.e., A to H) implemented to produce a gross sample. Next, we look in more detail at the most commonly used sampling methods. We also use symbols and formulas here, but we try to give descriptions of the methods so that the basic points can be understood by non-mathematicians too. This explanation is given in two steps: (1) everything is described for a single stage or phase or stratum, and (2) some of these are combined for our survey examples.

The first part concerns single inclusion probabilities for the most common types of sampling. They can be applied in the same way for strata, sampling phases, and sampling stages. For this reason, we do not use a subscript in the first part, but we do so later when the various methods put together. Any available subscript to indicate stratum, phase, or stage can be added if there is not one there.

4.5   Sampling and Inclusion Probabilities

In this subsection we present the most commonly used sampling selection methods and their inclusion probabilities (see also Lohr, 2010). These are both presented here without missingness so that if there is missingness, its mechanism is assumed to be ignorable, or MARS. The sample size, n, or its other forms are set separately, with the aim of achieving a good quality survey, but we do not discuss these issues here. The number of respondents is given the symbol r. The formulas in this subsection can be called 'design-based'.

Simple Random Sampling
The inclusion probability is constant for each k. The second term here, and later, is for the selection probability:

$$\pi_k = n\frac{1}{N} = \frac{n}{N}$$

If the assumption that the missingness mechanism is MARS holds true, the conversion to the respondents leads to the 'conditional' inclusion probability:

$$\pi_k = r\frac{1}{N} = \frac{r}{N}$$

Table 4.1   General outline of the probability sampling framework

Sampling question	Description
A. Frame(s)	If one frame only is required to get sampling/ sample units, it is called 'element sampling'. But if several frames are required to get those units, it is more complex; see Question B
B. Stage	Hierarchy used to approach the study/survey units by using probability sampling, initially going to the first-stage units (= PSUs), and then to the second-stage units (SSUs), and so on. *Terms:* one-stage sampling, two-stage sampling, three-stage sampling. The first-stage method is usually different from those used at later stages
C. Phase	First a probability sampling is applied for drawing a first-phase sample, and afterward a new sample is drawn at the second phase from the first sample. The method may vary in each phase. The number of phases is rarely more than two, except in panels
D. Stratification	The entire population is divided into several subpopulations, and the sample is drawn from each of them separately and independently. The inclusion probability of each stratum is thus equal to one. If the sampling design methods of two strata are different, this is called two-domain design
E. Sample allocation into strata	How has a desired (target) gross sample been shared into each stratum? Alternatives: equal, proportional, minimum, Neyman-Tschuprow. Anticipated response rates can be considered as well (by strata); see Question H
F. Panel vs. cross-sectional study	If a panel is desired, the sampling needs to be designed also for how to follow up the first sample units, and how to maintain the sample. Where a cross-sectional study is desired, it is good to design it so that a possible repeated survey can be conducted (thus getting a correct time series)
G. Selection method—leads to inclusion probabilities when sample size is decided	How to select the study units: – probability equal in all: simple random selection (SRS), equidistance, Bernoulli), or – probability varies unequally, typically by size, or = probability proportional to size (PPS)
H. Missingness anticipation or prediction	Trying to anticipate response and ineligibility rates and allocate a gross sample so that the net sample is as optimal as possible in order to get as accurate results as possible. Anticipation is good to do by strata if possible, but for the whole sample at a minimum

Bernoulli Sampling

Bernoulli Sampling (BS) is the same as SRS, but the sample size that is achieved is not necessarily of a fixed n because it varies randomly. The variation is relatively small.

Equidistance Sampling

The inclusion probability of Equidistance Sampling (EDS) for each k is constant:

$$\pi_k = \frac{1}{l} = \frac{1}{\frac{N}{n}} = \frac{n}{N}$$

Here l is the constant interval for the selection. The first k should be selected randomly. This interval is decided as soon as n is known, as can be seen in the preceding formula. The interval cannot be changed for the respondents, but some sample units are now missing. If this is not selective, it is possible to apply the same formula as for SRS. The conversion to the respondents gives the same formula as in SRS, assuming that certain k's are missing randomly.

▶   **Remark** We use the term 'equidistance' instead of the word 'systematic' that is often used in sampling literature. This is because 'systematic' is not as clear as 'equidistance,' since many strategies can be 'systematic' but do not have 'equidistance'.

Conclusion on Equal Inclusion Probabilities

Each $k \varepsilon U$ has an equal inclusion probability of being selected in a sample, whether we use SRS, BS, or EDS. This is a necessary condition for probability sampling.

How Is This Done in Practice?

1. If the frame is in an electronic form and an appropriate software package is available with a random number generator, a uniformly distributed random number in the interval (0, 1) for each k is needed to create a data file (e.g., the variable *ran*). This number can be used for EDS to select the first sample, and then, using the interval, to choose all the others so that the entire frame is covered. In the case of SRS, a technical option is to sort the units using the random ordering and then draw as many as are needed from an arbitrary place, working forward and/or backward. BS works such that if *ran* < the desired sampling fraction, the unit has been taken in a sample. For example, if *ran* < 0.01, then the sample size is about 1% of the sampling frame size.

Implicit Stratification

A common practice in some register countries is to use EDS with the order of the population register. Because the members of any particular dwelling unit appear one after the other, the length *l* is fairly long so that the method does not draw several people from the same dwelling. This often is considered to be a good point. The method also is called *implicit stratification*, but it has nothing to do with proper *stratification*, which it is best to call it *explicit stratification* to avoid misunderstanding.

2. If the frame is not in an electronic form, the best solution is to upload it into an electronic form and to continue as in the preceding. This is rarely possible if the survey concerns a large population. Still, it often is done at the PSU level, such as villages and blocks where the number is not too sizable (e.g., below 300). This strategy has been tried in several ESS countries when selecting addresses or dwellings, but there is no guarantee about how well it works. In Ethiopia, the houses with one or more households were marked on the first day of fieldwork, and then an equidistance selection was used to select the sample households. The interviewing started on the next day. This method could be considered ideal because it is really up to date if it is done carefully.
3. There are several other strategies using advanced technical tools in which, for example, coordinates are used and the 'sampling points' are selected randomly from these coordinates. GPS, Google maps, and satellite images might have advantages in this selection.
4. It is possible to select by individual without random numbers. Often, this is needed in the last stage of multistage sampling, when an interviewer needs to select a person older than 15 from all those who are over this age limit at an address or a dwelling that has already been selected by the survey organization. The most common method used by the ESS for this purpose is the *last birthday* method. A better version is one in which a survey interviewing day is randomized.

Unequal Inclusion Probabilities

Just for *clarification*: inclusion probabilities may vary by strata, quota, or phase. This most common case is not considered in this subsection but is discussed later in this chapter.

All methods require one or more auxiliary variables to be used for the inclusion, and thus to be taken from the sampling frame. In this subsection an example of this variable is in some sense '*size*', which is correlated therefore with the inclusion probability. The 'size' variable in most cases improves the precision of the estimates. There are other reasons for this, which are mainly the result of survey practice. We first present the case that has often been used in surveys where appropriate cluster PSUs are available.

Probability Proportional to Size

The size x_c is inserted in the inclusion and selection probability proportional to size (PPS), as follows:

$$\pi_k = n \frac{x_c}{\sum_U x_c}$$

The subscript x_c refers to a cluster PSU that is used at the first stage of sampling. The ESS clusters are generally small areas, whereas for PISA they are school classes. The PSU size n is thus decided separately. It is not usually necessary to convert to the respondents because the missing sampled PSUs rarely are accepted. The non-responses thus occur within these PSUs, concerning individuals.

This method seldom is used alone but is used in this way at the first stage. The denominator is the sum of the x's in the frame (e.g., the sum of all the school classes of the entire country, or the sum of the small area of PSUs, respectively), and does not relate to any figure for the target population units of the survey (e.g., the sum of the students in all schools). When the second-stage units are added, the sum will be the target population size, N, unless there are serious gaps in the survey fieldwork or statistical information system.

PPS Alone, Not Together with a Second- or a Third-Stage Inclusion

Probability proportional to size usually has not been used alone, but if there is a need to do it in this way, a special alternative should have been chosen. The most common such situation is that the sum of the weights is equal to the number of clusters in the target population. This is not achieved with the ordinary PPS strategy because it is not needed. The reason is that the target in most surveys is to create weights that have a sum equal to the target population, which consists of second-stage individuals. This target will be achieved after the later-stage inclusion probabilities. If the first- stage population is needed, the sampling method should be one that gives this target population. A common method for this purpose is PPS Sampford.

The PPS method can be used either *with replacement* or *without replacement*. The first of these is used in most surveys, such as the ESS. This may lead to an inclusion probability greater than one and therefore should not be accepted. How this problem can be avoided is discussed in the following box.

> **PPS with Replacement, with a Valid Inclusion Probability**
>
> If PPS is used in one-stage sampling, it usually is best to apply another selection method, but this is not necessary for ordinary surveys. The main option for avoiding probabilities greater than one is to create a cluster pattern so that the sizes do not vary too much. The following formula gives the conditions for the maximum cluster size:
>
> $$x_c < \frac{\sum_U x_c}{n}$$
>
> Or, respectively, for the sample size:

(continued)

$$n < \frac{\sum_U x_c}{x_c}$$

We can see that either the sample size or the maximum cluster size, or both, should not be too large. This problem is never encountered when the PSU clusters are census-enumeration areas; however, if administrative units (e.g., municipalities) are used, and there are both large and small municipalities in the country, there is a great danger of getting unacceptable probabilities. The best solution is either to divide up the large municipalities, or to use these as *explicit strata*.

Special PPS Cases

The inevitable practical reason why there might be unequal inclusion probabilities is that the frame units are available from a level other than the level of the study units. The following two cases are the most common in practice:

1. Let N be the size of the target population taken as individuals, but suppose that the purpose is to get a sample of households, thus of clusters of individuals, m_k. This is a good strategy if a frame of households is missing and difficult to create. Fortunately, it can be created for a sample so that a sample of individuals is selected and then a household is formed around the sampled person.

   A sample with n *individuals* is drawn from their clusters. The inclusion probability of each cluster varies by this cluster size at the target population level.

$$\pi_k = \frac{n}{N/m_k} = \frac{nm_k}{N}$$

The numerator of the second part of the formula indicates more clearly that the inclusion probability increases as the cluster size, m_k, increases. The cluster itself is such that it is available in the frame. It is not necessarily a household but is a dwelling, which can consist of one or more households. This inclusion probability is widely used in household surveys in countries with a central population register.

2. The study units k are individuals, but the frame consists of M clusters of these individuals. The cluster size, m_k, thus varies by the number of individuals in the target population. It is easiest to draw one k from each sampled cluster. This means that the inclusion probability of the individual k is linearly related to the cluster size:

$$\pi_k = \frac{nm_k}{M}$$

This formula resembles the formula in case 1, but the denominator is different. This inclusion probability is relatively common in the ESS, where either the address

Table 4.2 Example of inclusion probabilities in the third stage, selecting individuals

Number of individuals over 15 years old	Inclusion probability of the individual	Frequency	Percent
1	1.000	842	26.51
2	0.500	1595	50.22
3	0.333	423	13.32
4	0.250	246	9.25
5	0.200	49	2.20
6	0.167	15	0.47
7	0.143	3	0.09
8	0.125	2	0.06
9	0.111	1	0.03

Source: Test data (see Sect. 6.2)

register or the dwelling register is used to select a particular cluster and an individual over the age of 15 is drawn randomly from each selected address or dwelling.

Both options 1 and 2 have the disadvantage that the inclusion probability varies and does not always vary in the best way. It increases linearly with cluster size in the first case. This is a good thing if one wishes to get more sample units from large households, for instance. The number of single households will be smaller, but again that is not always a bad thing.

The individual inclusion probability is equal to the household inclusion probability in the second option. When the inclusion probability varies, it would be expected that the respective sampling weight would vary as well. The variation is one component of the accuracy of the survey estimates, and it is best to keep this variation at a suitable level. Example 4.1 illustrates this situation.

Example 4.1 ESS Sampling of Dwellings
Several countries use an address or dwelling register, then select the sampled addresses or dwellings, and then select the individuals aged over 15. This leads to varying inclusion probabilities at the second stage. Table 4.2 illustrates the practical situation from a dwelling register. We can see, for example, that the most common dwelling is one that consists of two people over 15 years old. The variability leads to variation in the inclusion probabilities at that level even though the first probabilities are equal to one. The coefficient of the variation of these inclusion probabilities is 43.7%, which is fairly common in countries using this design. This leads to the approximate *design effect* because of varying inclusion probabilities (DEFFp) at this stage—DEFFp = $1 + 0.437^2$ = 1.191. DEFFp will be considered more fully in Chap. 5, but for now it is enough to understand that if all the inclusion probabilities are equal, $DEFFp = 1$. This is therefore the design effect of simple random sampling without missingness. If the inclusion probabilities are not equal, this automatically leads to a larger DEFFp. It in turn leads to a greater confidence interval than in the case of SRS without missingness.

Stratification in Sampling

It is good to use stratification or, more exactly, 'explicit stratification', in almost all sampling. There is a reason for using full simple random sampling in the case when no auxiliary variable exists for stratification. Of course, it might be challenging to find a good stratification, but an attempt should still be made. In the simplest case, even when using proportional allocation, stratification requires certain statistics, particularly the target population figures. This thus sheds some light on what is going to be found in the final work.

Let us suppose that we have the target population statistics, N_h, in which $h = 1$, ..., H are explicit strata. How large H could be is not clear, but it must be at least ten or so. On the other hand, the maximum value for H also depends on the number of respondents achieved in each stratum. It is therefore necessary that each stratum contains enough respondents. It is not possible to give a simple answer to the question 'What is enough?', because the answer depends on many things.

If the gross sample size is n_h, then the inclusion probability, when using simple random sampling within strata, is:

$$\pi_k = \frac{n_h}{N_h}$$

This method also is called *stratified (simple) random sampling*. It is obviously the most common method and is used in all kinds of surveys, including business surveys where stratification is necessary so that the large businesses of each industry class, whose impact on most statistics is enormous, are included in the sample.

After the fieldwork, when the number of respondents is known for each stratum, the inclusion probability can be converted in straightforward fashion into this form:

$$\pi_k = \frac{r_h}{N_h}$$

If r_h is zero or small, there is a danger that the *basic sampling weight* is not plausible. This weight is thus the inverse of the inclusion probability of the respondents (assuming MARS):

$$w_k = \frac{N_h}{r_h}.$$

Naturally, if $N_h = r_h = 1$, the basic weight is not problematic but there would be problems if, for instance, N_h was equal to 10,000 and $n_h = 10$.

Inclusion Probabilities and Basic Weights for Designs with More than One Stage

In the case of pure simple random sampling, or its stratified version, the final inclusion probability is ready when the survey is implemented, and the respective design and basic weights are as presented earlier.

Nevertheless, if the sampling design includes more stages or phases, there are as many single-stage (single-phase) designs and, accordingly, inclusion probabilities (and not just one as there is in the preceding). Thus, the final inclusion probability needs to be calculated. There are two alternatives between the single-stage designs: (1) independent or (2) dependent. The reference for a dependent design is in Laaksonen et al. (2015), but here we only consider *independent designs* in detail.

The final inclusion probability, assuming that the single-stage inclusion probabilities are independent of each other, is in theory simple because the final inclusion probability of the multistage design is the product of all single-stage inclusion probabilities.

This simple product is not, in real life, simple because one or more probabilities cannot be known for all the sample units as a result of missingness. This should not occur in the first stage, as this would mean the whole sampling had problems. It should not be common in the second stage either, if register or other information is available. Unfortunately, in subsequent stages missingness is common because the units need to be contacted to get the information for the probability calculation. This means that the final inclusion probability can be calculated for the respondents only. Example 4.2 illustrates this problem with our test data.

Example 4.2 Inclusion Probabilities and Weights of the Test Data with Three-Stage Cluster Design

The example is based on the test data (see details in Sect. 6.2), which includes two domains. SRS is used in the first domain, meaning that the final inclusion probabilities are complete. By contrast, many inclusion probabilities of the third stage in the second domain are missing. This domain follows three-stage cluster sampling; see Table 4.3 (see also Sect. 6.2).

The final inclusion probability is therefore the product of these three probabilities. There are only two complete probabilities because the third is only given for the respondents. We thus do not know how many people over age 15 there are in dwellings that were not contacted, or, even if we by chance know this count for some units, this does not help much. Consequently, the product can be calculated only for 1573 respondents. Fortunately, our test data file is special because we have the full information about all probabilities. This gives us the opportunity to compare the realized and ideal probabilities. On the other hand, we know the first two probabilities completely, and thus the weights of dwellings. We see, for example, that the estimated number of dwellings in this population is 4.84 million (Table 4.4).

We can see that the realised and ideal figures, except the sums, are very close to each other but are not exactly the same. This means that the sampling works similarly for both the complete units and the respondents. We will see later that this does not hold very true for missingness. We have added the sum to the table; this is not informative concerning probabilities, but the sum of the

(continued)

Example 4.2 (continued)
weights should be the target population size. We can see that it is much too low for the realised weights but is correct when calculated with the ideal weight, which is without missingness.

Moreover, we can see from Table 4.4 that the sum of the realised design weights is much lower than the correct sum, but that the other figures do not differ substantially, with the minimums and the maximums being exactly equal. We can therefore believe that the weights could be adjusted to be closer to the correct ones, even to make the sums exactly the same, with the MARS assumption. We will continue from these weights to the basic weights in Sect. 7.

Table 4.3   Figures for single-stage inclusion probabilities in the cluster domain of the test data

Variable	Label	n	Mean	Minimum	Maximum	Coeff. of variation
PROB1	Inclusion probability of first sampling stage (PSU cluster)	3176	0.116	0.0015	0.813	145.2
PROB2	Inclusion probability of second sampling stage (dwelling)	3176	0.039	0.0007	0.417	175.2
PROB3	Inclusion probability of third sampling stage (individual person)	1573	0.596	0.1111	1.000	43.7

Table 4.4   Inclusion probabilities and weights of the cluster domain of the test data

Label	n	Mean	Minimum	Maximum	Coeff. of variation	Sum
Ideal inclusion probability of person	3176	0.000447	0.00006	0.00125	66.3	1.42
Realised inclusion probability of person	1573	0.000457	0.00006	0.00125	65.6	0.72
Ideal and realised weight of dwelling	3176	1523.8	802.5	1854.3	32.0	4,839,616
Ideal design weight of person	3176	3214.1	802.5	16,689	59.3	9,900,728
Realised design weight of person	1573	3119.2	802.5	16,689	58.9	4,906,545

4.6   Illustration of Stratified Three-Stage Sampling

A multistage sampling design is thus common in social surveys of individuals, but it is not easy for a beginner in surveys to understand. We illustrate this design in a case in which the target population is stratified, usually by geographic region, and then the sampling design within each stratum is used. This design can vary by stratum, but it follows the same strategy in each stratum. In some cases, it has been found to be effective to apply different designs for urban and rural regions. This is called a two-domain design.

The illustration is for a stratified three-stage sampling design so that the design strategy is equal in each stratum but all information naturally comes from each stratum (Scheme 4.1).

This scheme begins from six explicit strata; this number often can be enough, but a higher number of strata can work better, at least in larger countries. In the first sampling stage, primary sampling units of small areas are selected by PPS with replacement. Six out of 25 PSUs were selected here. These numbers often are higher in practice, but this is reasonable for illustration.

In the second stage, ten dwellings of PSU A2 are drawn using simple random sampling. The scheme does not indicate how many dwellings are in this stratum, but this number is usually in the hundreds or thousands, and in large strata it can be many more. Finally, just one individual is selected from each sampled dwelling, with simple random sampling. This selected individual is marked in a different way, rather than excluded, in the scheme. It is possible to take all individuals in the sample. This may lead to household surveys. On the other hand, only an individual of a certain age may be selected, like an individual over 15 in the ESS.

4.7   Basic Weights of Stratified Three-Stage Sampling

The basic weights are calculated based on the assumption that missingness is ignorable. We already have presented the methodology in the case of a stratified simple random sampling design. Example 4.2 earlier shows that the realised design weights are not correct because their sum is not consistent with the target population size. The only missingness in this example is in the third inclusion probability, but there may be more missingness in other designs. This example case is, however, relatively common and therefore we show how to get the correct basic weights in this case.

We must calculate the two inclusion probabilities, for both the complete units and the respondents. The subscripts of the following inclusion probabilities refer to stages 1, 2, and 3. First, we need the inclusion probabilities over stages 1 and 2, which are completely known and are thus for n units:

$$\pi_{12_k} = \pi_{1_k}\pi_{2_k} \tag{4.1}$$

Second, we find the inclusion probabilities for the respondents—there are therefore r units here, with r being less than n:

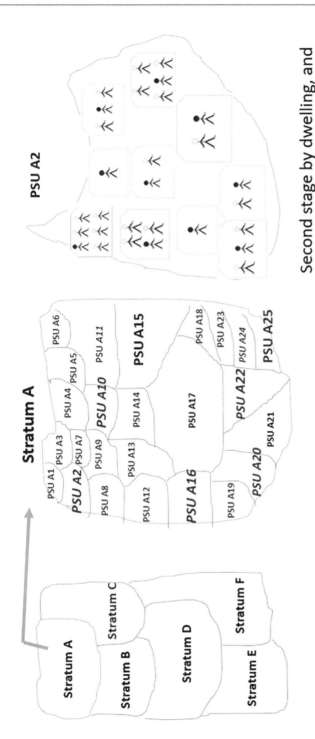

PSU A2

Stratum A

PSU A1
PSU A3
PSU A2
PSU A7
PSU A9
PSU A8
PSU A4
PSU A5
PSU A6
PSU A10
PSU A11
PSU A13
PSU A14
PSU A15
PSU A12
PSU A16
PSU A17
PSU A18
PSU A19
PSU A20
PSU A21
PSU A22
PSU A23
PSU A24
PSU A25

Stratum A
Stratum C
Stratum B
Stratum D
Stratum E
Stratum F

Stratification
All strata selected

First stage by 7 small area PSU's selected with PPS   (A2, A10, ..., A 25)

Second stage by dwelling, and
third stage by 10 individuals
SRS selection,   not selected

Scheme 4.1 Illustration of a stratified three-stage sampling design in which the study unit is an individual

$$\pi_{13_k} = \pi_{1_k}\pi_{2_k}\pi_{3_k} \tag{4.2}$$

We now want to calculate the best possible inclusion probabilities and the basic weights. We therefore start by calculating the preliminary basic weights after the second stage, which are without missingness, as the inverse of formula (4.1):

$$w_{12_k} = 1/\pi_{12_k}$$

On the other hand, we need the respective weights for the respondents, given that π_{3_k} is missing:

$$w_{12_k}(resp) = 1/\pi_{12_k}$$

Accordingly, we calculate the preliminary basic weights using formula (4.3):

$$w_{13_k}(pre) = 1/\pi_{13_k} \tag{4.3}$$

These correspond to the realised design weights (see table in Example 4.4) and are too small. Thus, we need to increase them so that their sum matches the ideal design weights if any information is missing. These basic weights are obtained using formula (4.4):

$$w_{13_k} = \left(\sum_n w_{12_k}(pre)/\sum_r w_{12_k}(resp)\right)w_{13_k}(pre) \tag{4.4}$$

These calculations, including weights, should be made by strata if strata are used. They work correctly if the missingness mechanism from stage 2 to stage 3 is ignorable, even though this is not necessarily the case. Example 4.3 illustrates the situation with the test data. It means that it is possible to improve the weights via reweighting, using the methods presented in Chap. 8.

Example 4.3 Basic Weights of the Test Data for the Cluster Domain (see Sect. 6.2)

We can calculate the complete inclusion probabilities and design weights for the dwellings by strata. Table 4.5 gives the results for the only two strata included in the data.

The ratio of the two sums in each stratum is used in calculating the final basic weights from the preliminary ones. Table 4.6 shows the results for the basic weights.

We can see that the sum of the final basic weights is basically ideal; that is, it matches the sum obtained from the ideal basic weights for which we knew all the inclusion probabilities. We can see that the variations of the weights (i.e., the coefficients of variation) are close to each other as well, but the means of the basic and ideal weights are very different.

Table 4.5 Figures for the Dwellings of the Cluster Domain in the Test Data

Strata	Weighted number of dwellings		Respondents
	Complete		
1	4,038,739.66		2,002,680.82
2	800,876.48		395,623.35

Table 4.6 Figures for the basic weights of the cluster domain in the test data

Weight	Number of observations	Mean	Minimum	Maximum	Coeff. of variation	Sum
Basic final	1573	6294	1625	33,656	58.9	9,900,728
Basic preliminary	1573	3119	802	16,689	58.9	4,906,544
Ideal basic	3176	3214	802	16,689	59.3	9,900,728

4.8 Two Types of Sampling Weights

The term 'sampling weight', 'sample weight', or 'survey weight' is a general label for the weights used in estimating the target population parameters. These parameters can be of two types:

1. They concern the totals of the target population or its sub-populations (domains), and are thus sums, amounts, or quantities.
2. They concern means, medians, percentages, or other relative parameters.

The sampling weights presented above work well in both these cases, but it is good to be careful with the software in order to know whether it is working correctly. This is one reason for gaining an understanding of another type of sampling weight, called the *'analysis weight'* or *'analytical weight'*. This is obtained from the *proper* or *ordinary sampling weight* w_k by dividing it by the average of all the weights of this target population. This weight is thus relative, whereas the proper sampling weight indicates 'amounts' or 'totals'.

$$w_k\_analysis = w_k / \left(\sum_r w_k / r \right) = w_k / \overline{\mathcal{W}}_k = w_k r / \sum_r w_k$$

The analysis weight is used more often than the proper (amount) sampling weight, since it works well enough in most analyses, but it does not work when the amounts are of interest. For example, the ESS weights are analysis weights only, but they can be transformed to proper weights (Chap. 9).

The sum of the proper sampling weights is thus *the target population size*, but the sum of the analysis weights is *the number of respondents*. The good thing about the analysis weights is that they make it possible to compare the weights of all types of

Table 4.7 Statistics for the weights in both the cluster domain and the srs domain of the test data

Weight	Number of observations	Mean	Minimum	Maximum	Coeff. of variation	Sum of ordinary weights
Gross sample of the cluster domain	3176	1.00	0.250	5.193	59.3	9,900,728
Basic of the cluster domain	1573	1.00	0.258	5.347	58.9	9,900,728
Gross sample of the SRS domain	1422	1.00	0.565	1.305	36.5	9,698,424
Basic of the SRS domain	605	1.00	0.497	1.425	42.2	9,698,424

surveys, since their average is equal to one. Table 4.7 gives the basic figures for the four weights. The first two rows are the same as in Table 4.4, but the next two rows are calculated from the simple random (SRS) domain of the same test data. The weights are analytical except the ordinary weights in the last column.

The weights are fairly different in these two domains. The variation of the weights in the SRS domain is much smaller than the variation in the cluster domain. The logical reason is that there are three inclusion probabilities in the cluster domain whereas there is only one in the SRS domain. In addition, there is some variation by strata, and this is slightly higher in the SRS domain because there are six strata.

Example 4.4 The Weights of the 2012 PISA Survey
The public PISA data are not the same as the public ESS data in all respects, even though all the methodological information can be found. The PISA survey instruction variables are complete for most countries, which is not the case for the ESS. This will be discussed further in the analysis in Chap. 14. The sampling weights, however, can be used in both PISA and the ESS. The main sampling weight of the ESS is analytical, and the average in each country is one, but the PISA weights are ordinary ones. Their sum is thus the target population of the country.

Table 4.8 gives an example for the 43 countries that participated in the problem-solving exam, not just in the mathematics, science, and reading ones. The analysis weights are computed from the initial student weights. It is useful to compare these with all other surveys that have analysis weights to show how the weights vary. The variation is often rather small, less than 40% for the coefficient of variation. Although it is higher in some countries, for several reasons, with the main one being that the country wants to get more precise estimates for certain regions or domains. If the weights do not vary much, it is possible to get relatively good point estimates even without weights in the estimation, although this is not recommended, of course.

Table 4.8 Statistics of the PISA 2012 weights for students in the countries that participated in most survey parts

Country	Weight	Mean	Minimum	Maximum	Coeff. of variation	Sum
United Arab Emirates	PISA student weight	3.5	1.0	22.7	71.4	40,612
	Analysis weight	1.0	0.3	6.4	71.4	11,500
Australia	PISA student weight	17.3	1.2	67.7	58.3	250,711
	Analysis weight	1.0	0.1	3.9	58.3	14,481
Austria	PISA student weight	17.3	1.0	81.5	36.9	82,225
	Analysis weight	1.0	0.1	4.7	36.9	4755
Belgium	PISA student weight	13.7	1.0	44.8	38.9	117,889
	Analysis weight	1.0	0.1	3.3	38.9	8597
Bulgaria	PISA student weight	10.3	4.8	27.0	20.5	54,255
	Analysis weight	1.0	0.5	2.6	20.5	5282
Brazil	PISA student weight	435.3	1.1	2837.7	72.4	2,397,036
	Analysis weight	1.0	0.0	6.5	72.4	5506
Canada	PISA student weight	16.2	1.0	116.1	111.1	347,987
	Analysis weight	1.0	0.1	7.2	111.1	21,544
Chile	PISA student weight	33.4	1.0	185.2	52.4	229,159
	Analysis weight	1.0	0.0	5.5	52.4	6856
Colombia	PISA student weight	61.7	1.2	478.0	101.9	559,674
	Analysis weight	1.0	0.0	7.7	101.9	9073
Czech Republic	PISA student weight	15.4	1.2	76.8	71.2	82,250
	Analysis weight	1.0	0.1	5.0	71.2	5327
Germany	PISA student weight	151.4	70.5	314.1	22.8	756,907
	Analysis weight	1.0	0.5	2.1	22.8	5001
Denmark	PISA student weight	8.8	1.0	77.5	81.7	65,642
	Analysis weight	1.0	0.1	8.8	81.7	7481
Spain	PISA student weight	36.4	2.5	144.7	101.1	370,862
	Analysis weight	1.0	0.1	4.0	101.1	10,175
Estonia	PISA student weight	2.4	1.3	8.0	44.0	11,627
	Analysis weight	1.0	0.5	3.3	44.0	4779

(continued)

Table 4.8 (continued)

Country	Weight	Mean	Minimum	Maximum	Coeff. of variation	Sum
Finland	PISA student weight	6.8	1.0	54.1	79.3	60,047
	Analysis weight	1.0	0.1	7.9	79.3	8829
France	PISA student weight	151.7	103.4	293.9	15.1	699,779
	Analysis weight	1.0	0.7	1.9	15.1	4613
United Kingdom	PISA student weight	138.5	47.6	457.9	31.8	579,422
	Analysis weight	1.0	0.3	3.3	31.8	4185
Hong Kong—China	PISA student weight	15.1	8.3	55.3	25.2	70,636
	Analysis weight	1.0	0.5	3.7	25.2	4670
Croatia	PISA student weight	9.1	4.1	23.4	24.6	45,506
	Analysis weight	1.0	0.5	2.6	24.6	5008
Hungary	PISA student weight	19.0	8.5	91.7	43.3	91,179
	Analysis weight	1.0	0.4	4.8	43.3	4810
Ireland	PISA student weight	10.8	1.4	31.9	32.3	54,010
	Analysis weight	1.0	0.1	3.0	32.3	5016
Israel	PISA student weight	21.4	14.0	65.8	27.5	107,990
	Analysis weight	1.0	0.7	3.1	27.5	5055
Italy	PISA student weight	95.0	1.3	871.2	64.4	521,902
	Analysis weight	1.0	0.0	9.2	64.4	5495
Japan	PISA student weight	177.6	57.3	381.5	20.2	1,128,179
	Analysis weight	1.0	0.3	2.1	20.2	6351
Korea	PISA student weight	119.9	49.7	251.6	13.1	603,632
	Analysis weight	1.0	0.4	2.1	13.1	5033
Macao – China	PISA student weight	1.0	1.0	1.2	1.7	5366
	Analysis weight	1.0	1.0	1.2	1.7	5335
Montenegro	PISA student weight	1.6	1.0	3.5	40.5	7714
	Analysis weight	1.0	0.6	2.1	40.5	4744
Malaysia	PISA student weight	83.1	11.5	151.1	22.9	432,080
	Analysis weight	1.0	0.1	1.8	22.9	5197
Netherlands	PISA student weight	44.0	7.2	161.1	47.3	196,262
	Analysis weight	1.0	0.2	3.7	47.3	4460

(continued)

Table 4.8 (continued)

Country	Weight	Mean	Minimum	Maximum	Coeff. of variation	Sum
Norway	PISA student weight	12.7	4.7	53.8	19.2	59,432
	Analysis weight	1.0	0.4	4.2	19.2	4686
Poland	PISA student weight	82.4	18.2	199.2	27.1	379,545
	Analysis weight	1.0	0.2	2.4	27.1	4607
Portugal	PISA student weight	16.8	2.3	71.3	51.2	96,034
	Analysis weight	1.0	0.1	4.2	51.2	5722
Shanghai—China	PISA student weight	16.4	4.1	52.6	22.7	84,965
	Analysis weight	1.0	0.2	3.2	22.7	5177
Russian Federation	PISA student weight	224.5	34.2	557.4	34.8	1,174,528
	Analysis weight	1.0	0.2	2.5	34.8	5231
Singapore	PISA student weight	9.2	1.1	19.0	25.0	51,088
	Analysis weight	1.0	0.1	2.1	25.0	5546
Serbia	PISA student weight	14.5	4.1	60.0	21.9	67,934
	Analysis weight	1.0	0.3	4.1	21.9	4684
Slovak Republic	PISA student weight	11.7	4.1	47.3	36.7	54,636
	Analysis weight	1.0	0.3	4.0	36.7	4678
Slovenia	PISA student weight	3.1	1.2	30.3	80.6	18,418
	Analysis weight	1.0	0.4	9.7	80.6	5911
Sweden	PISA student weight	20.0	3.2	80.6	18.4	94,936
	Analysis weight	1.0	0.2	4.0	18.4	4736
Chinese Taipei	PISA student weight	48.4	1.1	110.2	30.3	292,542
	Analysis weight	1.0	0.0	2.3	30.3	6046
Turkey	PISA student weight	178.8	2.8	394.1	16.7	866,681
	Analysis weight	1.0	0.0	2.2	16.7	4848
Uruguay	PISA student weight	7.5	2.8	17.7	28.7	39,771
	Analysis weight	1.0	0.4	2.4	28.7	5315
United States of America	PISA student weight	710.9	134.5	2597.9	41.2	3,538,783
	Analysis weight	1.0	0.2	3.7	41.2	4978

References

Baker, R., Brick, J. M., Bates, N. A., Battaglia, M., Couper, M. P., Dever, J. A., et al. (2013). Summary report of the AAPOR task force on non-probability sampling. *Journal of Survey Statistics and Methodology, 1*(2), 90–143. https://doi.org/10.1093/jssam/smt008.

Bethlehem, J. (2015). Essay. Sunday shopping—The case of three surveys. *Survey Research Methods* 9, 221–230. European Survey Research Association. Accessed May 2017, from http://www.surveymethods.org. https://doi.org/10.18148/srm/2015.v9i3.6202.

Heckathorn, D. D. (2002). Respondent-driven sampling II: Deriving valid estimates from chain-referral samples of hidden populations. *Social Problems, 49*(1), 11–34. https://doi.org/10.1525/sp.2002.49.1.11.

Laaksonen, S., Kemppainen, T., Kortteinen, M., Vaattovaara, M., Stjernberg, M., & Lönnqvist, H. (2015). Tackling city-regional dynamics in a survey using grid sampling. *Survey Research Methods, 9*(1), 45–55.

Lee, S., Suzer-Gurtekin, T., Wagner, J., & Valliant, R. (2017). Total survey error and respondent driven sampling: Focus on nonresponse and measurement errors in the recruitment process and the network size reports and implications for inferences. *Journal of Official Statistics, 33*(2), 335–366. https://doi.org/10.1515/JOS-2017-0017.

Lohr, S. (2010). *Sampling: Design and analysis* (2nd ed.). Boston: Arizona State University, Cengage Learning.

Lundquist, P., & Särndal, C.-E. (2013). Aspects of responsive design with applications to the Swedish Living Conditions Survey. *Journal of Official Statistics, 29*(4), 557–582. https://doi.org/10.2478/jos-2013-0040.

Valliant, R., Dever, J. A., & Kreuter, F. (2013). *Practical tools for designing and weighting survey samples, Statistics for Social and Behavioral Sciences*. New York: Springer.

Design Effects at the Sampling Phase

5

Clusters in two points of time

A 'design effect' is a useful and relatively compact term to indicate the influence of the sampling design on the uncertainty of each estimate. It was introduced by Kish (1994) and followed up on by other researchers (e.g., Gabler, Häder, & Lahiri, 1999; Shackman, 2001; and the ESS sampling team). This chapter to a great extent takes advantage of the work of this latter team (e.g., ESS Sampling Guidelines, 2017).

This effect can be estimated finally in the proper survey analysis when the data and all the required design variables are available (see Chap. 14). An attempt should have been made, however, to predict or anticipate this effect as much as possible when designing and implementing the sampling. This chapter focusses on explaining the core instruments for this anticipation. First, the key terms are presented.

© Springer International Publishing AG, part of Springer Nature 2018
S. Laaksonen, *Survey Methodology and Missing Data*,
https://doi.org/10.1007/978-3-319-79011-4_5

The general formula for the design effect, symbolized by *DEFF*, is as follows:

$$DEFF = var(S)/var(SRS)$$

where

- $var(S)$ = the variance estimate of the particular sampling design S, and
- $var(SRS)$ = the variance estimate of the simple random design, or another reference design

Both variances are estimated from the same data, and thus $var(S)$ is based on the real survey but necessarily $var(SRS)$ is not. The latter is used as a reference, giving information about how different the real variance is from that of the SRS design.

In practice, the latter variance, as well as the respective confidence intervals, is calculated here without taking the sampling design into account. This bias can be found in real life if everything is calculated as simply as possible. Unfortunately, this is often the case.

The effect DEFF is therefore a relative ratio. If it is greater than one, then the design S is less efficient than the SRS design; otherwise, it is more efficient. The DEFF is thus quadratic. If one wishes to compare the standard errors, the square root is needed. This is called *DEFT*, which stands for the square root of DEFF.

The DEFF varies with estimates that basically can be easily calculated in the survey analysis, and thus each point estimate may have somewhat fluctuating variance estimates or standard errors. There is therefore a need to find a compromise between all the survey estimates for anticipating the DEFF in order to choose the gross sample size. This also can be done for each stratum separately, but if too many factors are considered, the work will be demanding, and the anticipations may fail.

Thus, we present the general lines for anticipating DEFF for the whole population only, not for subpopulations. It is a good idea to divide the design effect in sampling design into the two components:

- DEFF because of clustering = *DEFFc*
- DEFF because of varying inclusion probabilities (consequently, attributable to weights) = *DEFFp*

The product of these is the whole design effect:

$$DEFF = DEFFc^* DEFFp$$

Next, we explain how each of these components is anticipated for the sampling design.

5.1 DEFF Because of Clustering, *DEFFc*

To introduce this, we use two scatter plots from the 2012 PISA (Fig. 5.1). On the *x*-axis is the mean of the success score for problem solving, and on the *y*-axis is the standard deviation of this score. The plots are the PISA sample schools, and the scales of the two graphs are equal so that they can be more easily compared.

The German scatter plot is much more stacked than the Finnish one. Figure 5.2 is taken from the test dataset (see Sect. 6.2), which is a partially artificial ESS data file. Now stratum 2 is more stacked than stratum 1, which slightly resembles the scatter in the Finnish PISA. These scatters illustrate some features of clusters; in particular, the *x*-axis shows the variation of the means of the clusters. Still, it is good to go forward and to implement indicators for homogeneity. This requires specifying a linear-mixed model and then estimating the intraclass correlation.

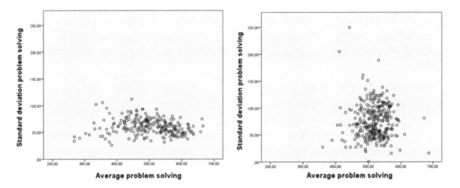

Fig. 5.1 Scatter plots between average scores for problem solving and their standard deviations in the PISA—Germany (*left*) and Finland (*right*). Plots are primary sampling units = PISA schools

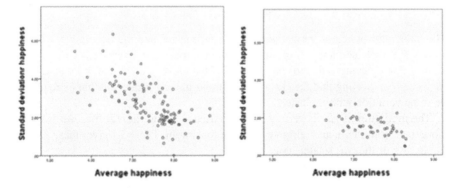

Fig. 5.2 Scatter plots between average 'Happiness' and standard deviation of 'Happiness' in stratum 1 (*left*) and stratum 2 (*right*). Plots are primary sampling units = small areas

▶ **Remark** The number of possible references for linear-mixed models is so vast that it is impossible to mention a fair list of the good ones, so we do not mention any references. On the other hand, there are many software packages available, including R, SAS, SPSS, and MATLAB. It is relatively easy to estimate the intraclass correlation in an ordinary survey case with any of this software.

The *intraclass correlation, rho* (sometimes known as *ICC*) can be estimated using a linear-mixed model. It is possible to estimate this conditionally so that explanatory variables are included in the model, but the basic specification is enough to estimate the ordinary *rho*. In this case, the model is without any explanatory variable, and its form is:

$$y_{ij} = \mu + \alpha_j + \varepsilon_{ij}$$

Here y_{ij} is the variable with a *rho* that is being estimated (i = individual and j = cluster), μ is an unobserved overall mean or intercept, α_j is the random effect shared by all values in cluster j, and ε_{ij} is an unobserved error term. The α_j and ε_{ij} are assumed to be normally distributed (mean = 0, variance = σ^2), and they are uncorrelated. When the model is estimated, we are especially interested in two variance estimates:

- s_α^2 = the cluster variance.
- s_ε^2 = the residual variance

The cluster variance indicates how much the cluster means vary (conditional to the mixed model) and can be found from the graphs. The residual variance reveals how much of the variation is not explained by this clustering when the clusters are used as random effects. Note that it is best to use the analysis weights when estimating the linear-mixed model.

The intraclass correlation is now:

$$rho = s_\alpha^2 / \left(s_\alpha^2 + s_\varepsilon^2 \right)$$

The numerator indicates the variation in cluster means, and the denominator is the sum of the explained and unexplained variations, thus a total variance. The *rho* is a kind of homogeneity indicator for clusters. If the clusters are equal in their means, *rho* is zero, indicating that the clusters are similar in their means but that there might be some variation within clusters.

The minimum of *rho* is zero and the maximum is one. In real life, *rho* is often close to the minimum, and fairly far from the maximum. Table 5.1 gives these values in the case of the two scatter plots.

The graphs already show clearer clusters for the PISA data on problem solving than for the ESS data on happiness. The scales of both graphs are equal, which facilitates interpretation. The intraclass correlations give the numerical indicators for

Table 5.1 Intraclass correlations in the cases of Figs. 5.1 and 5.2

Variable	Intraclass correlation
PISA problem solving for Germany	0.617
PISA problem solving for Finland	0.141
Happiness of stratum 1 in the test data	0.006
Happiness of stratum 2 in the test data	0.050

Table 5.2 Intraclass correlations and the DEFFs because of clustering for some variables in the ESS countries in Round 5, for the two-stage cluster design

Variable	*Rho*	*DEFFc*
Robbery rate	0.0294	1.43
Robbery fear	0.0198	1.29
Opinion: mothers should stay at home more, not go to work	0.0287	1.42
Opinion: talented students should be rewarded more	0.0028	1.04
Happiness	0.0005	1.01

the homogeneity or lack of homogeneity. The differences between these *rho*'s are huge. The largest *rho* is for the German PISA data, clearly implying that the differences between schools for problem solving are substantial, especially when German schools are compared with Finnish schools. On the other hand, the *rho*'s in the ESS between small area PSUs are much smaller. The variable 'Happiness' usually shows very little clustering within small areas. Stratum 1 is fairly ordinary for the ESS but stratum 2 is atypical because the highest intraclass correlations at the country level are at about this same level. Some examples are given in Table 5.2. This table also includes the design effects because of clustering, which are estimated approximately using Kish's formula:

$$DEFFc = 1 + (b - 1)\, rho \quad \text{where } b = \text{average net cluster size}$$

Intraclass correlation is therefore *important* in sampling when the PSUs are clusters. If the PSU is a single unit, such as a person or an enterprise, one does not need to worry about intraclass correlation because its value is equal to zero. Intraclass correlation may still be used for examining the *interviewer effect*, for example. Here, the interviewers form the 'class'; it is not good if the *rho* is high because this means that the interviewers are not doing their work with sufficient objectively or consistently. If clusters are used in the sampling design, the design effect must avoidably be considered. This is seen in the standard error, which in most cases increases because the DEFFc is greater than one. On the other hand, intraclass correlation also can be used in a special analysis if one wishes to estimate how certain groups or clusters are stacked together.

5.2   DEFF Because of Varying Inclusion Probabilities, *DEFFp*

The variability in sampling weights has an influence on standard errors. From this point of view, simple random sampling without unit non-responses is an ideal survey, but it is not really possible to achieve this. If two or more stages are used, it is difficult to achieve equal weights even for the design stage and thus for the gross sample. It is possible that the weights will vary more after the fieldwork, but if anticipation of unit non-responses is accurate, it is possible that the final DEFF will be decreased.

In the sampling stage, it is reasonable to anticipate the DEFFp using the expected weights in this approximating formula:

$$DEFFp = 1 + cv(w)^2$$

where *cv(w)* is the coefficient of variation of the weight, *w*. The first approximation of *w* could be the gross sample design weight based on the inclusion probabilities anticipated in advance or using the weight of the reference survey that is based on the same sample principles.

Still, it is better to anticipate by using the basic weights with the best realized response rates. Unless any assumptions about response rates can be made, this DEFFp is equal to the first version. Anticipation by explicit strata response rates can be considered at this stage but is not often used—for example, it is not used in the ESS.

Examples 5.1 and 5.2 illustrate the values of these design effects. The weights of the respondents for the test data do not vary much (see Example 5.1). The differences between the countries in Example 5.2 are rather large, but the median is about 1.2. If the DEFFp is much larger than this threshold, the design is unusual and far from being proportional. Even so, Slovakia is an outlier, so the design cannot be entirely trusted (i.e., the design and the inclusion probabilities should be checked). The United Kingdom's DEFFp is not low but can be trusted because it arises from the UK's three-stage design, in which the second stage in fact includes three stages (i.e., address, dwelling, and household) after PSU selection. Some designs are very proportional but do not include more than two stages.

Example 5.1 Design Effects Because of Unequal Weights in the Test Data, by Eight Strata

Stratum	Respondents	Coeff. of variation	DEFFp
1	1080	0.394	1.155
2	493	0.411	1.169
3	228	0.369	1.136
4	68	0.400	1.160
5	44	0.394	1.155
6	74	0.389	1.151
7	133	0.349	1.122
8	58	0.372	1.138

Example 5.2 Design Effects Because of Unequal Weights Based on the Design Weights in Some Countries of the ESS, Round 6; Countries with Simple Random Sampling Are Not Included Because Their DEFFp Is Equal to One

Country	DEFFp	Country	DEFFp
Hungary	1.003	Ukraine	1.228
Spain	1.011	France	1.230
Poland	1.019	Ireland	1.237
Iceland	1.031	Czech Republic	1.266
Israel	1.035	United Kingdom	1.271
Germany	1.109	Lithuania	1.333
Bulgaria	1.170	Russia	1.336
Cyprus	1.201	Portugal	1.375
Netherlands	1.207	Slovakia	1.921

5.3   The Entire Design Effect: DEFF and Gross Sample Size

The whole DEFF is thus the product of the two DEFFs we have looked previously. It is used when deciding on the gross sample size. In addition, one must consider two other components: (1) the anticipated ineligibility rate and (2) the anticipated unit non-response rate.

The concept of '*effective*' sample size *(neff)* is useful for benchmarking these components—that is, assessing how great their impact might be on the variance estimates (i.e., the squares of the standard errors). It would be possible to consider a fifth factor, 'stratification', as well, but this is not done by the ESS. There are two reasons for this:

- It is not easy to do because all anticipations should be made at the stratum level
- Its impact is not usually great (one example is shown later in this chapter).

The neff corresponds to the sample size for which the micro data of the respondents could give the same accuracy as the simple random design (SRS). Thus, if the net sample data really can be interpreted to be drawn from a target population with SRS, we do not even need sampling weights to get appropriate accuracy estimates.

Unfortunately, this is not the case in real life, but it is still good to compare the data that have been obtained with the SRS data. Thus, no estimate can be calculated based on an SRS design in real life. It is good to illustrate this, as shown next, using the SRS standard error of the mean:

$$stderr = sqrt\left(\frac{\sum_r s^2}{r}\right) \tag{5.1}$$

Here s^2 is the ordinary sample variance and the data consists of the r respondents. This formula holds true in the case of an SRS design with the MCAR missingness mechanism.

At the beginning of this chapter, we learned that the DEFF is determined with variances. Formula (5.1) in turn shows that the numbers of the sample units and the respondents have the same dimension. Thus, both DEFF components can be used in a straightforward manner when determining the gross sample size in Table 5.3. In addition to the anticipation of the two DEFFs, ineligibility and unit non-response rates need to be anticipated. None of these anticipations is easy, but if another similar survey (reference survey) is available, this may be a great help. Nevertheless, we cannot know in advance exactly how satisfactory our estimates will be.

5.4 How Should the Sample Size Be Decided, and How Should the Gross Sample Be Allocated into Strata?

The effective target sample size has been determined in Table 5.3, which corresponds to the minimum requirements of the ESS. This decision was based on many criteria. One criterion is that the accuracy of each country estimate is about the same. This gives good opportunities for comparing the results between countries. Because the minimum number of respondents required is 1500, appropriate

Table 5.3 Sampling design summary for determining gross sample size if the desired effective target sampling size is 1500

Operation	Example calculation (average-based, figures may vary by stratum or another domain)
1. Target for the effective sample size (neff)	1500
2. Anticipated missingness because of ineligibility (7%)	$1500/0.93 = 1613$
3. Anticipated missingness because of unit non-responses (35%)	$1613/0.65 = 2481$
4. Anticipated design effect because of clustering (DEFFc), including the anticipated intraclass correlation ($= 0.025$); if the average gross cluster size is 8, then the average net cluster size is $8 \times 0.93 \times 0.65 = 4.83$	DEFFc $= 1 + (4.83 - 1)*.025 = 1.096$ $2481 * 1.096 = 2719$
5. Anticipated design effect because of varying inclusion probabilities (DEFFp)—calculated for the anticipated respondents if possible	DEFFp $= 1.2$ $2719*1.2 = 3263$
6. Anticipated and, it is hoped, realised minimum gross sample size Anticipated net sample size	3263 $1973 = 3263 * 0.65 * 0.93$

estimates between many population groups or domains are possible, but then again these might be limited if the number of the respondents is not reasonably large.

The ESS is a general social survey without any specific target at the domain (i.e., subpopulation) level. If a survey has such a target, the best solution is to use stratification and to allocate a target for each stratum so that the accuracy target is achieved. This can be called *minimum allocation*; the other strata sizes can be allocated flexibly. The following are other common allocation methods:

- *Proportional* allocation, which therefore has been recommended for the ESS since Round 6. This does not allow the anticipated response rates to be considered. Still, such anticipation is usual in many other surveys. For example, it was anticipated in the Finnish Security Survey (Laaksonen & Heiskanen, 2014) that younger people and males would participate relatively poorly, while the target was to get precise estimates for these domains too. The sampling fraction was therefore higher for younger people and males. This anticipation was correct, so the results were satisfactory. Similarly, a relatively high sampling fraction may be used in urban areas, and a lower fraction in rural areas; such examples are very common, including the Polish ESS until Round 7.
- *Equal* allocation, in which case the neff of each stratum is equal; the ESS requirement by country therefore corresponds to this method of allocation.
- *Neyman-Tschuprow* (often called only *Neyman*) allocation in which the gross sample size (or neff) n_h of each stratum h is obtained with the following formula, which can be converted to the net sample if the anticipated net sample sizes are available:

$$n_h = n \frac{N_n S_n}{N_h S_h}. \tag{5.2}$$

Here n is the desired sample size of the whole sample, n_h is the respective gross sample size of stratum h, Nh is the size of the target population in stratum h, and S_h is the anticipated standard deviation of the study variable, y. This standard deviation can be taken from a similar previous survey, or it may be a proxy variable that is clearly correlated with the survey variable y. Naturally, a big problem is that most surveys have several y variables of interest. Thus, some type of compromise is needed.

Discussion on Minimum Sample Size

If a user knows his or her accuracy requirement concerning the standard error and/or the confidence interval, and if reasonable information about the expected variation exists, it is not difficult to calculate the required sample size in the case of simple random sampling. This follows from Formula (5.1) if the target population is large, say more than 10,000. If the population is small, a finite population correction term $= (N-n)/N$ needs to be included. Basic arithmetic now gives the required gross sample size in the case in which there is no missingness. Next, unit non-response and ineligibility must be anticipated in the best way possible, and then the fieldwork should function effectively to achieve these targets.

Nevertheless, it is difficult to anticipate the dissimilarity of the survey variables because this number might be huge (e.g., lying in the hundreds). The variation thus differs from one estimate to the next. Because the sample size still needs to be decided, it is good to think more practically. For example, if any estimates by domains are not needed, this suggests that one can be satisfied with a smaller sample size, which is rarely the case. The estimates usually are desired by gender and/or age group, and/or education, and/or region, for example. This means that each such category should have enough respondents. As a result, the overall sample size required increases.

It often is asked what the minimum required number of respondents really is in any domain category. This cannot be properly answered, but this author has heard the number 30 as a rule of thumb. If using this number, you will be responsible for the results. This means that if there are 10 domain categories in a small-scale survey used for estimation, then the sample size could be 300 respondents. If the missingness rate is 50%, the minimum gross sample size would be 600. This number was the minimum at the municipality level in the Southern Finland Grid-based Survey (Laaksonen et al., 2015).

Design effects will be considered to some extent in all the future chapters, particularly in Chap. 14—the analysis chapter. The present chapter ends with an example that illustrates the different components of the DEFF in the context of PISA. The example also includes stratification.

Example 5.3 Components of the Design Effect for the Variable 'Plausible Value of Science Literacy' in PISA, 2015

This example is calculated from the final micro data of the 2015 PISA. The two missingness DEFF components (i.e., ineligibility and unit non-response) therefore cannot be included, but, on the other hand, we have included stratification.

Table 5.4 includes the averages of the science literacy scores, with four alternative options and all the methods together:

- SRS = without any survey instruments, thus assuming that the sample is drawn by simple random sampling, and the respondents were selected accordingly
- Stratum = only stratification has been considered, no weights or clusters
- Cluster = only school clusters have been included
- Weight = only student weights are included
- All = all instruments (i.e., strata, clusters, and weights) are included in the analysis; therefore, the results are the best ones

The means of the results do not vary much. The reason is that the sampling is not far from being proportional in these countries. The standard errors vary more. As can be seen, this is largely because of clustering. Using design effects, DEFFs, it is easier to see the effects. This is shown in the second table, Table 5.5.

Table 5.4 Plausible value of science literacy, means and standard errors, by four alternative methods and all methods for some countries in the 2015 PISA

	Number of respondents	SRS		Stratum		Cluster		Weight		All methods	
		Mean	Std. error	Mean	Std. error	Mean	Std. error	Mean	Std. error	Mean	Std error
Germany	6504	512.2	1.18	512.2	1.18	512.2	4.21	509.1	1.23	509.1	4.31
Estonia	5587	535.6	1.14	535.6	1.11	535.6	3.18	534.2	1.25	534.2	2.82
Finland	5882	531.6	1.20	531.6	1.19	531.6	2.38	530.7	1.24	530.7	2.41
Japan	6647	538.8	1.10	538.8	1.08	538.8	4.46	538.4	1.12	538.4	4.41
Korea	5581	515.2	1.22	515.2	1.16	515.2	3.80	515.8	1.24	515.8	3.14
Russia	6036	486.4	1.01	486.4	0.97	486.4	2.94	486.6	1.13	486.6	2.66
Sweden	5458	493.0	1.33	493.0	1.31	493.0	3.20	493.4	1.40	493.4	3.13
USA	5712	495.8	1.25	495.8	1.24	495.8	3.51	496.2	1.35	496.2	3.67

Table 5.5 Design effects calculated from the standard errors of Table 5.4 for plausible values of science literacy in the 2015 PISA—Countries sorted by last column

	Number of strata	DEFF stratum	DEFF cluster	DEFF weight	DEFF all
Finland	10	0.99	3.95	1.07	4.05
Sweden	7	0.97	5.80	1.11	5.56
Estonia	3	0.94	7.74	1.19	6.08
Korea	4	0.90	9.66	1.03	6.58
Russia	42	0.92	8.47	1.24	6.94
USA	9	0.99	7.92	1.16	8.65
Germany	1	1.00	12.62	1.08	13.24
Japan	4	0.96	16.46	1.03	16.09

Table 5.6 Intraclass correlations for the same countries as in Tables 5.4 and 5.5 for plausible values of science literacy of the 2015 PISA

Country	Intraclass correlation
Finland	0.095
Sweden	0.177
Estonia	0.207
United States	0.210
Russia	0.240
Korea	0.272
Japan	0.483
Germany	0.510

The design effect is the ratio of the two variances, so the denominator is the variance of simple random sampling. The variance is the square of the standard error. The DEFFs of Table 5.5 thus are calculated from the standard errors of Table 5.4. This ensures that the DEFFs are correct, which is not necessarily true with all software. Now, we can see from the first column that the number of strata for Germany is one, which automatically gives the stratum $DEFF = 1$. In fact, Germany used several strata, but the data are not available in the public dataset. Thus, it is not possible to calculate the perfect DEFF in Germany; it would be expected that its overall DEFF is somewhat too large. This is because stratification most often reduces the DEFF, and it improves the accuracy, as occurs for all the other countries shown in Table 5.5. This is just one reason to use explicit stratification and to construct the strata so that they are more homogeneous than the full data without stratification.

Now, we can see clearly that the DEFFs because of clustering are the highest, particularly in Japan and Germany. By contrast, the Finnish DEFF because of clustering is relatively low. See Fig. 5.1 and Table 5.1, which show the same thing for Germany and Finland. This also indicates how large the differences are between schools in these countries. The DEFF because of unequal weights is highest for Russia. This means that the weights vary more than in the other countries listed in the table. The variation of weights depends on both the varying inclusion probabilities and the weighting adjustments; however, we do not go into detail about them.

To clarify the cluster effect with intraclass correlation, we present Table 5.6. This table tells quite a similar story to that shown in the DEFF Cluster column of

Table 5.5, but the order of the countries is not the same. The intraclass correlations are much higher here than when the clusters are small areas, as in the ESS, for example.

References

ESS Sampling Guidelines. (2017). Retrieved December 2017, from http://www.europeansocialsurvey.org/docs/round8/methods/ESS8_sampling_guidelines.pdf

Gabler, S., Häder, S., & Lahiri, P. (1999). A model based justification of Kish's formula for design effects for weighting and clustering. *Survey Methodology, 25*(1), 105–106.

Kish, L. (1994): Multipopulation survey designs: Five types with seven shared aspects. *International Statistical Review, 62*, 167–186.

Laaksonen, S., & Heiskanen, M. (2014). Comparison of three modes for a crime victimization survey. *Journal of Survey Statistics and Methodology, 2*(4), 459–483.

Laaksonen, S., Kemppainen, T., Kortteinen, M., Vaattovaara, M., Stjernberg, M., & Lönnqvist, H. (2015). *Tackling city-regional dynamics in a survey using grid sampling.* Survey Research Association. Retrieved June 2017, from http://www.surveymethods.org

Shackman, G. (2001). *Sample size and design effect.* Technical report, Albany Chapter of American Statistical Association. Retrieved May 2017, from http://faculty.smu.edu/slstokes/stat6380/deff%20doc.pdf

Sampling Design Data File

6

Designs in nature

The term 'sampling design (data) file' is not commonly used in survey sampling literature. The methodology behind it is used, but only implicitly. An exception is in the ESS sampling (ESS Sampling Guidelines, 2017) in which it was implemented for the first time in 2002. This chapter makes use of this experience, which has been described at a more general level by Laaksonen (2015).

The explicit determination of the sampling design file facilitates many things in survey practice, and also gives a clear target for the two major parts of a survey—that is, sampling and fieldwork.

© Springer International Publishing AG, part of Springer Nature 2018
S. Laaksonen, *Survey Methodology and Missing Data*,
https://doi.org/10.1007/978-3-319-79011-4_6

6.1   Principles of the Sampling Design Data File

The sampling design data file (SDDF) consists of all the gross sample units, and its variables include those that allow the creation of sampling weights and the analysis of survey quality. It is possible to complete the file after the fieldwork. Its most important characteristics, including sampling design variables and weights, ultimately will be merged with the real survey variables at the respondent level, then one is ready to start the survey analysis. Scheme 6.1 explains this situation.

This scheme focusses on the survey weights of the respondents, which are created from the sampling design file. We have already considered the basic weights in Chap. 4. Chapter 8 continues by considering more advanced weights. The input of all the survey weights is the sampling design data file. Scheme 6.1 does not include all the important variables that can be taken from the SDDF at the same time as the weights are merged with the survey's plain variables. These variables, and others, could be considered for merging:

- Other survey instrument variables, such as the codes of the strata and PSU clusters; if the data will be made public, these codes should be anonymous in the public file.
- If a particular SDDF variable is not included in the survey questionnaire, it can be used in the survey analysis; examples are gender, age, geographical variable, education, dwelling composition, housing characteristics.

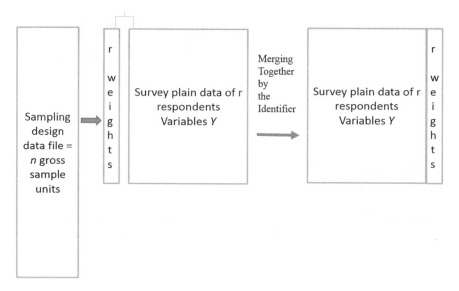

Scheme 6.1 The role of the SDDF in obtaining the survey data used in the analysis

The following is a list of the variables that should or could be included in the sampling design file, together with good meta data:

1. Include probabilities for each stage.
2. Other variables directly related to the sampling design (the PSU, which can be a cluster or an individual, explicit stratum, implicit stratum).
3. Outcome of the survey fieldwork (e.g., respondent, ineligible, non-respondent).
4. Macro auxiliary variables, statistics for the small area levels such as PSU, stratum, or grid square, statistics (e.g., population by gender or by age group or by degree of education).
5. Macro auxiliary variables—for example, rates for small areas like those listed in point 4: percentage divorced, percentage of undercrowding, percentage with 2 or more cars, percentage of owner occupation, percemtage of unemployed, percentage of long-term unemployed, percentage involved in social renting, percentage of highly educated.
6. Micro auxiliary variables for individuals and their groups, such as gender, age, degree of education, regional or areal codes, language, ethnic or other background, dwelling size, number of children, civil status, employment status, register income group (see also Sect. 2.5).

The auxiliary variables described in (4), (5), and (6) have the following roles:

- Quality analysis of the survey data themselves
- Quality analysis of the data-collection process
- Identification of reasons for non-responses and ineligibility
- Computation of ineligibility rate = number of ineligibles/gross sample size
- Computation of response rates = number of respondents/(gross sample size − ineligibles)
- Use of the data for weighting and reweighting
- Use of the data for checking and other editing
- Use of the data for imputations

We look at the details of these methodologies in the remaining chapters. At the end of this chapter we comment on the test sampling design data.

The minimum requirements are satisfied for the test file, SDDF because there are three inclusion probabilities, even though the probabilities are equal to one for the SRS domain (i.e., for strata 3–8). The file therefore gives the opportunity to calculate the final inclusion probabilities and the weights at the same time. Note, of course, that the stratum variable is needed as well.

The second minimum requirement is the fieldwork outcome variable, OUTCOME, which indicates those respondents whose weights are needed when two files are merged. The test SDDF includes a good number of micro auxiliary variables. Their quality and number are better than in ordinary surveys.

The file is without macro auxiliary variables, but the most important population figures by strata can be estimated via inclusion probabilities, as described in Chap. 4.

If the file does not include any other auxiliary variables, the advanced weights cannot be created. Thus, the basic weights are then the only weights that can be used. Therefore, these are correct if missingness is ignorable, or if the missingness mechanism is MARS (see Chap. 4); however, this rarely occurs in real life.

The test file is partially artificial, but it corresponds well to an ordinary ESS country file. Its auxiliary variables usually are derived from the proper survey, but most of them can be found from good registers or other administrative records, in particular. Among others, the following registers—the number of which is growing—can be used in the so-called register countries:

- Central population registers, which are the main source for the sampling variables but also include many personal, dwelling, and housing variables
- Employment registers
- Job seekers registers
- Formal education registers, which includes those who have been educated in the country
- Tax registers, which include income variables, although there are some constraints on their use for reasons of confidentiality

6.2   Test Data Used in Several Examples in this Book

This micro data file was created from the micro file of Round 6 of the European Social Survey (ESS). Its purpose is to illustrate an average country in this round based on several aspects:

- The target population size is 19.9 million
- The response rate is 51.6%
- The ineligibility rate is 8.3%

The sampling follows a stratified two-domain design so that the design for six urban strata is simple random sampling (target population 9.7 million); however, the design for the two rural areas is three-stage cluster sampling (target population 10.2 million). These two designs are the most common in the ESS, and some countries are even using a stratified two-domain design like this. We use the term 'test file' in the examples.

The pattern for the auxiliary variables is better than in any ESS country. Table 6.1 gives the list of the variables in the test file. These include sampling design variables and fieldwork outcomes that are mandatory, as well as a good number of micro and macro auxiliary variables that are used for reweighting, in particular (see Chap. 8). It is beneficial to recognize that the second- and third-stage inclusion probabilities are equal to one in the simple random sampling (SRS) domain. The sum of all margins = 19,906,273, which is the target population size (see Table 6.2).

Table 6.1 The micro variables of the SDDF of the test file

Variable	Label	Categories
IDNO	Respondent's identification number	Unique
PROB1	Inclusion probability[a] for the first sampling stage (small area)	Continuous
PROB2[b]	Inclusion probability for the second sampling stage (dwelling)	Continuous
PROB3[c]	Inclusion probability for the third sampling stage (individual aged over 15)	Continuous
age	Age of sampled individual	
citizen	Domestic versus other citizenship	2
common_law_marriage	Common law marriage	2
education	Education level	6
gndr	Gender of sampled individual	2
hinctnta	Household's total net income, all sources	10
maritalb	Legal marital status, post-coded	
member15	Household members below age 15	Count
members15Plus	Household members aged over 15	
outcome	Fieldwork outcome (1 = respondent, 2 = non-respondent, 3 = ineligible)	3
PSU	Primary sampling unit	
stratum	Explicit strata	8
agegroup	15–29, 30–44, 45–59, 60–74, 75+	5

[a]Inclusion probabilities: PROB1 = PPS without replacement
[b]PROB2 = simple random sampling in cluster domain; PROB2 = 1 in SRS domain
[c]PROB3 = simple random sampling in cluster domain; PROB3 = 1 in SRS domain

Table 6.2 The macro auxiliary variables (calibration margins) of the test file

Macro variable	Number of categories
Stratum	8
Gender	2
Age group	5
Education	6 education levels
Income	10 deciles

Table 6.3 illustrates the test file further, and we have included 20 random observations from the file. That is, the variables needed for calculating the sampling weights and the identifier needed to merge the respondents with the plain data. Some, but not all, of the auxiliary variables to be used for missingness analysis and for adjusted weights also are here.

Table 6.3 The first 20 observations of the test sampling design data file in the cluster domain

	Respondents with ID number	Inclusion probability of first stage, PSU	Inclusion probability of second stage, dwelling	Inclusion probability of third stage, individual	Explicit stratum	Outcome	Gender	People living in household	Legal marital status	Education level	Members below age 15
1	5053	0.05187397	0.01039591	0.33333333	1	2	1	3	1	3	0
2	3331	0.02356752	0.05287508	0.5	2	2	2	5	1	5	3
3	6153	0.00380864	0.14159292	0.5	1	1	2	2	1	5	0
4	2441	0.00256831	0.20997375	0.5	1	2	1	2	6	4	0
5	574	0.01312915	0.04107479	0.33333333	1	2	1	4	6	3	1
6	7265	0.02356752	0.05287508	0.5	2	1	2	2	1	6	0
7	3264	0.03046242	0.01770303	0.33333333	1	1	1	5	1	7	3
8	739	0.01468856	0.03671409	0.33333333	1	2	2	3	6	5	0
9	4270	0.06698721	0.00805045	0.33333333	1	2	1	4	6	3	1
10	4249	0.02832104	0.01904157	0.5	1	1	1	4	1	7	2
11	6794	0.01312595	0.09493671	1	2	1	2	1	4	7	0
12	7776	0.47625193	0.00261655	1	2	1	2	1	5	2	0
13	8002	0.31271783	0.00172448	0.5	1	2	2	2	1	2	0
14	5325	0.02799747	0.01926164	0.5	1	2	2	2	1	3	0
15	3487	0.09772151	0.00551851	0.5	1	2	2	2	1	3	0
16	6246	0.00152795	0.35294118	1	1	1	1	1	6	7	0
17	1699	0.02542467	0.02121078	0.5	1	3	2	2	1	7	0
18	6833	0.09753081	0.01277683	0.5	2	1	2	2	1	3	0
19	5994	0.01375831	0.03919647	0.5	1	2	2	2	6	6	0
20	1196	0.04804061	0.01122544	0.5	1	2	1	2	6	3	0

References

ESS Sampling Guidelines. (2017). Retrieved November 2017, from http://www.europeansocialsurvey.org/docs/round8/methods/ESS8_sampling_guidelines.pdf

Laaksonen, S. (2015). Sampling design data file. *Survey Statistician, 72*, 61–66.

Missingness, Its Reasons and Treatment

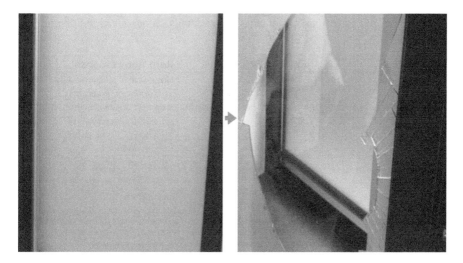

This reason is not common in surveys

We have described many things relating to missing values in the previous chapters but have not described them precisely. The focus of this chapter is how to deal with missing values. The outcomes of this are then used in the remaining chapters, particularly as they concern reweighting, imputation, and survey analysis. It therefore would be good to come back and look at this chapter if something is not clear when one is reading the later chapters. The examples here are mainly taken from the ESS, which includes missingness information. They thus have been calculated from the fieldwork data available. Other considerations and examples can be found in many sources and often in conference papers. We do not give many references, nonetheless it is good, for example, to compare the two ESSs (the European Statistical System, abbreviated to ESS). Stoop (2017) makes a useful comparison between the two. Gideon (2012) is also a good book to read, particularly the chapter

© Springer International Publishing AG, part of Springer Nature 2018   99
S. Laaksonen, *Survey Methodology and Missing Data*,
https://doi.org/10.1007/978-3-319-79011-4_7

by Stoop and Harrison (2012). Koch, Halbherr, Stoop, and Kappelhof (2004) focus on quality comparisons.

The methodologies for handling unit non-responses and item non-responses do not differ much from each other, but there may be substantial differences in what one should do after applying them. Thus, the analysis itself, in both cases, should be done roughly as set out in the following:

1. Investigate the reasons for missing values.
2. Create indicator variables for unit responses or item responses.
3. Calculate all the missingness rates, by reasons and by domains (background variables).
4. Report and interpret the results and publish the main findings of them.
5. Try to do everything better, if possible, in the next survey.

Nevertheless, there are many differences in the details, as described in Scheme 7.1.

Reason	Unit Non-response	Item Non-response
Non-contact due to incorrect data	Possible	Not possible since the data are for the respondents
Inability to answer correctly	It is possible because general disability	A correct answer might be difficult to get to all questions, also because he/she does not understand the question.
Hard refusal	Some are not willing to participate in any surveys, or not in this particular one since its topic is, e.g., not good.	Not possible
Soft refusal	Some answer most questions and they classifed as respondents	Some answers are missing, for various reasons, including a bad/unpleasant question
Screening question	Not any problem if the survey well designed	It is possible that some answers of the second part are missing that lead to some bias
Lost answer	Possible	Should not be possible concerning a particular question
Other or unknown reason	Possible	Should not be possible concerning a particular question

Scheme 7.1 General framework for the reasons for non-responses and how to handle them

7.1   Reasons for Unit Non-response

It is difficult to know the real reason for non-responses or ineligibility in self-administered surveys (web or mail), but it should be possible to determine the reason in interviewing surveys. Naturally, the codes can show more or less detail. If a gross sample unit cannot be contacted directly or a proxy interviewee is used, it might be difficult to know whether the unit is a non-respondent or is ineligible. The ESS can code unit missingness with three possible codes, as shown in Table 7.1. The main part of this table is from the third round when the response rates were higher than in the later rounds. This latter point can be found from the table's last column, which includes the response rate of a later round (i.e., either Round 6 or 7).

The response rates have declined in most of the countries that have participated in the survey (e.g., Estonia, Sweden, Slovenia, Ukraine, the United Kingdom, Germany, and Poland). This is an unfortunate tendency. Luckily, the rate has increased in a few countries (e.g., Spain, Switzerland, and France).

Table 7.1   Response rates and reasons for unit non-responses in some countries of ESS, Round 3

	Ineligibility rate (%)	Response rate (%)	Noncontact rate (%)	Refusal rate (%)	Response rate in a later round
Austria	1.7	62.5	7.8	28.6	51.9
Belgium	4.9	61.5	7.1	22.7	57.4
Denmark	6.4	65.1	5.6	23.9	51.9
Finland	1.5	70.8	2.8	21.2	62.9
France	7.1	44.2	12.1	39.5	51.6
Germany	7.2	52.7	6.2	27.4	31.4
Hungary	13.5	70.3	6.0	16.0	64.2
Ireland	8.1	62.5	9.5	22.3	60.7
Netherlands	3.0	64.5	2.7	28.0	58.6
Norway	3.4	66.2	2.1	25.5	54.3
Poland	3.8	74.4	2.3	18.2	66.0
Portugal	6.4	70.9	2.8	20.0	77.1
Slovenia	6.7	70.2	10.2	15.3	52.3
Spain	7.8	56.1	13.6	18.6	70.8
Sweden	2.3	66.5	4.3	22.6	50.5
Switzerland	6.5	47.1	2.9	39.7	52.7
United Kingdom	7.9	51.1	8.0	34.0	40.3
Estonia	12.7	79.5	5.1	11.4	60.0
Slovakia	4.6	63.4	1.6	21.6	74.1
Ukraine	0	66.6	6.3	16.1	59.1

Table 7.2 Possible codes for item non-responses

Reason	Positive code	Negative code
Respondent refused to answer	7 or 77 or 777	−1
Don't know	8 or 88 or 888 or 8888	−2
No answer	9 or 99 or 999	−3
Missing for other reasons	6 or 66 or 666	−4
Respondent not able to give a correct answer	5 or 55	−5
Question does not concern the respondent	3 or 33	−6
Not possible, or does not exist, or not applicable	6666	−9

7.2 Coding of Item Non-responses

It is not easy to know the reason for item non-responses in a self-administered survey, but it is quite easy if alternative reasons for non-responses are given as a category in the questionnaire. These alternatives should not be 'too easily' used. This is therefore a big issue in all survey questionnaires. This chapter does not address this problem, but it does discuss alternative codings. The list in Table 7.2 includes most of the commonly used alternatives, and two types of code for each. The negative codes are easier to recognize, but they are rarely used. Most of the positive codes given are the same as those used in the European Social Survey.

It is not good to include some of these codes in the questionnaire, thus they are given by the interviewer. She or he can include more codes too, as well as use textual coding that can later be coded in another way.

In what follows we are not concerned about the reasons for non-responses, but consider each missing value as belonging to just one category. This also includes completely empty cells.

7.3 Missingness Indicator and Missingness Rate

In the case of *unit missingness,* two missingness indicators can be created:

1. The *non-response indicator*, which takes the value 0 if the unit responds and the value 1 if the unit does not respond but belongs to the target population.
2. The *ineligibility indicator*, which takes the value 1 if the unit is ineligible, and the value 0 if the unit responds or does not respond.

These indicators can be considered as complements of each other in most cases, swapping the values 1 and 0. The first indicator is called the (unit) *response indicator*. The same label is sometimes given to the second case, where the zero category covers both the non-respondents and the ineligible units. This is the only option if there are difficulties in distinguishing between these two alternatives, which occurs if the unit cannot be contacted at all.

In the case of *item missingness*, only one type of indicator is needed, although this might be determined from either the positive or the negative direction. We present it from the positive direction here.

3. The *item response indicator*, which takes the value 1 if a valid answer to the question y is obtained, and the value 0 if the respondent does not give a valid answer. Note that this indicator concerns only the unit respondents. It means that the complete missingness indicators are a sort of sum of both indicators.

These missingness indicators can be used when calculating the missingness or response rates, respectively. The most important rate is the average of the indicator, which indicates the relative frequency of either missingness or response. These rates can be calculated from the background variables that have no missingness or only minor missingness.

Figure 7.1 is an example of item non-responses for 20 ESS countries (Round 7). The variable is 'Household's total net income, all sources'. The item non-response for this variable is relatively high, which is the reason for presenting this example. Country differences are fairly clear as well. The item response rate varies from 71% in Hungary to 95% in Norway. The rate has usually, but not always, grown from round to round.

Before proceeding to other examples, we present a general framework for analyzing missingness, whether this concerns items or units, in Scheme 7.2. The main objectives of this framework are:

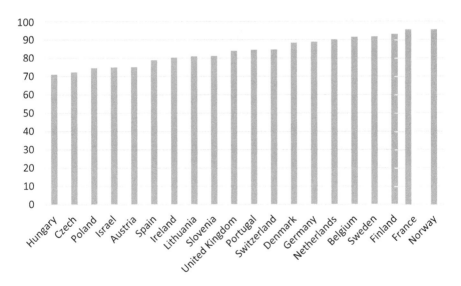

Fig. 7.1 Item response rates for income in 20 ESS countries, Round 7

1.	Calculate the one-dimensional rates of each indicator
2.	Calculate rates by categories of auxiliary variables including variables without missingness and variables with minor missingness
3.	Estimate the multivariate response propensity model in which the response indicator is the dependent variable and the explanatory variables and their combinations are selected from the auxiliary variables
4.	Estimate the predicted values, called response propensities, from the response propensity model

Scheme 7.2 A framework for analyzing missingness

Table 7.3 Unit response rates by domains in the test data

Domain	Observations	Mean (%)
Cluster	3176	49.5
SRS	1422	42.5

1. To understand the missingness of a survey
2. To learn from this about missingness for future surveys
3. To exploit the missingness information for post-survey adjustments of this survey

For more detail, see Chap. 8 for unit non-response and Chap. 12 for item non-response.

We now concentrate on response indicators because they are more easily used in the next steps. Thus, we take the response indicator and calculate its averages for some auxiliary variables. First, the response rates for two test data domains are presented, SRS and Cluster, in Table 7.3. The response rate of the three-stage cluster design data is higher than that of the simple random design. Both rates are fairly low, but lower rates are found when calculating the rates by auxiliary categories. We do not present separate figures by domain but only figures for the whole dataset. These results are shown in the graphs in Fig. 7.2.

The unit response rates vary fairly substantially by both education and age group, but vary less by marital status. Note that the counts of some categories of marital status are small, particularly the count for registered civil unions. The rates for education are fairly similar to those in many other surveys: those with little education are often the worst respondents, whereas the highly educated are the best. We give another example in Fig. 7.3 based on a real survey in which the categories are about the same as in Fig. 7.2. This figure clearly illustrates how the rates vary by survey mode, with the highest differences being when using the web mode.

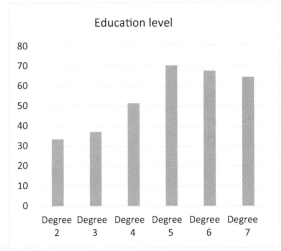

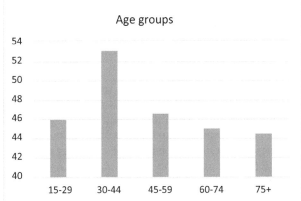

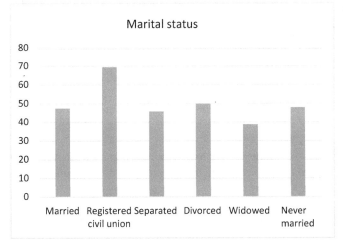

Fig. 7.2 Unit response rates by 'Education' level, 'Age group', and 'Marital status' in the test data

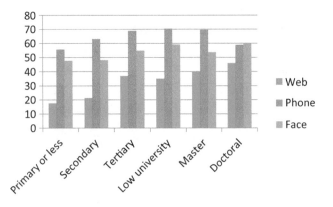

Fig. 7.3 Unit response rates by education and survey modes in the Finnish Security Survey (Laaksonen & Heiskanen, 2014)

7.4   Response Propensity Models

A *response propensity model* is usually a binary regression model in which the link function is a logit, probit, log–log, or complementary log–log function. Refer to the graphs in Fig. 7.4.

Another alternative is to build a *classification tree model* with similar variables, but we do not go into detail here about this model. Instead, we describe and apply response propensity models with the two most common links—that is, the logit and probit functions. These can be implemented in the same way as any other statistical model, trying to find the best explanatory variables for the response indicator, both additively and with interactions. The first purpose is to obtain the model that best illustrates which variables explain the response behaviour. The second purpose is to predict the probabilities as effectively as possible; these predictions are then utilized in both reweighting (Chap. 8) and imputation (Chap. 12).

Figure 7.4 does not include the log–log function, which is the mirror curve to the *Cloglog* function. Logit and probit are symmetric, whereas the other two are asymmetric. A linear function may give unacceptable estimated probabilities (i.e., probabilities that are negative or greater than one). We find the curves to be fairly linear within the interval (0.3, 0.7), but far from linear at the margins. Thus, the linear function does not work at all in the marginal areas (i.e., where the probabilities are small or large).

The estimates of the response propensity model can be interpreted in the usual way, but it is also good to calculate the *estimated response probabilities*, which are also called the *response propensities* or the *propensities* or the *propensity scores*. We begin to illustrate these models and scores using two examples, one for *item response* (Example 7.1) and the other for *unit response* (Example 7.2). Both examples continue from previous examples.

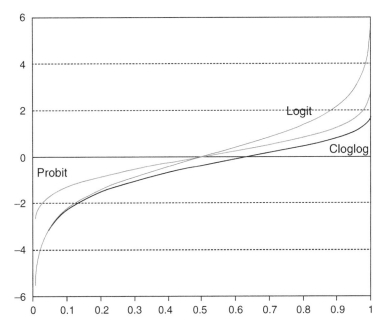

Fig. 7.4 Logit, probit, and complementary log–log (Cloglog) link functions for binary regression models

Example 7.1 Propensity Model for Item Response
This example uses the same ESS data as shown in Fig. 7.1, which gives the response rates for 20 countries for income. We move forward by estimating a *logit* regression for this response indicator, choosing the number of explanatory variables in the model. The best variables are those without missing values. There are not many of these, but, in addition to country, the following can be used:

– Age
– Gender
– Household size
– Interviewing time

On the other hand, it is also possible to test variables with missingness that is minor. We find these three variables:

– Happiness (item non-response rate = 0.3%)
– Marital status (1.0%)
– Subjective income—feeling about household's income nowadays (0.9%)

(continued)

Example 7.1 (continued)

If all three variables are included in the model, we lose 2% of the observations. Thus, we can analyze the item response for 'Objective' income more or less completely.

The estimation of the model indicates that only one explanatory variable is not significant. This is 'Subjective income'. It means that the item non-responses for it does not depend on Subjective income. We use this information in the example in Chap. 11 (see 'Aggregate imputation' in Sect. 11.4, including Table 11.1 and Fig. 11.1).

By contrast, the other explanatory variables are significant. We do not present all the details of this result, but some of the main ones are as follows:

- Males were able to communicate the income of their households better than females (odds ratio = 1.12)
- Those in the middle age groups gave their income much more often than those in the oldest and youngest age groups
- When the household size increases, item non-responses decline
- It was most difficult to get a response on income from those in the 'Never married' group, but the differences between the marital status groups are not large
- Happiness and Interviewing time are positively related to the responses on income

Example 7.2 Response Propensity Probit Model of the Finnish Security Survey

This second example is for *unit response*. It comes from the Finnish Security Survey, which includes a good number of auxiliary variables from two registers—the central population register and the formal education register. Figure 7.3 includes the response rates by formal education for the three survey modes. We do not present the respective estimates from the multivariate model: They are not exactly the same, but neither are they significantly different. We also do not present the regional estimates because these are not interesting for outsiders. Table 7.4 does not include age, either, but these probit estimates are given in a separate graph in Fig. 7.5. This is more illustrative than the four age estimates only. We use the four age variables, age itself, and three of its powers in the model. One can see what this means graphically in Fig. 7.4. The following variables are not included—Living area, Formal education, and Age—however, Age is included in Fig. 7.5.

The categories are compared against one category. If the probit estimate is greater than 0.1, it is roughly significant. None of the estimates are strongly

(continued)

Example 7.2 (continued)
significant for gender, but the differences by mode are still interesting. Partnership is a specially created variable that is rarely used and that categorizes marriage into four groups. This is done because one marriage variable is too heterogeneous. Since the register includes the wedding year, this re-categorization is possible, with the number of years since the wedding (Old, Medium and Recent) being added, while people with more than one marriage are included in their own group. We would have been happy to categorize the group of single people as well, but this was not possible with this register.

The differences between the modes are evident in several categories of Table 7.4, but they are clearer for age, as demonstrated in Fig. 7.5. To understand the y-axis, it should be noted that probit = 0 corresponds to the estimated response probability of 50%. This scale of the y-axis is good for a graphical representation, whereas a linear scale could cause misunderstanding.

We present more examples in Chap. 8, where we apply response propensity modelling for post-survey adjusted weights. In that chapter we estimate the predicted values for each respondent from this model and use these in reweightings.

Table 7.4 Probit estimates of the unit response model for the Finnish Security Survey

Auxiliary variable	Web	Phone	Face-to-face
Male vs. female	−0.0565	−0.0256	0.1038
Native language			
Finnish vs. Russian	0.2599	0.2319	−0.1071
Other vs. Russian	−0.1135	−0.1085	−0.3186
Partnership			
Widowed vs. old marriage	−0.2224	0.1060	−0.1071
Single vs. old marriage	−0.3414	−0.2130	−0.3115
Many vs. old marriage	−0.1236	−0.2956	−0.1181
Recent vs. old marriage	−0.3011	−0.0946	−0.2245
Medium vs. old marriage	−0.1526	−0.1472	0.1363
Children			
No children vs. 1+ children	0.1835	−0.1360	−0.0015
Housing			
1 room vs. 4+ rooms	−0.0427	−0.4151	−0.1458
2–3 rooms vs. 4+ rooms	−0.0374	−0.1151	0.0062

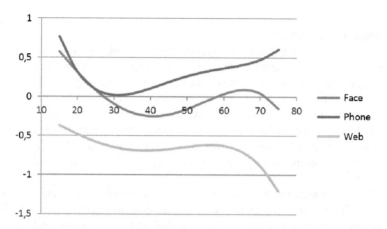

Fig. 7.5 Probit estimates by age for the three survey modes in the Finnish Security Survey (Laaksonen & Heiskanen, 2014)

References

Gideon, L. (Ed.). (2012). *Handbook of survey methodology for the social sciences*. New York: Springer.

Koch, A., Halbherr, V., Stoop, I., & Kappelhof, J. (2004). *Assessing ESS sample quality by using external and internal criteria*. Working Paper. Retrieved January 2017, from https://www. researchgate.net/publication/316043128_Assessing_ESS_sample_quality_by_using_external_ and_internal_criteria

Laaksonen, S., & Heiskanen, M. (2014). Comparison of three modes for a victimization survey. *Journal of Survey Statistics and Methodology, 2*(4), 459–483.

Stoop, I. (2017). *The other ESS: The European social survey and the European statistical system*. New Techniques and Technologies for Statistics (NTTS). Retrieved December 2017, from https://www.conference-service.com/NTTS2017/documents/agenda/data/abstracts/abstract_ 238.html

Stoop, I., & Harrison, E. (2012). Classification of surveys. In L. Gideon (Ed.), *Handbook of survey methodology for the social sciences*. Heidelberg: Springer.

Weighting Adjustments Because of Unit Non-response

8

Weights and curves in nature

Advance Reading
It is good to understand the following methodologies and tools before going into this chapter, in addition to the terms and concepts of Chap. 2:

– Chapter 4: Sampling Principles, including inclusion probabilities, missingness mechanisms
– Chapter 5: Design Effects at the Sampling Phase, including design-based weighting from which we continue in this chapter to create better weights, called reweights

(continued)

- Chapter 6: Sampling Design Data File, including auxiliary variables; the new weights are created from this file or its supplements
- Chapter 7: Missingness, Its Reasons and Treatment gives a priori information for reweighting

8.1   Actions of Weighting and Reweighting

Weighting and reweighting can be considered to cover the following seven actions:

1. Sampling design before the fieldwork
2. Weights for the gross-sample (n units) using (1), the result being the 'design weights'
3. Creation of the sampling design data file (SDDF) before and after the fieldwork
4. Computation of 'basic weights' for the net sample or for the respondents (r units), assuming missing at random under sampling design (MARS)
5. Reweighting assuming MAR(c): specification, estimation, outputs, checking trustworthiness
6. Estimation: point-estimates, variance estimation = sampling variance + variance because of missingness
7. Critically look at the results, including benchmarking these against recent results (how plausible are they?)

Toward Reweighting
Reweighting starts from the valid basic weights that need to be improved so that the estimates will be less biased than those obtained by the basic weights. Usually, the aim is not to improve all estimates but at a minimum some key estimates. The other estimates are often improved at the same time, but not all of them may be. As it is recognized, good auxiliary data are necessary to make reweighting successful. If you have a small amount of good auxiliary variables, you cannot do much. So, you must work actively with an auxiliary data service during the survey process. This may require resources but not as much as often thought. An important point is that auxiliary data are useful to include in the SDDF all the time during the survey process.

8.2   Introduction to Reweighting Methods

We do not try to explain all the possible reweighting methods because there are too many of them. Yet, it is difficult to recognize any specific method given that so many different terms are used. This book is no exception. The terms here are rather new but, in the author's opinion, they are clear and logical.

Therefore, we concentrate on the two core methodology families: (1) response propensity weighting and (2) calibration weighting. Nevertheless, the strategy or framework here is broader than is usually presented because calibration can start either from basic weights or from response propensity weights. If the basic or other simple weights are used as the starting weights in the calibration, this method is known as '*pure calibration*'; this calibration the one that is most commonly used in practice. If the propensity weights are used, the strategy is known as '*joint propensity and calibration weighting*'; however, it is not necessary to use this term. The most important thing is to specify which weights are the starting weights for the calibration.

Because the simplest and most common calibration is post-stratification, we first describe its principles, and then present response propensity weighting. Finally, the methodology of calibration is described, one part of this being joint propensity and calibration weighting.

The purpose of calibration, in general, is to create weights that give certain benchmark values to macro auxiliary variables. If the benchmarks are true values, these 'estimates' are definitely correct. For example, if the population figures are correct after estimating by gender, age groups, and large regions, this increases confidence about the results. Naturally, these true values can only be achieved for those benchmarks; nothing is guaranteed for the other estimates, including the proper survey estimates. One common drawback is that these benchmarks are not true values but are approximations because true values are difficult to obtain. All weighting methods lead to some true (or nearly true) values—for example, the sum of the weights is (or should be) equal to the target population size. Accordingly, pure response propensity weighting gives true values by explicit strata or post-strata as well.

▶ **Real-Life Case**
Some statistics, such as the gender distribution, are well known. If a survey shows that there are 45% males and 55% females in the target population, and it is known as a fact that there are about as many males as females, it might be difficult to trust the survey at all. Calibration is useful here to give a valid gender share. Thus, this does not mean that all the other estimates automatically will be as correct. Similarly, some regional statistics might be relatively well known, and it may be good to calibrate for these estimates. Age group is also used as a benchmark in calibration. This is good, but age distribution is not as well known by ordinary people.

8.3   Post-stratification

Post-stratification is a basic calibration method that is useful to apply if there are population-level data (macro auxiliary data) that have not yet been utilized in the sampling design. This is often the case. The following are the targets:

- To reduce the bias because of frame error if the post-strata statistics (margins) are more correct than the initial ones; if an updated frame exists, this helps because it means that the frame error can be corrected to post-strata levels.
- To calibrate estimates at a more detailed level than initially, thus into post-strata levels.
- To reduce the bias because of unit non-responses, although this it is not automatically ensured.
- To reduce the sampling errors that occur if the post-strata are more homogeneous than the initial strata.

The best known paper on post-stratification is by Holt and Smith (1979), but it also would be good to read Smith's 1991 paper. All these targets definitely cannot be achieved but at least some should be reachable.

Post-stratification, unfortunately, is not simple because it is *conditional* on the initial sampling design. This means that there may be difficulties in computing appropriate post-stratified weights. A sizeable problem is often that the data are too few in some post-strata, which means that there is no opportunity to create a high number of post-strata. This is obviously the main reason why the other calibration methods, which we consider later in this chapter, have been developed. First, however, we explain how post-stratification can be implemented, or how to create the post-stratified sampling weights.

If the sampling design is *simple random sampling*, we can very flexibly create the post-stratified weights, provided that (1) the data file consists of one or more categorical variables with target population statistics that are available, and (2) the number of respondents is big enough, as required for ordinary stratification. The post-stratified weights have the same form as the stratified weights, that is,

$$w_k = \frac{N_g}{r_g}$$

where g is a post-stratum $g = 1, \ldots, G;$ the number of post-strata thus is G.

This method is often used even when it is not known how close to simple random sampling (SRS) the sampling design is. For example, when several respondents are obtained by computer-assisted interviewing (CATI) more or less randomly, the weights are calculated on the assumption that the respondents are selected randomly within post-strata. This very commonly is applied by market survey institutes that also decide the post-strata in advance and call them 'quotas'. Early-stage researchers act in a similar way when the target of generalising the results is imposed suddenly and enough data from the respondents are available; however, there is no proper sampling design. This gives some possibilities for estimation, but it is difficult to know how biased the estimates will be.

The Most Common Post-stratification

Most commonly, the sample is drawn by explicit stratification and with a certain allocation. The strata or *pre-strata* are symbolised by h. When the respondents are

known, problems with responses are found. For example, if the stratification is
regional, as is often the case, the basic weights adjust for regional representativeness,
not for anything else. Nevertheless, it may be found that females participate better
than males, and educated people better than those with less education. This may lead
to post-stratification, given that the target population statistics are available by the
same categories as in the survey data file. Table 8.1 illustrates the situation.

This is not the most common strategy because it is easier to create post-strata by
cross-classifying the pre-strata and post-strata. This is not necessary because they
can be created more flexibly, as we have done here. In this case it was found that the
non-response varies greatly by the two education categories in pre-stratum 'Region
1', whereas gender is the best auxiliary variable in 'Region 2'. Finally, it was found
that both gender and education predict non-response in Region R, as shown.

Naturally, the other regional pre-strata may need different post-stratification. This
flexible strategy also allows one to use some initial pre-strata if it is believed that
there will be no benefit from post-strata. These requirements therefore are revealed
by the non-response analysis (see Chap. 7). The form of the post-stratified weights is
like that of the stratified weights:

$$w_k - \frac{N_{hg}}{r_{hg}}$$

More up-to-date target population figures 'N_{hg}' of the post-stratum cells 'hg' may
be available than the initial ones, and these should be used in this case (using the
updated frame population). The number of the respondents, r_{hg} is calculated from the
sampling data file. It is important to avoid post-strata that are too small because then,
in particular, the denominator is too small. There is no problem, however, in the case
when $N_{hg} = r_{hg} = 1$ because the weight is equal to one.

▶ **Special Post-stratification Case**
A special case occurs if explicit stratification is applied and, after the
fieldwork, outliers (extremely rich people or big businesses) are found in
one or more strata while the basic weights are large. This may have a
great impact on some estimates and mean that the initial stratum is not
homogeneous at all, thus such units are not in the correct stratum.

It is possible to try post-stratification so that such outliers are moved
into one special post-stratum and the others remain in the initial stratum,

Table 8.1 Example of post-stratification after regional pre-stratification when true values are
available by gender and education

	Initial stratification = Pre-stratification						
	Region 1		Region 2		Region R		
Post-strata within pre-strata	Less educated	More educated	Males	Females	Less educated males	Less educated females	More educated males and females

which is now classified as a post-stratum. The weights for the latter might be obtained easily by reducing N_h but the weights for the special post-stratum might be more difficult if no auxiliary information is available. Such information could be the number of extremely rich people or big businesses in this domain. Clearly, the minimum sampling weight is equal to one if only one outlier is found and is moved to the post-stratum. It follows that, in the case of several outliers derived from the same pre-stratum, the weights will be larger.

Example 8.1 Post-stratification in the Test Data of the SRS Domain
The SRS domain of the test data is applied in this example. The initial sampling design is stratified simple random sampling with six regional strata, or pre-strata. Using the ordinary procedure, the basic weights are computed. A decision is then made to improve the weights by post-stratification with one auxiliary variable, 'gender', because of a peculiar variation by gender that is shown in Table 8.2. Females respond better in all the strata other than stratum 11.

Post-strata are made to adjust for gender differences in particular. It is easy to create 2×6 post-strata as in Table 8.3, using the above formula. The first two digits of the post-stratum in the table refer to the pre-stratum, and the third digit refers to the gender (M = Male, F = Female).

There are enough respondents in each post-stratum, although not very many in some. In Table 8.4 we continue to analyse these weights against the basic weights.

The coefficient of variation (CV) of the initial weights is 42%, which is relatively high, but the CV for the post-stratified weights is higher, as expected. The analysis weights (relative weights) clearly can be compared, even though the absolute (amount) weights cannot be compared easily.

Table 8.2 Response rates by gender and six pre-strata of the SRS domain in the test data

Stratum	Gender	Observations	Response rate
10	Male	278	0.367
	Female	307	0.410
11	Male	83	0.470
	Female	80	0.363
12	Male	39	0.385
	Female	49	0.592
13	Male	87	0.402
	Female	81	0.481
14	Male	159	0.415
	Female	139	0.482
15	Male	59	0.407
	Female	61	0.557

Table 8.3   Twelve post-strata and their respective reweights

Post-strata	Respondents	Target population size	Post-stratified weights
10M	102	2,619,122	25,677.67
10F	126	2,587,880	20,538.73
11M	39	708,021	18,154.38
11F	29	742,842	25,615.24
12M	15	385,323	25,688.20
12F	29	397,965	13,722.93
13M	35	318,346	9095.60
13F	39	328,790	8430.51
14M	66	564,684	8555.82
14F	67	583,212	8704.66
15M	24	227,390	9474.58
15F	34	234,850	6907.35

Table 8.4   Basic and post-stratified sampling weights and their analysis weights on the same basis as in Table 8.3

Weight	Number of respondents	Mean	Coeff. of variation	Minimum	Maximum	Sum
Basic	605	16,030	42.2	7970	22,837	9,698,424
Basic analysis	605	1	42.2	0.50	1.43	605
Post-stratified	605	16,030	45.1	6907	25,688	9,698,424
Post-stratified analysis	605	1	45.1	0.43	1.60	605

Now, we can see that the ratio of the maximum to the minimum of the basic weights is 2.87 and that of post-stratified weights is 3.72. Such ratios are not problematic. For example, the ESS only takes care of the weights, so analysis weights above 4 are truncated into 4.0. This corresponds to the minimum weight $1/4 = 0.25$, but many ESS weights are below this limit. If we calculate the similar symmetric ratio, the acceptable ratio would be $4/0.25 = 16$, which is much higher than that of this post-stratified example.

8.4   Response Propensity Weighting

This weighting begins from the analysis of unit non-responses using the auxiliary variables available in the sampling design data file (SDDF). Chapter 7 considers the core principles of this analysis. First, the analysis is done for every single auxiliary variable, but then a multivariate response propensity model is estimated. The main goal of this model is to predict response behaviour so that the estimated response propensities are calculated in the output file, which includes the identity code of each respondent (see also Scheme 6.1, Chap. 6). The model itself takes advantage of the non-respondents as well. It is not clear whether ineligible units also should be included in the model, but this is not usually done.

To illustrate the modelling, we use the same test SDDF file as we did for post-stratification (thus the design is stratified SRS), and then we build the model. This SDDF is relatively good because there are more auxiliary variables than is usual in surveys. Table 8.5 gives the results when using the logit, or logistic regression, link. The data source for Table 8.5 and Fig. 8.1 is the test file in Chap. 6.

Table 8.5 does not give interactions, but we created the interaction between the degree of education and gender. This is illustrated in Fig. 8.1, which shows that the gender differences vary even though females replied slightly better in all groups. Some differences are small. The whole interaction term is significant, and we decided to keep it in the model used for reweighting. Note that it is not necessary to include only the significant auxiliary variables there because an insignificant variable has only a minor influence on the weight if the variables are categorical, as they are here. Continuous variables with outliers might be problematic, however.

It is useful to look at response propensities by population groups to understand their distribution. One appropriate way is to calculate their cumulative frequencies, as in Figure 8.2 (see also Table 8.5 and Fig. 8.1). The categories of this figure are the rounded estimated propensities (propensity scores) by 3%. The most dramatic

Table 8.5 Parameter estimates of the logistic regression model

Parameter		Estimate	Standard error	p-value
Intercept		1.31	0.2966	<0.0001
Gender	Male	−0.3824	0.1292	0.0031
	Female	0	0	
Education	Degree 2	−2.7349	0.2483	<0.0001
	Degree 3	−1.2829	0.2072	<0.0001
	Degree 4	−0.4259	0.2814	0.1301
	Degree 5	0.8743	0.3071	0.0044
	Degree 6	−0.1133	0.2623	0.6657
	Degree 7	0	0	
Citizen of the country	Yes	0.2044	0.3011	0.4972
	No	0	0	
Members of household	1	0.5642	0.2985	0.0587
	2	0.7966	0.2803	0.0045
	3	0.0772	0.2745	0.7785
	4	0.1825	0.2749	0.5068
	5	0	0	
Members below 15	0	−0.5185	0.1981	0.0089
	1	0	0	
Common law marriage	No	−0.5015	0.1392	0.0003
	Yes	0	0	

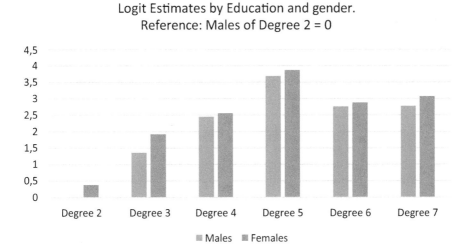

Fig. 8.1 Logit estimates of the response propensity model by education and gender

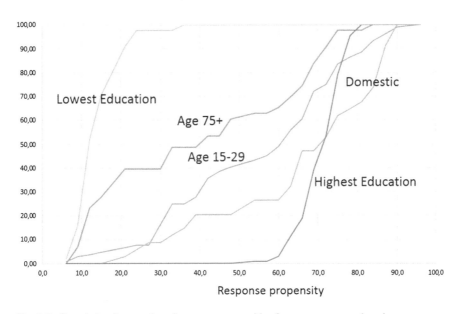

Fig. 8.2 Cumulative frequencies of response propensities for some response domains

difference is found between the lowest and highest degrees of education. The highest propensities of the lowest group are below 40%, whereas the lowest propensities of the highest education group are about 50%. The propensities of the other groups vary much more than these, beginning at about the same level as those of the lowest education group, but continuing to approximately the same level as those of the highest education group.

As soon as a survey data 'cleaner' knows the response behaviour well enough, it is possible to go forward to calculate the response propensity weights. This consists of the steps set out in the following for the case of a stratified simple random design.

Steps for Response Propensity Weighting When the Response Model Is Estimated (see e.g., Laaksonen, 2007; Laaksonen & Heiskanen, 2014)
This procedure is for stratified simple random sampling:

1. Assume that the response mechanism within each stratum is ignorable and that the initial (basic) weights thus have been calculated on this basis. These are available only for the respondents k and are symbolized by w_k.
2. Take those initial weights and divide them by the estimated response probability of each respondent, which is obtained from the probit or logit model and is symbolized by p_k.
3. Before going forward, check that the probabilities, p_k, are realistic—that is, that they are not too small (which might mean below 0.05), for instance. All probabilities are below one, naturally.
4. Given that the sum of the weights from the second step does not match the known population statistics by strata h, they are calibrated, or scaled, so that the sums are equal to the sums of the initial weights in each stratum. This is done by multiplying the weights from the second step by the ratio in each stratum h:

$$q_h = \frac{\sum_h w_k}{w/p}$$

5. It is also good to check these weights, comparing them against the basic weights and possibly against the post-stratified weights. If the weights are not plausible, the model should be revised.

Example 8.2 The Response Propensity Weighting of the Test SDDF Data
We continue from the SDDF with the stratified SRS domain. It is possible to continue both from the basic weights and from the post-stratified weights. We do both, using the response propensity model of Table 8.4 and Figs. 8.1 and 8.2. The results, including the earlier ones, are shown in Table 8.6.

We find that the variation of the weights increases after moving to more advanced weights, with one small exception. When using the post-stratified weights as the starting weights in the response propensity adjustment, the variation is about the same. It is interesting that these weights are somewhat smaller. The overall variation is fairly large; the reason for this lies in the big differences between the response propensities predicted by the significant auxiliary variables. It is expected that the new weights will give less biased estimates.

Table 8.6 Response propensity adjusted weights and their characteristics from the SDDF of the stratified SRS

Sampling weight	Respondents	Mean	Minimum	Maximum	Coeff. of variation	Sum
Ordinary/amount						
Basic	605	16,030	7970	22,838	42.2	9,698,424
Post-stratified	605	16,030	6907	25,688	45.1	9,698,424
Adjusted basic	605	16,030	3163	137,329	78.3	9,698,424
Adjusted post-stratified	605	16,030	2273	108,195	78.0	9,698,424
Analysis/relative						
Basic	605	1.0	0.5	1.4	42.2	605
Post-stratified	605	1.0	0.4	1.6	45.1	605
Adjusted basic	605	1.0	0.2	8.6	78.3	605
Adjusted post-stratified	605	1.0	0.1	6.7	78.0	605

▶ **Comment on Weighting with Response Homogeneity Groups**
The response propensity weights in this chapter are applied to each individual (i.e., every respondent). Naturally, because the auxiliary variables most often are categorical, some weights may be equal for more than one individual. As we have warned, continuous variables with outliers might be problematic and therefore should be avoided. Individual-level adjustments are naturally the most flexible and would be expected to be the best; however, the results are not very different if everything has been done at the aggregate level, given that the aggregates are not small.

Response propensities are applied even more often at the aggregate level than at the individual level. In this context, the aggregates are called the *response homogeneity groups, response homogeneity cells* or *adjustment cells*. In this case, the response propensities are constant for each such aggregate/cell. These constant propensities are either like the predicted values, as in the methodology, or they are empirical relative frequencies, which is simpler. We recommend the first option. The advantage of response homogeneity group weighting is that such aggregates are easier to get in many surveys. The aggregated response propensities are applied widely, including by Brick (2013), Brick and Jones (2008), Haziza and Lesage (2016), Ekholm and Laaksonen (1991), and Little (1986).

8.5   Comparisons of Weights in Other Surveys

To allow a greater understanding of these adjusted weights, we present two tables, Tables 8.7 and 8.8. The first (Table 8.7) is from the ESS, Round 6, when the post-stratified weights were published for the first time. This table thus provides an opportunity to compare these two weights. The analysis weights can be compared in a straightforward fashion because they are standardized so that their average is equal to one.

The variation in weights does not correspond to reality in Table 8.7 because the highest basic weights are truncated at 4.0. This means that the post-stratified weights cannot be much greater than 4 either because the basic weights are the starting weights for the post-stratification. The CV of the post-stratified weights, in all countries other than Slovakia, is higher than that of the basic weights. The exception of Slovakia is hard to explain, since the variation in most cases increases after adjustment. If the sampling design takes into account the anticipated response rates, it is expected that the change would be minor.

The second weighting comparison, in Table 8.8, includes the response propensity adjusted weights (Laaksonen & Heiskanen, 2014; Laaksonen et al., 2015). It also contains the response rates. It is expected that the variation of the well-adjusted weights is high when the response rate is high. This is observed for both the web survey and the grid-based survey, which have relatively low response rates. Because there were good auxiliary variables, it was possible to carry out a beneficial adjust-ment for the weights and to reduce the bias in the point estimates. As is shown in the final example of this chapter, weighting does not always solve the non-response bias problem.

Note that it is possible to calculate the approximate values of DEFFp from the last column, in this way:

$$\text{DEFFp} = 1 + (\text{CV}/100) \times (\text{CV}/100).$$

We see that the values for DEFFp vary from 1.13 (phone sub-survey) to 1.46 (Southern Finland Grid-based Survey). The variation of the last weights arises from two main reasons: (1) there is a very disproportional sample allocation, and (2) the weighting adjustment itself. The adjusted weights thus depend very much on the response propensities.

The sample allocation includes a special case—that is, two special strata, one of so-called 'poor people grids' (250 × 250 m), and the other of 'rich people grids'. The sampling fraction was relatively high in both these strata and was highest in the rich people grids. This allocation ensured that enough respondents were obtained of both types because the study was focussed specifically on comparing the differences between people living in these spacial domains. The largest domain—grids between rich ones and poor ones—was not a focus here, and these people were well represented even using relatively low sampling fractions.

Table 8.7 The two analysis weights of the ESS by country, Round 6

Country	Sampling weight	Respondents	Minimum	Maximum	Coeff. of variation (CV)
Bulgaria	Basic	2260	0.20	3.09	41
	Post-stratified	2260	0.16	4.00	59
Cyprus	Basic	1116	0.40	2.85	45
	Post-stratified	1116	0.22	4.01	60
Czech Republic	Basic	2009	0.04	4.00	52
	Post-stratified	2009	0.00	4.03	63
Germany	Basic	2958	0.54	1.24	33
	Post-stratified	2958	0.02	4.00	57
Spain	Basic	1889	0.70	1.66	11
	Post-stratified	1889	0.50	4.00	31
France	Basic	1968	0.21	4.00	53
	Post-stratified	1968	0.16	4.01	63
United Kingdom	Basic	2286	0.51	4.00	52
	Post-stratified	2286	0.29	4.01	57
Hungary	Basic	2014	0.87	1.17	5
	Post-stratified	2014	0.57	1.70	21
Ireland	Basic	2628	0.45	3.63	49
	Post-stratified	2628	0.28	4.00	53
Israel	Basic	2508	0.78	3.39	19
	Post-stratified	2508	0.42	4.00	34
Iceland	Basic	752	0.91	1.92	18
	Post-stratified	752	0.83	2.09	19
Lithuania	Basic	2109	0.23	4.00	58
	Post-stratified	2109	0.13	4.02	60
Netherlands	Basic	1845	0.26	4.00	46
	Post-stratified	1845	0.25	4.00	54
Poland	Basic	1898	0.62	1.27	14
	Post-stratified	1898	0.53	1.61	18
Portugal	Basic	2151	0.12	4.00	61
	Post-stratified	2151	0.06	4.04	74

(continued)

Table 8.7 (continued)

Country	Sampling weight	Respondents	Minimum	Maximum	Coeff. of variation (CV)
Russia	Basic	2484	0.16	4.00	58
	Post-stratified	2484	0.10	4.00	59
Slovakia	Basic	1847	0.06	4.00	96
	Post-stratified	1847	0.04	4.04	72
Ukraine	Basic	2178	0.29	4.00	48
	Post-stratified	2178	0.23	4.00	54

Table 8.8 Characteristics of the weights of the two Finnish surveys based on the response propensity model

Survey	Response rate	Respondents	Minimum	Maximum	Coeff. of variation
Finnish Security Survey					
– Face-to-face sub-survey	50	366	0.10	4.01	48
– Web sub-survey	25	971	0.05	17.60	58
– Phone sub-survey	62	1866	0.08	4.79	37
Southern Finland Grid-based Survey	36	9618	0.17	10.10	68

8.6   Linear Calibration

The basic idea of calibration is to find reweights so that certain margins (macro auxiliary statistics) are as correct as the data given. There are several strategies that can be used to achieve this target. Usually the algorithm is such that the distance between the so-called starting weight and the calibrated weight is minimized. There are various technical and methodological tools for this. The French INSEE software CALMAR 2, uses Lagrange multipliers that give a mathematically easy way to apply several distance functions; however, in the case of linear functions other tools obviously are simpler (Deville & Särndal, 1992; Deville, Särndal, & Sautory, 1993; Särndal, 2007, Särndal & Lundquist, 2014, Estevao & Särndal, 2006; Kott & Chang, 2010; Le Guennec & Sautory, 2005; Lundström & Särndal, 1999; McCormack, 2006; Sautory, 2003). Here we first apply the linear distance function that is most frequently used. This can be called *linear calibration*.

The macro auxiliary variables are needed for calibration. We therefore wish these to be true values or true margins of the target population. These variables are symbolized by x_p, with the number p being small—say between 3 and 7. Each such variable includes several categories with these true values, thus they are vectors. The weight w_k is the variable that will be calibrated and the calibration weight is, respectively, c_k. Both these weights are therefore for the respondents.

The first requirement is to minimize the distance function

$$D(c_k, w_k) = \sum_U w_k G\left(\frac{c_k}{w_k}\right)$$

In the case of linear calibration, the distance function is

$$G = \frac{1}{2}(x_n - 1)^2$$

Finally, minimization is done so that the p calibration equations hold true,

$$\sum_r c_k x_p = \sum_U x_p$$

Some constraints can be added, so the ratio $\frac{c_k}{w_k}$ is within a desired interval.

The first step in calibration is to find the correct 'true values' of the desired auxiliary variables. The following variables are often used in social surveys:

- Gender (two categories)
- Age group (5 to 10 categories)
- Large region (5 to 10 categories)
- Education level (4 to 7 categories).

These aggregates are then saved in a specific file and used in the calibration software, so that the software does its best to get weights that satisfy these calibration margins. The algorithm usually succeeds, but there is no guarantee that the calibrated weights are desirable. It may be possible that they are negative or below one.

> **Example 8.3 From the Basic Weights to Linear Calibration in the Test Data (Continued from Example 8.2)**
> The following calibration margins are used here:
>
> - Two genders
> - Five age groups
> - Six explicit strata (regions)
>
> The margins definitely are true values because we take them from the same databases. We thus do not expect to meet any problems. The weights are fairly large and, less obviously, do not lie below one. All starting weights give the true values for the explicit strata, but calibration does not ensure that this benchmark will be met again unless the same margin is included in the

(continued)

Example 8.3 (continued)

calibration process (i.e., minimization of the weight changes). We therefore have only the real calibration margins shown in Table 8.9. The three calibration margins used are Gender (2 categories), Age group (5) and Stratum (6).

When comparing this with Table 8.8 without calibration, we see that the variation increases slightly after calibration but the order is the same, except that the CV of the calibrated results with adjusted post-stratified weights is now the largest, and their maximum weights are the highest. On the other hand, all the weights are plausible and we can go forward to estimation.

As we have said, plausible weights are not guaranteed with linear calibration. In this case, negative weights are obtained easily. One strategy is to add a fourth auxiliary margin. We do this using six education levels. The consequence is that 2% of the weights are below one. In the analysis, there is no fair solution; nonetheless, it is possible to increase the bad weights subjectively above one, or to use a calibration that does the same thing so that the constraint for the ratio between the initial and the calibrated weights is met. This is still subjective, and there is no guarantee that the calibration algorithm always will work.

Table 8.9 Linear calibration weights with four starting weights, stratified simple random domain of the test data

Starting sampling weight	Respondents	Mean	Minimum	Maximum	Coeff. of variation	Sum
Ordinary						
Basic	605	16,030	4877	35,424	49.8	9,698,424
Post-stratified	605	16,030	4344	61,579	58.4	9,698,424
Adjusted basic	605	16,030	2103	106,926	79.6	9,698,424
Adjusted post-stratified	605	16,030	2342	120,717	81.0	9,698,424
Analysis						
Basic	605	1	0.30	2.2	49.8	605
Post-stratified	605	1	0.27	3.8	58.4	605
Adjusted basic	605	1	0.13	6.7	79.6	605
Adjusted post-stratified	605	1	0.15	7.5	81.0	605

8.7 Non-linear Calibration

Linear calibration seems to work often, but not always. The constraints for the calibrated weights may be met, but this is not an objective solution. A more objective solution is to use a distance function that does not lead to weights that are negative or below one. The most common of such solutions is raking-ratio calibration. This originated in the 1940s (Deming & Stephan, 1940), but now is implemented in a different way. It is one calibration option in the French INSEE software, CALMAR 2, where the distance has the following logarithmic form:

$$G(x) = x \log x - x + 1$$

CALMAR 2 offers another non-linear solution, called 'sinus hyperbolicus'. We only present the raking ratio here because it is used most commonly. It is close to post-stratification, but more flexible than this. Raking ratio calibration allows one to include the auxiliary margins in the calibration equation in the same way as linear calibration methods.

We illustrate the case of negative weights derived from linear calibration in Table 8.10. This example uses four calibration margins, so Education level has been added to the six categories in Table 8.9. We thus can see that linear calibration may result in negative weights even if one calibration margin is added. This is awkward even though the value is not large. Fortunately, the raking ratio solves this problem technically, but gives a higher variation of the weights. Both weights vary more than when using only three calibration margins. This may be a general rule, meaning that a calibration provider should be careful when trying to use many calibration margins.

Figure 8.3 shows that the negative weights of the linear calibration have not been moved far by the raking ratio calibration. The scatter is not linear, but is more or less logarithmic, as expected. A few very high weights appear in both, but this is to a great extent because of the high starting weights that are the basic weights here.

Table 8.10 Linearly calibrated and raking-ratio weights, stratified simple random domain of test data

Sampling weight	Respondents	Mean	Minimum	Maximum	Coeff. of variation	Sum
Ordinary						
Linearly calibrated	605	16,030	−2541	113,062	92.9	9,698,424
Raking ratio calibrated	605	16,030	2079	165,733	99.7	9,698,424
Analysis						
Linearly calibrated	605	1	−0.16	7.05	92.9	605
Raking ratio calibrated	605	1	0.13	10.34	99.7	605

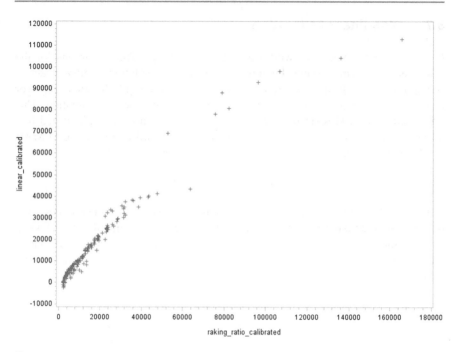

Fig. 8.3 The scatter plot between the raking-ratio weights and the linearly calibrated weights; compare the results with those shown in Table 8.10

It is vital to find the best possible weights for estimation, but what these are is not automatically clear. In any case, if the available auxiliary variables (both micro and macro) are used completely for reweights, it is expected that the bias in the point estimates will be reduced. The standard errors usually will be increased slightly, while the variation in weights is increased. It is best to get an optimal solution between these targets. Nevertheless, it is not clear how to achieve this.

If several weights are created, it is benefical to discuss these within the working team and to decide which weight really may be the 'best'. At the end of this chapter, we present a case study that illustrates the situation. In this case we know the true estimates, so it is possible to decide which weights are best fairly easily.

Analysis examples are given in Chap. 14. These include ones in which the weights of the complete test data are used, thus covering both the SRS and the cluster domains of the test data.

Example 8.4 Comparison of Four Weights in Simulated Data
The data behind this simulated dataset come from a real survey, the Finnish Security Survey (FSS), which was considered in Chap. 7 (see Example 7.2) and earlier in this chapter when considering unit non-responses.

(continued)

Example 8.4 (continued)

The simulation universe here is extended to the respondents of the FSS, consisting of nearly 200,000 persons. The missingness of this universe is as close as possible to that of the real survey. The sampling design was stratified simple random. The following four weights were created:

– Basic weights assuming that unit non-responses within strata is ignorable
– Linear calibration starting from the basic weights
– Response propensity weighting using eight micro auxiliary variables (see Example 8.2)
– Linear calibration starting from the response propensity weights.

The three calibration margins were used in both calibrations: (1) four explicit strata, (2) five age groups, and (3) two genders.

This pattern is easy to obtain in most countries because such margins can be found as known population totals. Fortunately, they do not lead to negative weights even when linear calibration is used; thus, we do not need to go on to any non-linear distance function. More margins, or other types of margins, may be problematic, as shown by the calibration method of the European Social Survey (2014). The ESS found education level to have a significant influence on response behaviour and wanted to apply this macro auxiliary variable. It was possible to obtain a satisfactory variable only from another sample—the EU Labour Force Survey. This therefore is not a true value, but it is harmonized in some sense, so it was used. It was considered to be the 'best solution'. Fortunately, the weights were plausible because raking-ratio calibration was applied.

One may wonder about the selection of explicit strata because this already has been used in both the basic weights and the response propensity weights. So why should it be included again? The reason is that this benchmark does hold true then when calibrating only to two new margins (i.e., age group and gender).

Eight different indicators were used in the estimation comparisons. We do not present the initial estimates here, only their relative deviation from the true value, corresponding to the relative bias. This is the most illustrative way to compare results. These comparisons are presented in Table 8.11. The order is by the success of the joint response propensity and linear calibration (last column).

The last row of Table 8.11 shows an overall ranking of the methods. If we interpret this in a straightforward way, we can see that the best method is the combination of response propensity and calibration, with pure response propensity coming second, and pure basic weighting being the worst. Yet, there are exceptions. Pure basic weighting actually is the best for Violence by

(continued)

Table 8.11 Results for the relative bias with basic and response propensity weights, both continued with linear calibration (see Laaksonen and Hämäläinen, 2018)

Indicator	Basic weight		Response propensity	
	Pure	Calibration	Pure	Calibration
Violence by ex-partner	**0.60**	−2.72	−0.83	−1.21
Harassment ever	−1.36	−2.22	−0.53	**−0.42**
Worry	0.76	−0.84	0.16	**−0.02**
Violence by stranger recently	−1.03	**−0.10**	0.12	0.15
Harassment recently	6.91	0.55	0.62	**0.32**
Income	2.06	1.79	0.39	**0.33**
Violence by partner	7.24	**4.22**	4.68	4.52
Violence by stranger ever	6.50	**2.39**	4.86	5.27
Average success ranking by four methods	3.38	2.50	2.25	**1.88**

Best estimates are bolded in the Table

Example 8.4 (continued)

ex-partner, for which no method works well. Pure calibration works well for another difficult indicator, Violence by partner. This indicator seems to be the most difficult to estimate well with any method. We cannot explain why the combined method is as bad as it is for this indicator, but it does work better than basic weights, fortunately.

Another indicator that is difficult to estimate correctly is Violence by stranger ever. It needs to be understood that it is not appropriate to use the auxiliary variables to predict missingness if no method is reasonably good. Fortunately, we see that the joint response propensity and calibration method succeeds relatively well with some indicators, the best ones being Worry, Income, Violence by stranger recently, and Harassment recently. In all these cases, the basic weights do not lead to reliable estimates.

These weights are created without any auxiliary variables except region (explicit stratum), which is used in the sampling design. It is clearly understood that the bias in income can be reduced using the micro auxiliary variables available. It is interesting that a similar reduction is found for Worry as well. The joint method even gives slightly better results than the pure response propensity weighting method.

In general, almost all weights with adjustments improve the estimates to some extent, but they can be biased either upward or downward. Second, it seems that even sophisticated weights do not always improve accuracy substantially. A good point is that they do not lead to worse accuracy either, although the improvement is minor. In some cases, therefore, no weighting methods give a guarantee that the bias because of missingness is reduced substantially. This means that one should pay attention to finding auxiliary variables that are tailored to each survey situation. This is easy to say, but not to implement.

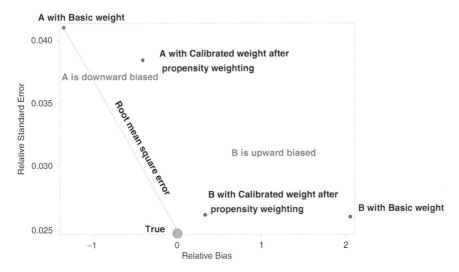

Scheme 8.1 Illustration of the concepts 'bias', 'standard error' and 'mean square error' based on the case in Table 8.11

Bias, Standard Error and Mean Square Error

The concepts here are used commonly in sampling, but the standard error can be estimated more or less effectively from ordinary data. It is good to try to assess the extent and the direction of the bias, even though it cannot be estimated explicitly. Here we explain the two concepts of bias and standard error, as well as their 'sum', which is called the mean square error (MSE). The MSE is presented in the following formula, in which $var(s) =$ the variance estimate of the parameter estimated using the best possible information:

$$MSE = Bias^2 + var\,(s).$$

The square root of the MSE is often more illustrative, although it cannot be published in most cases. Fortunately, we can do so in the case in Example 8.4. This illustration is presented in the graph in the following scheme, where estimate A concerns Harassment ever and estimate B Income in Table 8.11. We can see clearly that the estimate is approaching the true value when using the best possible weights. The standard error does not change much, but the root MSE naturally will be reduced; only one of these lines has been drawn on the graph, with the worst result (Scheme 8.1).

8.8   Summary of All the Weights

Scheme 8.2 includes all the weights introduced in Chaps. 4 and 8. This scheme does not distinguish between the ordinary sampling weights, of the amounts or totals, and the analysis weights, and does not cover how to choose between these. The scheme includes seven actions that can be alternatives, and thus it is not usually necessary to develop all of these in one survey. The best final weights always include some calibration, but they can be calculated via the different preceding actions, the shortest

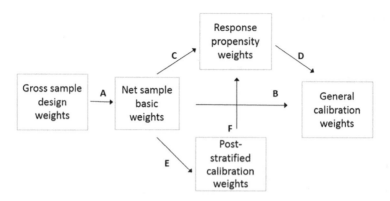

Scheme 8.2 Summary of all the sampling weights of this book

chain being first A and then B. This is called *pure calibration*. This is the only option if no micro auxiliary data are available but only valid macro variables, that is, some good calibration margins.

Calibration is thus a benchmarking technique that gives the desired margin values, but it is not realistic to include too many margins. What 'too many' means should be examined in each case. The target is that the margin values are as true as possible. They are thus the best possible macro auxiliary variables for this particular survey.

The scheme shows that the starting weights for calibration can be of three types. Response propensity weights are the best option, since they are straightforwardly related to the response behaviour of the gross sample units (proper sample). These auxiliary variables should be available at micro level but can include macro variables as well. In addition, they are benchmarked to the margins that are in the sampling design, typically to the pre-strata. The method also works after post-stratification, when the benchmarking is to post-strata margins.

What the final weights can be is the big question. They are often the basic weights that are calculated assuming the response mechanism is negligible or is *MARS*. These weights are naturally the only alternative if there are no auxiliary variables other than those applied in the sampling design.

Nevertheless, it is possible that afterwards some macro auxiliary variables can be found from statistics and exploited in post-stratification and in other calibration. Only one requirement must be met: there must be true statistics for the benchmarking margins for such variables that are in the same format in the survey data. These benchmarks make the benchmarked estimates correct, but they do not ensure that all the other estimates will be unbiased. The response propensity weights before calibration can be assumed to lessen the bias further, since it is now possible to take advantage of all the micro and macro auxiliary variables. It is possible that the results will not change much, but everything has now been done to ensure a high quality survey, using reweights.

Note that linear calibration may give implausible weights that are negative or are less than one. This may occur more often if one tries to use 'too many' calibration margins (or their categories). Post-stratification, raking ratio and sinus hyperbolicus methods never give implausible weights. Post-calibration corrections that technically remove the implausible weights to make them plausible are not recommended.

It is good to construct as many weights as possible, including by using different variable patterns and link functions in the response propensity modelling, and then to analyze them and to test some key survey estimates. Finally, a decision needs to be made on which weights to insert into the final survey file. Usually, only one alternative is accepted by ordinary users. This is not a difficult problem, since some weights can easily be dropped out and rejected. On the other hand, some of the best weights may not give substantially different estimates, and it might be difficult to make the final decision. However, the survey team should ultimately find a consensus.

Observation

We present examples in Chap. 14 using our test data file. We use the following labels for the weights in these examples:

– The methods A and B correspond to 'pure calibration', which is recommended if no micro auxiliary variables exist that have not already been used.
– Calibration after propensity weights includes the following weights: A, C, and D.
– The chain A, E, F, and D is not possible for a stratified simple random domain but adding this partial post-stratification does not change those results very much, and hence this weight is not shown in any example. However, see Table 8.6, which includes weights A, E, and F for the 'SRS' domain.

References

Brick, J. M. (2013). Unit nonresponse and weighting adjustments: A critical review. *Journal of Official Statistics, 29*(3), 329–353.

Brick, J. M., & Jones, M. E. (2008). Propensity to respond and nonresponse bias. *METRON – International Journal of Statistics, LXVI*(1), 51–73.

Deming, W. E., & Stephan, F. F. (1940). On a least squares adjustment of a sample frequency table when the expected marginal totals are known. *Annals of Mathematical Statistics, 11*, 427–444.

Deville, J.-C., & Särndal, C.-E. (1992). Calibration estimators in survey sampling. *Journal of the American Statistical Association, 87*(418), 376–382.

Deville, J.-C., Särndal, C.-E., & Sautory, O. (1993). Generalized raking procedures in survey sampling. *Journal of the American Statistical Association, 88*(423), 1013–1020.

Ekholm, A., & Laaksonen, S. (1991). Weighting via response modelling in the Finnish Household Budget Survey. *Journal of Official Statistics, 7*(2), 325–337.

Estevao, V. M., & Särndal, C.-E. (2006). Survey estimates by calibration on complex auxiliary information. *International Statistical Review, 74*(2), 127–147.

European Social Survey. (2014). *Documentation of ESS post-stratification weights*. Retrieved April 2016, from http://www.europeansocialsurvey.org/docs/methodology/ESS_post_stratification_weights_documentation.pdf

Haziza, D., & Lesage, E. (2016). Discussion of weighting procedures for unit nonresponse. *Journal of Official Statistics, 32*(1), 129–145.

Holt, D., & Smith, T. M. F. (1979). Post-stratification. *Journal of the Royal Statistical Society, Series A (General), 142*, 33–46.

Kott, P., & Chang, T. (2010). Using calibration weighting to adjust for nonignorable unit nonresponse. *Journal of the American Statistical Association, 105*(491), 1265–1275.

Laaksonen, S. (2007). Weighting for two-phase surveyed data. *Survey Methodology, 33*(2), 121–130.

Laaksonen, S., & Hämäläinen, A. (2018). Joint response propensity and calibration weighting. *Journal of Statistis in Transition New Series, 19*(1), 45–60. https://doi.org/10.21307/stattrans-2018-003.

Laaksonen, S., & Heiskanen, M. (2014). Comparison of three modes for a victimization survey. *Journal of Survey Statistics and Methodology, 2*(4), 459–483.

Laaksonen, S., Kemppainen, T., Kortteinen, M., Vaattovaara, M., Stjernberg, M. & Lönnqvist, H. (2015). *Tackling city-regional dynamics in a survey using grid sampling.* Survey Research Association. http://www.surveymethods.org

Le Guennec, J. & Sautory, O. (2005). *CALMAR 2: Une Nouvelle Version de la Macro Calmar de Redressement D'Échantillon Par Calage.* Retrieved February 2016, from http://vserverinsee. nexen.net/jms2005/site/files/documents/2005/327_1-JMS2002_SESSION1_LE-GUENNEC-SAUTORY_CALMAR-2_ACTES.PDF[Read 2014}

Little, R. J. A. (1986). Survey nonresponse adjustments for estimates of means. *International Statistical Review, 54*, 139–157.

Lundström, S., & Särndal, C.-E. (1999). Calibration as a standard method for treatment of nonresponse. *Journal of Official Statistics, 15*(2), 305–327.

McCormack, K. (2006). The calibration software CALMAR – What is it?. Central Statistics Office Ireland. Retrieved March 2014, from http://vesselinov.com/CalmarEngDoc.pdf

Särndal, C.-E. (2007). Calibration approach in survey theory and practice. *Survey Methodology, 33* (2), 99–119.

Särndal, C.-E., & Lundquist, P. (2014). Accuracy in estimation with nonresponse: A function of degree of imbalance and degree of explanation. *Journal of Survey Statistics and Methodology, 2* (4), 361–387.

Sautory, O. (2003). CALMAR 2: A new version of the calmar calibration adjustment program. *Proceedings of Statistics Canada's Symposium: Challenges in Survey Taking for the Next Decade.*

Smith, T. M. F. (1991). Post-stratification. *The Statistician, 40*, 315–323.

Special Cases in Weighting

Special weights

So far, several sampling weights have been presented, particularly in Chap. 8. The general goal is to try to utilize all possible auxiliary variables to reduce any possible and obvious bias in the point estimates by using weights that are as advanced as possible. Not much can be done without appropriate micro and macro auxiliary variables. This chapter does not continue any further into improving these weights, but we present some special cases that can be used with any available weights—that is, the best possible weights naturally lead to the best results. We thus write the weights in this chapter more generally, using the symbols $w_\_$ or w_k. Four different cases are presented.

9.1 Sampling of Individuals and Estimates for Clusters Such as Households

Question How can household level estimates, such as household composition or average household size, be estimated if the sampling units are individuals?

This problem has been encountered in the European Social Survey (ESS), and it is possible that a user will just make estimates the same as for individuals. Yet, this leads to incorrect estimates. Why?

Given that the individual weights are summed up to the population of those aged 15 or over (15+), the estimates using these weights concern these individuals. We need to know the estimates for the households, however. The number of households for each unit is obtained by dividing the individual weight by the number of people over 15. Thus, nothing is needed if the 15+ size is one; however, in the case of larger households, the respective weight will be smaller. Table 9.1 is based on the ESS individual basic (or design) weights, dividing these by the number of members of the household age 15 or over for each responding individual:

$$w\_basic\_Households = w\_basic\_individuals/members\ 15+$$

Table 9.1 shows clearly that the pure individual weights in every country lead to an average household size that is too high, although the difference varies to some extent. The countries are sorted by how correct the estimates are.

The highest average household sizes nevertheless look quite large. They might be biased, with the reason being not incorrect weighting but the selectiveness of the

Table 9.1 Average household size by country with correct and incorrect weights, ESS Round 7

Country	Individual weights	Household weights
Austria	3.05	1.89
Finland	2.36	1.98
Estonia	2.50	2.06
Sweden	2.61	2.10
Denmark	2.55	2.16
Norway	2.62	2.19
Germany	2.84	2.19
Switzerland	2.76	2.30
Netherlands	2.84	2.42
Belgium	2.95	2.45
Czech Republic	2.83	2.46
Slovenia	3.14	2.55
Ireland	3.13	2.60
Poland	3.31	2.68
France	3.20	2.81

respondents. This could be because of the low response rates of single people, for example. Further interpretation remains for the reader to evaluate.

9.2   Cases Where Only Analysis Weights Are Available Although Proper Weights Are Required

It is fairly common for survey researchers not to need proper sampling weights for which the sum corresponds to the target population size. The reason is that these weights are not necessary in estimating relative figures (e.g., averages and percentages). They are not necessary, for ordinary multivariate analysis either. We therefore use the term 'analysis weight' for the weights that are used.

Nevertheless, the proper weights often are needed to gain an understanding of the estimates at the target population level. If such weights are not in the dataset, they can be obtained easily if the average of the weights of the respondents is known. This gives the following simple formula:

$$w_k = w_k\_\text{analysis} \times (\text{the average of the proper weights}).$$

It is not automatically clear how to get that average. It can be obtained by dividing the target population size by the number of the respondents. In this phase, it therefore is necessary to decide on and get to know the target population, if this has not been done already.

The ESS micro file does not include these proper weights directly, but they can be calculated because the file includes the so-called *population weights* for each country. If one multiplies the population weight by 10,000, the target population size is obtained. This, in turn, gives the proper weights with this formula:

$$w_h = 10,000 \, w_p d_k$$

where d_k = the ESS analysis weight and w_p = the ESS population weight.

This weight can be used in all analyses if the estimates for the population domains in the ESS countries (i.e., not the countries themselves) are of interest. Such analysis is much less common because the country differences are more interesting. Nevertheless, if it is only ethnic or socioeconomic groups, among others, that are of interest, these weights are correct. Chapter 14 includes two examples of the use of such weights—see Tables 14.6 and 14.7.

9.3   Sampling and Weights for Households and Estimates for Individuals or Other Subordinate Levels

Here we have the correct household-level weights, w_k, used for household estimation, concerning *income*, for instance. The file also includes the number of household members, with their ages and positions in the household. It is possible to estimate some figures so that their importance can be seen at an individual level or another subordinate level. The weights for individuals are obtained by *multiplying by the number of household members* (or equivalent consumption units). This therefore means that the sum of the weights is equal to the sum of individuals in the target population, or to the sum of equivalent consumption units.

This weighting generally is applied when analysing household income differences because otherwise the household income depends on the composition of the household. For instance, an increase in the number of income recipients increases the disposable income, but an increase in the number of children, and other economically inactive persons (without income or with low income), leads to increasing consumption. Disposable or cash income per consumption unit is thus the ordinary indicator in studies of income differences. The weights therefore need to be converted at the same time.

Another question is which estimates can now be calculated if these variable values differ within households but we do not present details about this point here.

9.4   Panel Over Two Years

Let the weights of year t be $w_k(t)$, and those of year $t+1$ be $w_k(t+1)$. The number of respondents in the year t is $r(t)$ and the number in year $t+1$ is $r(t+1)$. Note that the period from 1 year to the next might be greater than one. Because of unit non-responses, $r(t+1) < r(t)$. Here, we discuss the weighting for the panel analysis—that is, income or other changes from the first wave of the panel to the next. This weighting can be done using the balanced or the unbalanced panel approach, but we concentrate on the balanced case because this is the most common. In this case, the weights $w_k(t)$ are not concerned with the number of respondents in the second wave, thus $r(t+1)$. These weights thus need to be converted first for this number of respondents. We do not present all the possible weighting strategies here because these also are dependent on the auxiliary data available. For example, it often is difficult to get updated auxiliary data for the non-respondents of both years. We thus assume here that both weights are such that their sum corresponds to the target population of each year—t and $t+1$.

The weights concern the same households, but the household composition may have changed. Moreover, we need to calculate the changes at unit level from t to $t+1$. What is the best way to do this?

Three alternative weights can be applied: (1) the weights for year t (corresponding to Laspeyres' index), (2) the weights for year $t+1$ (corresponding to Paasche's index), and (3) the (geometric) average of the two weights (Fisher's ideal index). Which should be chosen?

The answer depends on the target of the study. Case (1) is a good choice for a cohort-type study, or a follow-up, and is commonly used in ordinary index calculations as well because survey-period weights (for the period $t+1$) are difficult to obtain. Case (2) corresponds to a retrospective approach. It is interesting to compare these two estimates and to learn how the phenomenon progresses. The

Table 9.2 Income differences and changes with two types of weights

Weight	Coefficient of variation, year t	Coefficient of variation, year $t+1$	Mean income change
Weights of year t	0.540	0.529	0.190
Weights of year $t+1$	0.529	0.535	0.107
Geometric average of two weights	0.534	0.532	0.143

weights in (3) are between these two alternatives and are best comparable with cross-sectional estimates; these estimates can be considered to be the most 'neutral'.

Example 9.1 Income Changes in a Two-year Panel

This example comes from the Finnish income distribution survey that was performed in the mid-1980s (1984–1986) (Laaksonen, 1991). This survey was for a two-year panel, so every year a new wave was added while an old wave was omitted. The age of the data is not important because similar principles apply everywhere to income panels. Because this is a two-year panel, the principles are easier to observe given that the changes are more substantial.

It is not important how the weights were created, but the first panel year (= t) weights were updated for the second year in order to make their sums equal to the target population size of $t+1$ (i.e., concerning households). In turn, the weights for the second year (= $t+1$) were calculated to correspond to the same target population. Naturally, these latter weights are more closely related to the sampling design (i.e., stratified SRS with unequal inclusion probabilities). The first year weights for the second year were calculated for the respondents of the first panel year, but it was assumed that the inclusion probabilities were on the same basis (even though the composition of the households often had changed). The weights are thus a type of conditional weight, but they are the best possible ones.

The survey was interested both in the cross-sectional figures and in the panel results, which are changes at an individual household level. To calculate these, the weights are needed. Table 9.2 presents the main results for households. Income differences are measured with the coefficients of variation. We find that the first year weights show decreasing differences, whereas the second year weights show increasing ones. When calculating the same with the average weights, the change is small, but slightly decreases. This difference is not significant.

The last column of Table 9.2 is for income changes (Laaksonen, 1991). These are fairly different with the two weights. The result resembles the changes in the index calculation. The first year weights are similar to Laspeyres' weights, which also lead to a higher change in the index field. On the other hand, the second year weights give results in the opposite

(continued)

Example 9.1 (continued)

direction, in the same way as Paasche's weights in index theory do. Consequently, the geometric average weight (i.e., Fisher's ideal index) would be recommended for cross-sectional purposes.

Reference

Laaksonen, S. (1991). *Comparative adjustments for missingness in short-term panels. Applications to questions of household income distribution.* Studies 179, 66 pp. Helsinki: Central Statistical Office of Finland.

Statistical Editing

10

Nicely edited?

Statistical editing, or statistical data editing, is a significant and important part of a survey process. If the raw data has not been edited in any way, editing may require a great deal of time and resources. Typically, this is the case if a paper questionnaire has been used; all other modes give an opportunity to do some *pre-editing*, therefore the *final editing* ought to be easier.

This chapter presents the core methods and tools for editing; we start with its main purpose. This topic has been specified more thoroughly and theoretically and practically determined since the 1990s, the paper by Granquist (1997) being one pioneer document. Later, much work in the field has been done as part of the United Nations Economic Commission for Europe (UNECE) work sessions. The UNECE published a useful document on data quality in 2006. Moreover, it maintains a glossary of terms on statistical data editing, which is available on the Internet.

© Springer International Publishing AG, part of Springer Nature 2018   141
S. Laaksonen, *Survey Methodology and Missing Data*,
https://doi.org/10.1007/978-3-319-79011-4_10

This chapter uses this Commission's work, but unlike the UNECE we do not concentrate on this topic from the point of view of official statistics. For example, we only use some key terms from the UNECE's glossary (2017).

Statistical editing is a crucial part of the quality assurance of survey data as well as survey processes. The first point is related to the quality control and improvement of data, and we focus on it now. Yet, it also is necessary to look forward and to document the strong and weak points of the survey process so that lessons can be learned for future surveys. This often has been forgotten, and thus the same errors or mistakes are repeated. In addition, it is useful to look at other similar types of surveys, to take a glance at how they are edited, and to make use of the information gained in the best way.

Specific tasks of statistical editing
– Evaluating and developing the survey process for the future, with the goal of 'learning by doing'. It is good if similar surveys follow what has been done in your specific one.
– Developing a system that helps to reduce the manual work in editing—by using selective editing, for instance. The purpose of this is to concentrate on detecting the most fatal errors in the data, such as those that may have a significant impact on data quality.
– Detecting, checking, and correcting errors at the micro level so that the results at the macro (aggregate) level also are plausible and reliable.
– Paying special attention to missing values so that they are coded with as many codes as possible or are left as missing. At the same time, a preliminary decision needs to be made on what to do about missing values in the data analysis. If a decision is made to impute these partially or entirely, it is valuable to do this at this stage, because thought also needs to be given to which auxiliary variables could be used in imputation.
– Providing indicators that describe the changes made during editing and explaining how some core estimates have been revised ('improved') by editing.
– Estimating the workload of the editing (and imputation).

10.1   Edit Rules and Ordinary Checks

Edit rules are the guidelines for checking the correctness of individual variable values. The UNECE glossary (2006) describes an edit rule more broadly: 'A condition or algorithm used to detect, and possibly prescribe treatment for, anomalous and erroneous data. Edit rules can be applied at unit or aggregate level.'

Edit rules may be more or less strict; this can be determined by *gates* given for each value to be checked. If the gate is narrow, the values are checked more precisely than in the other cases. This means that if the gate is wide, editing does not lead to many changes or possible improvements. Thus, the edit workload depends significantly on the width of the gates for editing.

The quality is expected to be better if the gate is narrower, but everything depends on how well a possibly erroneous value can be corrected. If it is possible to check all suspect values with the respondent (using the list of suspect values), this is excellent; however, it is not possible in most human surveys. Fortunately, it often is possible in the case of surveys at large businesses.

If the suspect values cannot be checked against the true values, the only strategy is to make the suspect values believable, plausible, or logical. This means first that they should be at the correct level or (i) *within the predetermined range* of each variable. It is relatively easy to do this as early as the time of data entry, thus as part of pre-editing. This is the first edit rule and always should be followed, nonetheless it is not always clear which values can be accepted. In the case of closed questions in computer-assisted questionnaires—that is, when only certain categorical values are accepted—it is quite easy to check whether the values are acceptable, but for continuous variables it may be more difficult.

It is possible to have different acceptable values for different subgroups (e.g., gender, age, or education level). According to the UNECE, this is (ii): the second edit rule, which states that *one value may depend on the value of another variable.* This is a bit more demanding in computer-assisted surveys, but it is possible to apply it. There is a danger that a respondent would not like it if his or her answer was not accepted because of another answer the individual gave. The rule therefore should be used carefully in pre-editing, but in the post-fieldwork editing stage it should be applied; the solution may not be nice always because it will be necessary to change one or both values in order to obey this edit rule.

To generalise, a third edit rule, (iii), thus *can be one-, two-, three-, or multidimensional.* The number of suspect values obviously is growing at the same time; consequently, the workload for checking and correcting implausible values is increasing. Usually, the logic for various values seems to be more important than that the value is absolutely right—for example:

- If the age of a person is 10, and he or she has a child, it may be best to change the age but to keep the child there.
- If the age of a person is 20 and he or she is a university professor, either the age is wrong, or the occupation is wrong.
- If a person is unemployed but has a wage of €5000, one of these values obviously is incorrect. It is good to look at the other answers as well before correcting one value.
- If a person's occupation is a cleaner and he or she is well educated, this may be possible but it also is possible that one of the answers is not correct. It is good to look at the other answers before altering one of them, unless it is not possible to ask the respondent again.

A special multidimensional edit rule—that is, rule (iv)—uses a *linear or another multivariate regression model* in which the dependent variable is the one that researcher wants to check, or the variable of interest; several explanatory variables are selected, and the model is estimated. The residuals are then calculated and ordered. The extreme residuals are examined first. It is possible that these are the result of an error in the dependent variable or an error in one or more explanatory variables. Of course, all the extreme residuals are not errors, but they are still interesting. If the responses are from a paper questionnaire, it is possible to check these answers. By doing this, it may be found that there has been a data entry error. This is easy to correct.

10.2   Some Other Edit Checks

Identifiers may play a significant role in surveys, particularly for survey institutions. They are unique identifiers such as a personal identity code or business entity code. In addition, an identifier may consist of several variables (e.g., first name, second name, date of birth, and birth year). All these are confidential and should not be released to outsiders without permission. On the other hand, they should be correct, thus they should be checked and, if necessary, corrected. All correct identifiers should be maintained in the survey institution's files for as long as feasible.

Moreover, the *confidential identifiers* may be converted into a protected form so that this file can be released to outsiders as well. The conversion rule should be stored because it may be needed later. It is good to use some type of randomisation in this conversion. Because of mistakes in data entry, it is possible, for example, that when two sets of data are merged, the same two identifiers (duplicates) are found in the new file. One of these should be deleted. This is part of the editing work.

Extreme or other exceptional values may be awkward. These are often called *outliers*. On the other hand, the data file also contains *inliers* that look like ordinary values until they are controlled against one or more other variables, then they no longer look ordinary. In editing, it is most important to detect values that are not correct. An erroneous outlier is called an *out-error*, and an erroneous inlier an *in-error*. It is to be hoped that such errors will not exist in the cleaned data.

Unless the questionnaire and the data entry already have been given good codes for missing values, such coding should be made at the editing stage. One rule is that a missing value should never be coded as 'zero' because zero is usually a proper value. Instead, the best codes for missingness are negative ones (e.g., -1, -2, -3, -4). The ESS and many other surveys use codes that are very different from the proper codes (e.g., 7, 8, 9, 77, 88, 99, 6666).

▶   **Comment on Correcting Outliers** It is important, of course, to correct outliers if they are erroneous, but many such extreme values are correct. How should these values be handled?

   1. The best solution is to handle them in the same way as the other values in relation to the aggregate statistics that are based on the complete target population or the register, in particular.

2. Although the complete target population is used, the average is not always the best indicator for variables with a skewed distribution. The median or another more robust indicator is better than the average in the case of income or wages, for example. Laaksonen et al. (2015) used the median and then determined 'poor grids' and 'rich grids' using register-based tax incomes; if they had not done this, it would have been possible that one rich household would have determined that a grid was 'rich'.

3. In the case of a sample survey, one outlier can affect the estimate significantly, especially if its sampling weight is large (e.g., in the thousands). One solution is to change this weight so that it corresponds to its share in the target population. The minimum weight is naturally one, but often it may be somewhat higher. If correct information is available, it is possible to determine this.

4. The simplest solution for handling an outlier is to categorise this continuous variable into an appropriate number of categories so that the last group includes all values above a certain threshold. This does not work if, for example, one wishes to measure income differences with the Gini coefficient or a similar good indicator.

10.3   Satisficing in Editing

In Chap. 3 we considered problems of replying and introduced the term 'satisficing'. One consequence of satisficing is 'straightlining', and the other is 'item non-response' with no real reason. These may be found if editing is done well, but it is not necessarily easy to do so.

What should be done if satisficing, or straightlining, has definitely been detected? One reaction could be to mark the whole answer as a non-response because too many answers are implausible, therefore code it as a unit non-response. If half of the answers are not plausible, it is possible to change these to missing answers (i.e., item non-response) and to use an applicable meta data code such as 'deficient'.

10.4   Selective Editing

Selective editing is used successfully in business surveys where the fact variables are common. It is possible to use it for other variables as well. There are several approaches to selective editing, but the basic idea is *to construct a model*, which can be a statistical model or a mathematical model such as a function, that *predicts the probability* that a certain value is erroneous (i.e., error-localisation). In editing, the values with the highest error probabilities are first checked and corrected the most carefully, and those with low probabilities are checked less carefully or even left as they are or allowed to be corrected automatically.

When developing a selective editing model, it is good to train it with a so-called training dataset that has first been checked against a smaller dataset, often more manually, to test the workability of the model. When the model has been found to work, it can be run over all the data.

Selective editing can be used more manually as well, keeping in mind those values that may have a significant influence on the core estimates of the survey. In practice, this can be organised so that the team members look separately at individual values from various parts of the data and collect possible problematic values, at least taking a (stratified) random sample. When a list of problematic cases is available, it is possible to check for similar cases in the whole dataset using a computer program.

10.5   Graphical Editing

Graphical editing often is useful because it helps with detecting outliers that can be out-errors or in-errors. Nowadays, there are more and more multidimensional statistical graphs that can identify possible errors. Unfortunately, it still is not easy to check whether it is just these values that are erroneous or whether there are others connected with them.

Figure 10.1 shows a simple example of graphical editing. Its scatter plot is from the ESS, the x-axis being for 'Happiness' and the y-axis for 'Life satisfaction'; these variables are well correlated (coefficient of correlation $= 0.71$). The graph also

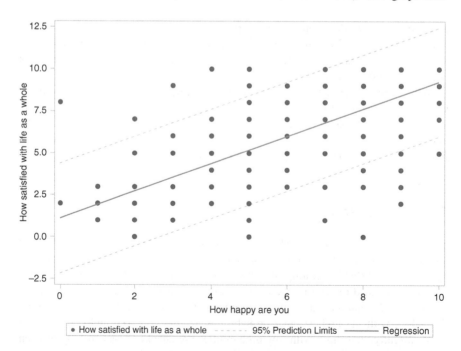

Fig. 10.1 Graphical presentation for editing of the ESS Round 7

includes the 95% confidence intervals of the linear predictions. It is obvious that the values outside these intervals are often erroneous; however, which are the ones that are errors and should they be corrected? It is difficult to answer this, and we do not have a good answer. Anyway, it is good to look at and report such cases.

10.6   Tabular Editing

Table 10.1 shows the graph in Fig. 10.1 in tabular form, which may help when thinking about whether to revise some values and how to handle them further in the analysis. The values that are far away from the diagonal are not plausible. It is difficult, for example, to understand that the score for Happiness could be 10 but the score for Life satisfaction is 0. Fortunately, the number of such cases is relatively small. To the author's knowledge, most analysts do not revise these values, but it would be possible to omit the strangest ones shown in Table 10.1.

10.7   Handling Screening Data during Editing

It is useful to create two variables if one filter is used, one for the entire target population and the other for the restricted population with the filter variable (e.g., for those who replied 'yes'). Table 10.2 shows this case and continues from the example on designing the questionnaire (see Example 3.2 in Chap. 3). The quantity estimates are equal, but the prevalence is, in most cases, more interesting. We can see that the prevalence is essentially different for the whole population and the population with one or more cars.

10.8   Editing of Data for Public Use

Ordinary editing checks the range of individual values for each variable to see whether it is plausible. It is more difficult to edit the data conditionally (i.e., checking that the values of two or more variables are plausible). This means that the end-user should do this checking himself or herself and therefore continue the editing if implausible values are found.

Table 10.1 Tabular comparison to be used with Fig. 10.1, ESS Round 7

Table of happy by stflife

Happy (How happy are you?)	stflife (How satisfied with life as a whole)											Total
	0	1	2	3	4	5	6	7	8	9	10	
0	262	40	21	21	12	19	5	4	6	4	14	408
	0.51	0.08	0.04	0.04	0.02	0.04	0.01	0.01	0.01	0.01	0.03	0.79
1	88	143	61	44	17	29	16	7	8	7	5	425
	0.17	0.28	0.12	0.09	0.03	0.06	0.03	0.01	0.02	0.01	0.01	0.82
2	116	115	227	129	60	68	27	18	18	15	5	798
	0.23	0.22	0.44	0.25	0.12	0.13	0.05	0.03	0.03	0.03	0.01	1.55
3	105	120	299	487	216	195	65	47	44	20	12	1610
	0.20	0.23	0.58	0.95	0.42	0.38	0.13	0.09	0.09	0.04	0.02	3.12
4	57	65	191	407	532	356	134	107	49	20	16	1934
	0.11	0.13	0.37	0.79	1.03	0.69	0.26	0.21	0.10	0.04	0.03	3.75
5	193	128	298	565	714	2135	694	485	281	89	123	5705
	0.37	0.25	0.58	1.10	1.39	4.14	1.35	0.94	0.55	0.17	0.24	11.07
6	45	31	98	260	356	1057	1447	962	432	85	70	4843
	0.09	0.06	0.19	0.50	0.69	2.05	2.81	1.87	0.84	0.16	0.14	9.40
7	36	35	93	232	314	948	1430	3487	1892	416	168	9051
	0.07	0.07	0.18	0.45	0.61	1.84	2.78	6.77	3.67	0.81	0.33	17.56
8	42	28	58	138	178	640	706	2406	6421	1975	674	13,266
	0.08	0.05	0.11	0.27	0.35	1.24	1.37	4.67	12.46	3.83	1.31	25.74
9	24	23	18	57	51	179	188	499	2050	3899	1226	8214
	0.05	0.04	0.03	0.11	0.10	0.35	0.36	0.97	3.98	7.57	2.38	15.94
10	46	16	31	58	57	228	120	263	585	817	3055	5276
	0.09	0.03	0.06	0.11	0.11	0.44	0.23	0.51	1.14	1.59	5.93	10.24
Total	1014	744	1395	2398	2507	5854	4832	8285	11,786	7347	5368	51,530
	1.97	1.44	2.71	4.65	4.87	11.36	9.38	16.08	22.87	14.26	10.42	100.00

Table 10.2 Example of the use of editing for screening: Car stolen in the last 5 years

Prevalence, %			Number of stolen cars
	Unweighted	Using adjustment weights	Adjustment weights
The entire target population	2.25	2.34	268,174
Households with one or more cars	2.55	2.66	268,174

Example 10.1 Cross-Tabulation of the Two Categorical Variables for Logical Checking (Two-Dimensional Edit Rule)

This example is from the ESS in which two variables were checked to see how logical the values are. Both variables are for time spent watching TV; the rows are for total watching time, and the columns are for time spent watching politics, news, and current affairs. It is clear that the total watching time should be at least as great as the time spent watching a particular type of program. By cross-classifying the answers, it can be seen that not all the answers are logical. This therefore shows that even when using face-to-face (f2f) interviewing not everything works correctly (Table 10.3). The answers in red are not logical.

We may wonder about several things in the table, for example:

– Positive values in the upper right corner are not logical
– What does 'not applicable' mean because it is non-zero only in one cell; does it mean that the respondent has no TV?
– 'Don't know' for the total time spent watching TV looks strange if an answer is given for the time spent watching TV news and so on.

How should the TV watching variables be edited? It is at least possible to change all the values for total time watching TV to the same level as that for time watching politics, news, and current affairs.

It is possible to use a specific categorisation based on the subject matter targets of the study so that the missingness codes are in the group of 'others'. If 'not applicable' means that the respondent has no access to TV, this could be a specific small-scale study. We checked what this conveys, and the result is shown in Fig. 10.2. Most rates are rather low, but the one for Israel (IL) resembles an outlier. We do not try to interpret this result here, but it would be good to try to do so in a proper survey analysis. For example, if this 'No TV_rate' is correct, would it be useful to explain why it is so high in Israel?

A categorical variable, such as 'TV_Watching', can be changed to a continuous form, but this cannot be done very precisely, mainly because the

(continued)

Example 10.1 (continued)

last alternative has no upper limit. We carry out one transformation to give a better understanding of the logic between those two variables. This transformation is as follows:

if tvtot = 0 then TV_Watching_All = 0;
else if tvtot = 1 then TV_Watching_All = 0.3;
else if tvtot = 2 then TV_Watching_All = 0.8;
else if tvtot = 3 then TV_Watching_All = 1.3;
else if tvtot = 4 then TV_Watching_All = 1.8;
else if tvtot = 5 then TV_Watching_All = 2.3;
else if tvtot = 6 then TV_Watching_All = 2.8;
else if tvtot = 7 then TV_Watching_All = 3.5;

The same transformation is made for 'TV_Watching_Politics'. These transformations can be criticised, but it is now possible to compare the countries with each other, for example—see Table 10.4. The countries are sorted by the last column.

The table clearly shows that watching news and politics on TV is much less common than watching everything else on TV. These mean aggregates are logical, although some individual answers were not. We do not interpret these results further.

Table 10.3 Cross-tabulation of the ESS Data for Time Spent Watching TV

TV watching, total time on average weekday	TV watching, news/politics/current affairs on average weekday												
	0 Not at all	1 Less than 0.5 hours	2 0.5 to 1 hour	3 More than 1 hour up to 1.5 hours	4 More than 1.5 hours up to 2 hours	5 More than 2 hours up to 2.5 hours	6 More than 2.5 hours up to 3 hours	7 More than 3 hours	66 Not applicable	77 Refusal	88 Don't know	99 No answer	Total
0	0	0	0	0	0	0	0	0	2342	0	0	0	2342
1	664	2204	85	24	14	3	3	9	0	1	15	0	3022
2	826	3350	2552	84	25	5	11	13	0	0	16	0	6882
3	605	2887	2867	948	58	17	5	8	0	0	14	4	7413
4	617	2744	3670	1075	581	26	15	8	0	0	21	2	8759
5	426	1784	2882	1283	489	313	31	16	0	0	15	2	7241
6	330	1378	2605	1225	618	257	277	27	0	0	14	2	6733
7	688	1801	3780	2272	1375	663	454	971	0	0	45	4	12053
77	0	0	4	0	0	0	0	0	0	1	0	0	5
88	20	46	39	11	6	2	0	4	0	0	57	0	185
99	2	6	11	2	1	1	0	1	1	0	0	13	38
Total	4178	16200	18495	6924	3167	1287	796	1057	2343	2	197	27	54673

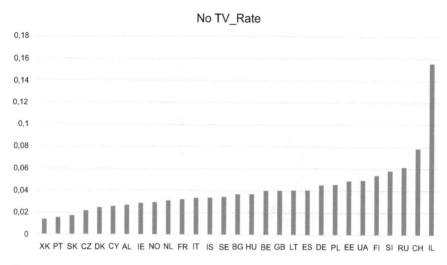

Fig. 10.2 ESS countries by the rate of 'not applicable' (no TV) as an answer to the question about watching TV news, politics, and current affairs.

Table 10.4 Averages of total TV watching and TV watching of news and politics for the ESS countries, Round 7

Country	Total TV watching	TV watching politics	Share of TV watching politics
Hungary	2.09	0.59	0.28
Czech Republic	2.24	0.66	0.30
Ireland	2.06	0.68	0.33
Austria	1.89	0.63	0.33
United Kingdom	2.21	0.78	0.35
Belgium	1.92	0.69	0.36
Slovenia	1.61	0.60	0.37
Switzerland	1.38	0.52	0.38
Lithuania	2.11	0.80	0.38
Germany	1.80	0.68	0.38
Netherlands	2.03	0.83	0.41
Poland	1.73	0.73	0.42
Israel	1.64	0.70	0.43
Estonia	1.87	0.81	0.43
Sweden	1.59	0.70	0.44
Denmark	1.90	0.86	0.45
Finland	1.66	0.78	0.47
Spain	1.86	0.87	0.47
France	1.95	0.92	0.47
Norway	1.70	0.81	0.47
Portugal	1.72	0.85	0.49

References

Granquist, L. (1997). A new view on editing. *International Statistical Review, 65*(3), 381–387.

Laaksonen, S., Kemppainen, T., Kortteinen, M., Vaattovaara, M., Stjernberg, M., & Lönnqvist, H. (2015). Tackling city-regional dynamics in a survey using grid sampling. Survey Research Association. Retrieved June 2017, from http://www.surveymethods.org

UNECE. (2006). *Statistical data editing. Volume 3: Impact on data quality.* Retrieved March 2017, from https://webgate.ec.europa.eu/fpfis/mwikis/essvalidserv/images/1/1b/SDEVolume3.pdf

UNECE. (2017). *Glossary of terms on statistical data editing.* United Nations Statistical Commission and Economic Commission for Europe, Conference of European Statistician Methodology. Methodological Material. Retrieved March 2017, from https://webgate.ec.europa.eu/fpfis/mwikis/essvalidserv/images/3/37/UN_editing_glossary.pdf

Introduction to Statistical Imputation

11

Impute or not, Athens

Chapters 11 and 12 are concerned with imputation methods and tools. The first of them gives an introduction that explains the term itself and looks again at missingness issues that have been considered already. Now the main concern is whether to use imputation. Imputation is not automatically recommended: it should be used only if the results are expected to become better.

The next chapter presents a framework for imputation methods and techniques. We do not try to present all the possible methods, but we cover the subject in such a way that a competent user can apply imputation with adequate knowledge of informatics or by using a general or specialized software package. It is worth studying other approaches to imputation as well, using the references of Chaps. 11 and 12.

© Springer International Publishing AG, part of Springer Nature 2018
S. Laaksonen, *Survey Methodology and Missing Data*,
https://doi.org/10.1007/978-3-319-79011-4_11

Advance Reading

It would be good to understand the following methodologies and tools, in addition to the terms and concepts of Chap. 2, before going further into this chapter:

– Missingness mechanisms (Chap. 4)
– Item non-responses and the reasons for them (Chap. 7)
– Importance of auxiliary variables (Chaps. 2, 5, 6, 7, 8, 9)
– Linear regression models (Statistical books)
– Logistic (logit) regression models (Chap. 7)
– Probit regression (Chap. 7)
– Response propensity (Chap. 7)

Survey data can be complete in theory and, in simple cases, in practice. The sample then covers all the target population units without any missing values (i.e., the MN mechanism, see Chap. 4). Even if the inclusion probability is one, but not everyone replies, the case might be awkward unless the response mechanism is ignorable. Most surveys are sample-based, thus missingness is intentional. If the sampling design follows the correct probability rules, the gross sample allows one to estimate the desired point and interval parameters without problems.

These formulas work well even in cases in which the response mechanism is missing completely at random (MCAR). The only drawback is an increased interval estimate (i.e., standard error, confidence interval) given that the number of respondents is smaller than the number in the gross sample. There are basically three techniques for dealing with non-responses: (1) weighting and reweighting (see Chaps. 5–8), (2) analysis so that missingness is considered by modelling, and (3) imputation.

We do not include any details in this book about (2) (see, e.g., Heckman, 1979; Pfefferman, 1993; Vannieuwenhuyze et al., 2010), but do present a framework for using imputation. This field is very broad, and there are many frameworks, approaches, and methods for imputation that are applied both in theory and in practice. It is not possible to include everything in one chapter, so readers should look at the books and articles in the reference list as well.

The main 'competitor' for imputation is obviously '*data deletion*', which could be considered as the baseline method for imputation. In this case only the observed values are used in the analysis. In one-dimensional analysis we leave out only the missing values for this particular variable; however, in ordinary multivariate analysis we only include those statistical units with variable values that are fully observed. Thus, the amount of data may be reduced dramatically. Data deletion works, to some extent only, if the response mechanism is MCAR, although standard errors will increase.

In this chapter first defines the term *imputation* and the targets for imputation, and then presents some data-handling tools that do not require any proper imputation.

The main purpose of the chapter is to present an appropriate framework for imputation so that we can apply this in practice in the next chapter using concrete real-life examples.

11.1   Imputation and Its Purpose

Imputation is the insertion of a value into the data in a more or less fabricated way (i.e., 'best proxy') for the following reasons:

- There is no value in this cell—that is, it is completely missing.
- The existing value is partially missing (e.g., it is given as an interval), and there is a desire to replace this with a unique value to get a more valid estimate of the distribution (including percentiles, standard deviation, and coefficient of variation).
- The existing value does not seem to be correct; consequently, there is a desire to get a more reliable value by replacing it with a more plausible imputed value.
- The current value seems to be too confidential so that the identity of this individual unit would be disclosed. The fabricated (i.e,, imputed) value can be considered less problematic, even though it is clear that it is not a true value.

Imputation can be performed for both macro and micro data, but here we only consider the imputation methods for *micro* data. Nevertheless, basically the same methods can be applied to macro data; usually, this imputation is more limited so that simpler methods are enough.

A missing, or other inappropriate value, can be imputed once, which is called *single imputation* (SI), or many times, leading to varying imputed values—that is, *multiple imputation* (MI). We present SI methods first, and MI after that. We do not concentrate on imputation because of confidentiality; thus, we focus mainly on replacing a missing value with a best possible proxy.

▶   **Imputation Because of Data Confidentiality** Although we do not really address this issue, it is worth remarking that multiple imputation might be advantageous in this case. The reason is that there are then several imputed values in the dataset, and it is therefore more difficult to identify a respondent unless all the values are close to each other. This, of course, also depends on the imputation methodology (see, e.g., Reiter 2010). The following is the big question.

To Impute or Not to Impute?

It is possible that one survey party is more willing to perform imputation than another. It, however, is easier to perform imputation within the survey institute that is taking care of data quality. An outsider, who is also an end-user, sometimes still has to impute values if he or she is not happy with the results. The reality is that the insiders have more auxiliary and other variables available, partly because some data might be confidential, so cannot be given to outsiders. The insiders are also more familiar with the data process. Yet, the most important reason to impute values is:

> The pattern of the imputed values should be of a standard that means that the estimate using the partially imputed variable is more valuable than the data without imputation. Thus, if imputation is advantageous from an estimation point of view, it should be used. This leads to certain requirements for the imputation methodology.

Naturally, surveys have several estimation tasks, and it can be the case that a certain imputation is not advantageous in all respects. Thus, it is possible that some estimates are computed with, and some others without, imputed values. On the other hand, a big question is which imputation is best for each estimate. It also should be noted that a bad imputation may lower the quality of the estimate. Users should therefore be careful and will need to convince themselves and their clients that imputation leads to some improvement.

Note, however, that all users and clients are happy if the number of missing values is decreased. It thus is not always necessary to impute all the missing values, but only those that have an impact on the estimates are influential. Moreover, much depends on the estimate being of interest. The next subsection specifies this question in more detail.

▶ **Reasons and Strategies for Imputation**
   The following are various imputation reasons and strategies:

   1. The first reason is the number of missing values and the impact if there is no imputation. This is the most important practical question:
      - If the missingness rate is high, say above 50%, the data quality is in most lcases bad if data are deleted, so users are unhappy. If the missingness mechanism is ignorable, the results obviously are moderately good. On the other hand, imputation would be easier in this case than in the case of a nonignorable mechanism.
      - If the missingness rate is low, say below 5%, but it has been found that one or more influential respondents are missing (e.g., big businesses in business surveys, or extremely rich people in income surveys), everything possible should be tried to improve the data quality. Imputation might be the only option.
      - A high missingness rate is not usually as awkward for categorical variables as it is for skew continuous variables, given that the categories are determined optimally. For example, if the respondents with extremely high incomes are in the same category as the ordinary high-income respondents, it is not fatal if some values are missing. On the other hand, these missing values can be quite easily imputed into this high-income category.

2. There may be aesthetic reasons, in the sense that a data file with an 'ugly' pattern of missing values does not convince users about the data's quality. Nonetheless, this also can be a good point—that is, if the quality is bad, the user might be more careful in his or her analysis. Of course, if the quality of the imputation is high, this is the best result.
3. The worst strategy is to complete the data without giving proper attention to the quality of the imputation and to give no indication as to which values are imputed.
4. In all cases, the imputation methodology should be documented so that the user knows how much the data can be trusted.

11.2 Targets for Imputation Should Be Clearly Specified

The first one in this list is quite trivial but the next ones often are more realistic (Chambers 2003):

1. A user will be happy if the imputed values are as close as possible to the correct/ true values—that is, there is *success at an individual level*. Another point is that it is difficult to know how close the imputed values are to the true ones, except in a few cases. This often may be too demanding a target, thus somewhat lower standards are more realistic in practice.
2. A user will still be relatively happy if the distribution of the imputed values is close to the distribution obtained from the true values (*success at a distributional level*). Of course, it is difficult to check this, as well, but easier than in case (1).
3. Meeting a target of *success at an aggregate level* also is satisfactory, specifically in statistical institutes, or other survey institutes, where estimates, such as average, total, ratio, median, point of decile, and standard deviation, are typical. These can be checked, to some extent, particularly in when surveys are repeated.
4. Some users hope to get the *order of imputed values* as correct as possible, but examples of this are rare in journals.
5. Finally, *success in preserving relationships* (e.g., correlations and covariances) also is important in many studies.

Target (5) often is simpler to satisfy using weighting methods because the data's individual relationships remain the same; however, the weights change them to some extent (and, it is hoped, in the correct direction) in the indicators. Target (1) is difficult to check in cross-sectional surveys unless there are excellent auxiliary variables (as seen later in this chapter). In practice, *targets* (2) and (3) *are preferred* because indicators for their performance often can be found, particularly in repeated surveys. Thus, we mainly use these criteria in the empirical imputation exercises.

11.3   What Can Be Imputed as a Result of Missingness?

The following possible imputation situations can be found:

– Undercoverage requires a new up-to-date frame. This is very seldom possible.
– The units with missing data are not selected for the sample. This is done in theoretical or simulation studies, but not really in practice.
– There are unit non-responses for all or some variables. Then we can use mass imputation, which competes with weighting methods. The purpose of mass imputation is to complete the data in order to estimate everything from one dataset. This helps to make all the estimates consistent with each other. It is enough to achieve success at the aggregate level in such cases.
– There is item non-response. This is the most common case in practice, and we only present examples of this.
– There are deficient and sensitive values. This is quite common, but we do not present any examples of it.

11.4   'Aggregate Imputation'

It is not always possible to perform adequate imputation, but it is good to know something about the missingness categories. One possibility is to analyse missingness at the aggregate level. Here, we give an example from the European Social Survey (ESS) in which 'Objective income' was one of the more demanding variables. Its quality in the first three rounds (2002–2006) was fairly inferior, and the values were even completely missing in some countries; however, since then the quality has greatly improved. The strategy since Round 4 has been to use ten categories, by income deciles, for each country. These income categories are all that is needed for most analyses, although the ESS documents indicate the deciles in currencies as well.

Nevertheless, there are four categories for missing answers: 'Refusal', 'Don't know', 'Other missing', and 'No answer'. The first three of these are in the questionnaire, but the last was added later because some missing values were still found. Table 11.1 gives the counts of the respondents in each category for 14 countries in the ESS Round 7. We can see that the 'No answer' group is very small but that the other three are about as large as the proper income decile groups.

The missingness rate for Objective income is relatively high, at 14.7%. This means that we will lose this number at a minimum in all the multivariate analyses in which Objective income is included. It therefore would be nice to know something about those missingness categories. One strategy is to use auxiliary variables without missingness or for which the missingness rate is low. We test one variable, 'Age', without missingness here and another with a low missingness rate, 'Subjective income'. The missingness rate for Subjective income is 0.8%. This latter variable

Table 11.1 Examination of missing objective income groups of the ESS Round 7 for 14 countries

Objective income group	Respondents	Mean Subjective income	Age
1st_Decile	2083	48.2	51.8
2nd_Decile	2329	58.6	55.1
3rd_Decile	2280	63.3	54.4
4th_Decile	2439	68.6	51.8
5th_Decile	2421	72.1	50.2
6th_Decile	2432	75.8	49.7
7th_Decile	2448	79.5	46.7
8th_Decile	2301	82.5	45.7
9th_Decile	1832	87.6	45.8
10th_Decile	1885	93.7	46.6
Don't know	1645	76.2	36.6
No answer	19	62.9	48.5
Other missing	2051	58.3	53.1
Refusal	2056	66.8	58.2

at the same time could be considered to be close to Objective income; thus, it is a good auxiliary variable.

The Subjective income of the ESS is computed from the answer to the following question: 'Which of the descriptions on this card comes closest to how you feel about your household's income nowadays?'

Living comfortably on present income = 1
Coping on present income = 2
Finding it difficult on present income = 3
Finding it very difficult on present income = 4
(Don't know) = 8

We have rescaled this variable linearly so that it varies from 0 (very difficult) to 100 (comfortably). Table 11.1 also includes the averages of this variable and 'Age' for 'Objective income groups'. 'Subjective income' and 'Age' have been tested as auxiliary aggregate variables. Now, it is possible to see which types of groups form the missingness categories. Figure 11.1 facilitates this comparison.

Figure 11.1 shows that the Objective income for 'Refusal' is between the 3rd and 4th deciles, but these respondents are older than the other groups. The group of 'Other missing' is close to the 2nd decile but is a bit younger on average. The group of 'No answer' is very small but not far from the 'Other missing' group. The last fairly large group, the 'Don't know', seems to be the youngest; however, on average their Objective income is relatively high. We can conclude that this 'aggregate imputation' sheds some light on the missing categories for objective income. It is possible to use these two auxiliary variables for micro-level imputation as well, but we do not give any examples in this book.

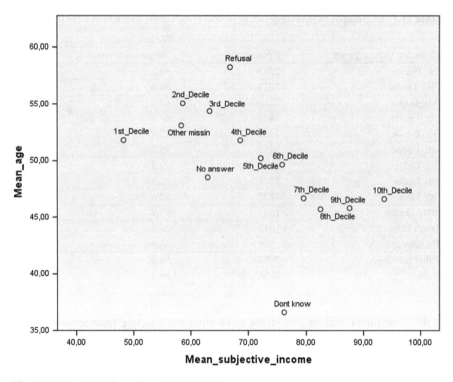

Fig. 11.1 Graphical illustration of Table 11.1

Another conclusion is that aggregation is a useful tool for reporting some results because it also gives the opportunity to continue toward statistical graphing. It often is useful to gather several results under the same file, with the same row aggregates, and this may be a good summary of the results. 'Aggregate imputation' is a tool for reviewing missingness without proper micro imputation. There are other tools that can be used for the same purpose, as described in the next section.

11.5   The Most Common Tools for Handling Missing Items Without Proper Imputation

The following list summarises the most common imputation tools:

1. In the case of mass missingness, the weighting, or the reweighting, is generally exploited. This is possible only for the respondents. The respective imputed data therefore cover the non-respondents too (or those non-respondents whom one wishes to include in the estimation). Note that one imputation strategy is a kind of weighting method but with more flexible weights than the standard reweighted sampling weights (see Real-Donor Imputation in Chap. 12)

2. Item non-responses are marked with a coding that gives good coverage, such as:
   - $-1 =$ respondent candidate not contacted—a problem here may be that we do not know whether this unit belongs to the target population; such cases are rarely imputed
   - $-2 =$ respondent refused to answer (main reason for imputation)
   - $-3 =$ respondent was not able to give a correct answer (possible to impute)
   - $-4 =$ missing for other reasons
   - $-6 =$ question was not asked of the respondent (imputation using logical rules); see the screening case in Chap. 9
   - $-9 =$ question does not concern the respondent

These codes are not used often, but codes, such as 7, 8, 9, 66, 77, 88, and 99, 6666, are used too. Negative values are easy to observe. A zero (0) *must not* be used as a missing code.

Good and illustrative codes also are useful when deciding on the imputation method itself. When one is performing imputation, it is beneficial to try another imputation technique for each missingness category because the nature of these units might be different. This is rarely applied in this way in practice.

Moreover, it is good to state that the coded variable is then full, without missing values. This kind of categorical variable can be used as an explanatory variable in standard linear and linearized models, among others. Example 11.1 illustrates this case in detail. If one wants to use a continuous variable, proper imputation is required.

3. The values with missing codes are excluded from each analysis so that the observation number may vary by variable.
4. This tool is like case (3), but now the units with missing values are excluded from each analysis. In this latter case, the number of observations is always the same. Standard multidimensional analysis does this automatically for those variable patterns used in such an analysis. This strategy, 'case deletion', gives results that are consistent with each other. This is still a relatively common strategy.
5. This tool uses pair-wise analysis for multivariate purposes, with the correlations being the basis for further analysis. This operation first computes pair-wise correlations as in case (3), then continues from the correlation matrix toward multivariate analysis. We lose less information here than in case (4), but consistent results are not easy to get.

Example 11.1 Multivariate Linear Regression for 'Happiness by age' Using the ESS
Happiness by age is an interesting research topic among economists, psychologists, and social scientists. Blanchflower and Oswald (2008) found that happiness by age is U-shaped. This result has been obtained by others as

(continued)

Example 11.1 (continued)

well, although not in all studies. The estimation is not based on any simple frequency calculations, but on a linear regression model with some control variables for personal characteristics. The explanatory variables can be different, but usually they are things such as gender, education, and income. General subjective health is used in some studies as well, but this is not accepted by all researchers (Laaksonen, 2016).

We do not try to address the possibly critical questions here, but just compare the Happiness by age with two types of model:

1. Applying case deletion, thus excluding all respondents without the complete information.
2. Including the control variables in the model with missingness codes—that is, with all variables being complete and without missing values. This strategy is appropriate because all the control variables are categorical.

The dependent variable, Happiness, includes missing values. Fortunately, this rate is low, less than 1%. The three control variables (i.e., Country, Gender, and Age) are complete. We thus lose observations only in model (1), even though there are missing codes in the other control variables.

Using the 2016 ESS data for 20 countries, the number of the observations is 37,845 in model (2) and declines by 16.7% to 31,551 in model (1). This decrease is not very large, but it is still good to compare these alternative models. We use a small model with the following control variables:

– Country
– Gender
– Age
– Age-squared
– Education level, with five codes and one missing category
– Objective income, with ten deciles and three missing categories

The Age variable thus includes two components that are commonly applied in studies of Happiness by age (e.g., Blanchflower & Oswald, 2008; Laaksonen, 2016). This easily gives the possibility of checking whether Happiness by age is U-shaped.

The variable Happiness is measured so that the minimum is 0, for 'Extremely unhappy', and the maximum is 10, for 'Extremely happy'. This variable is a dependent variable in the linear regression model. Its *R-square* increases slightly when the missing categories are deleted, from 11.4 to 12.6%. When comparing the regression coefficients of the missingness codes of model (2) against the codes of model (1), we find that the closest category for the

(continued)

Example 11.1 (continued)

'Refusal' and 'Don't know' groups is the 5th decile, whereas the closest for the 'Other missing' group is the 1st decile. In the case of education level, the only missingness group is close to the lowest education group. We can therefore conclude in general that the happiness of the respondents who do not want to state their income, or who do not know it, are well educated and their income is either average or lower.

The estimates of the observed categories do not differ much from each other. Consequently, the age estimates also are relatively close. The U shape is found with both models, as Fig. 11.2 shows. The minimum age for model (2) is 55.3 years, whereas the minimum age is 53.7 years for model (1).

This difference is so small that we could be happy with both models if we were only interested in whether there was a U shape. On the other hand, we find that the model with missingness categories works correctly and gives additional information about the behaviour of the happiness of the missingness groups. The following colours are used in the graph:

Red = Model with missingness categories for education and income
Blue = Model without non-respondents

In addition, we estimate the same model only for those with missing categories, the 16.7% of respondents mentioned earlier. Their U curve is compared with that for all the respondents in Fig. 11.3. Now the minimum is higher, 61.9 years, and the happiness level is a bit lower. Still, the U curve is found fairly easily. Now we can conclude that the handling of missingness in this way matters, but not dramatically. The following colours are used in the graph:

Red = All respondents
Blue = Respondents with missing codes for income and education

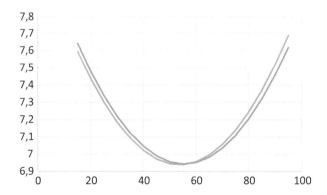

Fig. 11.2 'Happiness by age' in ESS Round 7 for 20 countries

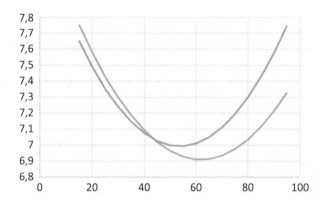

Fig. 11.3 Happiness by age in the ESS Round 7 for 20 countries, for the missing category respondents

11.6   Several Imputations for the Same Micro Data

We present a number of appropriate imputation methods in Chap. 12, but often the practical problem in surveys is to decide whether several incomplete variables should be imputed on the same occasion. Naturally, one or two key variables might be of the most interest. We cannot give any 'perfect' advice for those who are concerned with the quality of micro data; nonetheless, we give some suggestions using a general example first and follow them with comments.

> **Example 11.2 Possible Imputation Strategies in the Case of Item Non-responses of Five Variables**
>
> This artificial example includes six variables altogether. Variable $x1$ is such that it is completely observed. The data file can include other such variables as well. They also can be used for weighting if they are available for the non-respondents or for the target population. Here they can be used for imputation. There are five variables—$y1$, $y2$, $y3$, $y4$, and $y5$—with item non-responses that are of interest to users. The dataset includes 2000 respondents.
>
> The ordinary task is to examine missingness. This is done here so that the averages of the item response indicators are calculated. These indicators are symbolised with the ending '_resp'. The last row of Table 11.2 gives these item response rates. The order of the variables in the table is by these rates. We

(continued)

Example 11.2 (continued)

find that the rates for the first three variables are very high, but those for the other two are much lower. Nevertheless, we can say that all the single rates are relatively high and that it is therefore possible to think about imputing the missing values. By contrast, if the rate was very low, say below 50%, it would be more challenging to impute these values.

Complete responses are received from 73.2% of the unit respondents. Multivariate analysis with these variables (case deletion) could thus violate the estimates. The item response rates for each of the five variables are substantially higher, but clearly vary. We should therefore think seriously about imputation; Table 11.2 is a good starting point for this. Rows 13, 15, and 16 of the table cover 21.7% of the observations, and only one variable is missing for each. We thus have the opportunity to use all the complete variables as auxiliary variables and to hope that they will help with imputation. It is possible to continue to impute all the missing values, or if the completion rate of 94.9% after the first three imputations is enough, to use these observations only. Yet, it does not matter much if some imputations are not very successful in all the analyses.

Row 1 in the table requires one imputation only, with the '$x1$'s as the auxiliary variables. In practice, it can be necessary to impute more than one value, as with this small artificial dataset. Using the table, it is helpful to recognize the term '*sequential imputation*', which means imputing one variable first, then taking these imputed values as a new auxiliary variable when imputing the second variable, and so on. Various strategies could be followed for sequential imputation in the Table 11.2 case. For example, it would be possible to impute row 16 (i.e., $y5 = 0$ of it). These 207 values thus would be the new auxiliary values when imputing row 15, and possibly the whole of the column $y5 = 0$. If the imputed variables are used as auxiliary variables, their quality should be sufficiently high, or the imputation may deteriorate the estimates. We do not present an example of sequential imputation in this book (see, e.g., Kong, Liu, & Wong, 1994; Little & Rubin, 2002).

Table 11.2 Response pattern for the artificial data with six variables (2000 units)

Observations	x1_resp	y1_resp	y2_resp	y3_resp	y4_resp	y5_resp	Count	Percentage
1	1	0	0	0	0	0	1	0.1
2	1	0	1	1	0	0	1	0.1
3	1	0	1	1	0	1	2	0.1
4	1	0	1	1	1	0	1	0.1
5	1	0	1	1	1	1	1	0.1
6	1	1	0	0	0	0	3	0.1
7	1	1	0	1	0	0	1	0.1
8	1	1	0	1	0	1	12	0.6
9	1	1	0	1	1	1	1	0.1
10	1	1	1	0	0	0	7	0.5
11	1	1	1	0	0	1	7	0.4
12	1	1	1	0	1	0	15	0.8
13	1	1	1	0	1	1	36	1.8
14	1	1	1	1	0	0	52	2.6
15	1	1	1	1	0	1	190	9.5
16	1	1	1	1	1	0	207	10.4
17	1	1	1	1	1	1	1463	73.2
Item response rate, percent	100.0	99.7	99.1	96.6	86.2	85.6		

References

Blanchflower, D., & Oswald, H. (2008). Is well-being U-shaped over the life cycle? *Social Science and Medicine, 66*, 1733–1749.

Chambers, R. (2003). Evaluation criteria for statistical editing and imputation. In *Euredit Project Papers*. Retrieved October 2006, from http://www.cs.york.ac.uk/euredit/

Heckman, J. J. (1979). Sample selection bias as a specification error. *Econometrics, 47*(1), 153–161.

Kong, A., Liu, J. S., & Wong, W. H. (1994). Sequential imputations and Bayesian missing data problems. *Journal of the American Statistical Association, 89*(425), 278–288.

Laaksonen, S. (2016). Research note: Happiness by age is more complex than U-shaped. *Journal of Happiness Studies*. https://doi.org/10.1007/s10902-016-9830-1.

Little, R. J. A., & Rubin, D. B. (2002). *Statistical analysis with missing data, Wiley, probability & mathematical statistics* (2nd ed.). Hoboken: Wiley. 408 pp.

Pfefferman, D. (1993). The role of sampling weights when modeling survey data. *International Statistical Review, 61*, 317–337.

Reiter, J. P. (2010). Multiple imputation for disclosure limitation: Future research challenges. *Journal of Privacy and Confidentiality, 1*(2), Article 7. Retrieved November 2014, from http://repository.cmu.edu/jpc/vol1/iss2/7

Rubin, D. B. (2004). *Multiple imputation for nonresponse in surveys*. Hoboken: Wiley Interscience.

Vannieuwenhuyze, J., Loosveldt, G., & Molenberghs, G. (2010). A method for evaluating mode effects in mixed-mode surveys. *Public Opinion Quarterly, 74*(5, 1), 1027–1045. https://doi.org/10.1093/poq/nfq059December.

References

Imputation Methods for Single Variables

12

Seasonal imputation

This chapter considers imputation methods for single variables. Naturally, it may be necessary to impute the values of several variables in each dataset and to carry out several imputations for each dataset. It is essential to understand the basics of Chap. 11, which presents the starting point for imputation methods. It is helpful to look at that chapter for the core terms, but an important question is also why one should, or should not, use imputation. Before answering this question, it is necessary to analyse the missingness and the reasons for it thoroughly. Then again, it is good to remember that the imputation methodology always depends on the case; thus, each variable should be separately imputed even though the principles of the method used can be similar. Successful imputation therefore is 'tailored' to the specific case, and the best results are obtained if the 'imputation team' has sound knowledge of the basis of the data and its quality.

It is not advisable to put too much trust in automatic and mechanical imputation software. It, technically, can be used if its quality has first been checked. Such software easily can fill in the data gaps for several variables during the same run, but this should not be a core target. As noted in Chap. 11, the minimum target is to estimate some aggregates and distributions reasonably well using partially imputed data. This possibly can be achieved using automatic tools; however, the user first has

© Springer International Publishing AG, part of Springer Nature 2018

S. Laaksonen, *Survey Methodology and Missing Data*,

https://doi.org/10.1007/978-3-319-79011-4_12

to convince himself or herself, and then the main users of the results, that the estimates are less biased than if there had been no imputation.

The framework for imputation is not standard, but largely follows the terms of Rubin (1987, 1996, 2004), for example. It also is worth reading other books and articles—for example, those by Allison (2005), Carpenter and Kenward (2013), Enders (2010), Muñoz and Rueda (2009), Laaksonen (2003), Laaksonen and Piela (2003), Laaksonen et al. (2004) and Laaksonen (2016a, 2016b), Here, we approach imputation methods more generally first, describing the imputation process.

12.1 Imputation Process

Imputation is part of the data-cleaning process. It can be considered to include the following *six actions*:

1. *Basic data editing*, during which it is determined which values it is desired to impute.
2. The *acquisition* and *servicing* of auxiliary data, including preliminary ideas to exploit these. This mainly concerns those variables that are not in the survey dataset, and thus also includes variables used for the unit non-respondents, which may need to be downloaded from the same sets that contain the ordinary survey variables. On the other hand, each micro data file includes other useful auxiliary variables, and it is good to identify such values that are not completely missing (item non-responses).
3. *Imputation model(s)*: One or more models are needed for each imputation. At this stage, the model should be specified and estimated, and the outputs saved for further use.
4. *Imputation task(s)*: The outputs of the imputation models and other tools are used to impute the desired missing values. It is possible that new editing will be needed if the imputed values do not match the edit rules.
5. *Estimation*: That is, point estimates, with the imputed values used as well. In addition, the variance (i.e., sampling variance plus imputation variance) is estimated.
6. *Creation of the completed dataset, or several datasets*: This includes good meta data and information about the imputed values; if possible, the imputed values should be flagged unless data confidentiality is an issue. The documentation for the imputation process and the methodology should be available as well. It is not necessary to include all the details in public files, but everything should be available inside the survey institution.

This chapter now focusses on actions (3) and (4), but action (5), relating to the results after imputation, repays attention. We only include estimates of the imputed values in most examples because these better illustrate the performance of the imputation method.

These two core actions (i.e., imputation model and imputation task) should be integrated appropriately into the imputations. This means, for example, that both are programmed thoroughly, and that the imputation results can be immediately checked if the model specification has changed. Next, we present the basic principles behind these two actions.

12.2   The Imputation Model

There are two *alternative imputation* models:

1. The model may be determined using *smart logical information* so that it gives a good prediction for the case for which imputation is required. It may use a deterministic (or stochastic) function, such as $y = f(x)$ (+ *a stochastic term e*), or a rule (as in editing) such as 'if this but not the other, then the missing value is that'.
2. The model may be *estimated using either the same data for which imputation is required or other data* that is similar (at least in its structure and model variables) to the present data.

The following is a recommended strategy. First, try to impute values using alternative (1) as far as possible—this is called *logical or deductive imputation*. Second, impute the remaining values using alternative (2). We do not present any concrete examples of alternative (1) because its applications are closely related to the specific survey. We thus concentrate on alternative (2).

Imputation model (2) is always a model with a purpose that is to *predict* something, using auxiliary variables as independent variables.

The dependent variable of the imputation model being estimated can be of two types:

(A) The variable being imputed *or*
(B) The missingness/response indicator of the variable being imputed.

Case A can cover all possible forms of variables, both categorical (including binary) and continuous, but in Case B the dependent variable is binary. The model is 'single-level' in the examples here but multilevel modelling can be used as well (see, e.g., Lago & Clark, 2015).

These two models are estimated from two different datasets:

(A) from the respondents (observed units) and
(B) from the respondents and the non-respondents. Still, the explanatory variables should be available from both the respondents (observed units) and the non-respondents (unobserved units) in order to estimate the predictions of the units without missing values.

The *predictions* are of various kinds. In Case A, they correspond to the values of the variable being imputed. In Case B, the predictions are the estimated response probabilities or response propensities, which is like the position in reweighting (see Chap. 8). Note that a categorical explanatory (i.e., auxiliary) variable with missingness codes may work reasonably well in the imputation model (see Example 11.1).

If Case A concerns a continuous variable, then the most common model is *linear regression* or its *logarithmic* version. Recently, linear-mixed models also have been applied, and these models may be better than linear ones if the measurements are from two levels.

Regression models are easy to use, and the *model fit* (*R-square*) is a good general indicator for the performance of it. It is therefore good to recognize this indicator when searching for the best auxiliary variables, or covariates, in the model specification phase. This will be the first real operation when carrying out imputation. Its result can be used in the imputation models in Case B as well. The model fit also is useful when comparing various methods.

It is, however, good to repeat that the predictions of the model are used later. For this reason, their quality should be equal over all values of the variable. Case B concerns a binary variable (1 = responded/observed, 0 = not), but a similar model can be used for Case A if the dependent variable is binary (e.g., 1 = employed, 0 = unemployed).

When using a binary model (i.e., either Case A or Case B), the link function needs to be selected, as in reweighting (see Chap. 8). This can be logit, probit, log–log, or complementary log–log. There are no dramatic differences in explaining the models between these link functions, but they are not exactly alike of course. Imputation thus requires using this model for predicting the response propensities for all units (i.e., respondents and non-respondents). That is, the first outputs are values between 0 and 1. In Case A when a binary variable is being imputed, the predicted values are also between 0 and 1, but these indicate estimated relative frequencies.

In addition to ordinary models, such as linear regression or probit regression, the imputation model can be nonlinear and nonparametric. An interesting example of the latter type is *tree modelling*. If the dependent variable is categorical, we talk about a *classification tree* (*random forests* is its newer version), whereas the model for a continuous dependent variable is a *regression tree* (see the AUTIMP project in Chambers et al., 2001).

Moreover, neural nets often create analogous groups of the gross sample. This kind of a group is called an *imputation class* or *imputation cell* in imputation terminology. Imputation cells also can be constructed manually or by using smart statistical thinking. For example, *strata* or *post-strata* can be relatively good imputation cells. Given that the imputation cells are homogeneous from the 'imputational' point of view (especially if MCAR holds true within cells), they offer many advantages. Thus, imputation cells can be constructed with 'smart thinking'— for example, so that the model of Case A or Case B can be estimated twice by gender if one thinks that the predictions vary by gender. Regions and age groups can be suitable imputation cells as well.

Concluding Points About Imputation Models

Predicted values will have a big role when beginning to impute—that is, at the stage of the imputation task. The *important point* is that the predicted values should be available both for respondents and non-respondents; specifically, the auxiliary variables should be complete given that it is desirable to impute all missing values. All the previous predictions can be attempted. We have observed that there are many similarities as well as essential differences; however, we cannot say for sure which method is finally going to be the best, or even whether there is a best method.

It would be expected, however, that some methods, even though they are used in real life, are not good. If the imputation model is to be sound (i.e., to predict well), most imputation task choices work quite well. Thus, if the imputation model is effective, it does not matter much which imputation task is used. Still, most real-life applications are not as easy, and imputation models therefore do not fit very well with the empirical data. Nevertheless, it often is necessary to perform imputations. This means that the best choice of methodology is frequently a compromise.

12.3 Imputation Tasks

Two alternatives can be utilized after the imputation model has been estimated:

- The *model-donor* approach, in which the imputed values are computed deterministically (or stochastically) from the predicted values of the model (adding noise in the stochastic case).
- The *real-donor* approach, in which the predicted values (or the values with added noise) are used to find the nearest or a near neighbour of a unit with a missing value from whom an imputed value is borrowed.

The imputed values in the first case are *not necessarily observed*, except that they often are for categorical variables—although they can be converted to possible values after preliminary imputation. On the contrary, the imputed values of the second case are always *observed values*, being observed at least once among the respondents.

	(a) Model-donor approach	(b) Real-donor approach
A The variable being imputed itself	Yes	Yes
B The missingness indicator of this variable	No	Yes

Scheme 12.1 Integrating the imputation model and the imputation task

To *integrate the model and the task*, we have the options of those set out in Scheme 12.1. This means that the predicted values of the missingness indicator cannot be used directly for model-donor imputation.

▶ **Comment on the Terms** We can find the terms 'hot deck' and 'hot decking' in the imputation literature. This mystic concept is derived from the 1950s, when some US surveyors would randomly select a donor from the observed values. This looked like a hot deck in which the possible donors were moving around and suddenly one was selected to replace the missing value.

 The term 'hot deck' is not clear. It is historical, and it is good to know its origin. In later years it also was used even when the donor was not selected at random—for example, when the real donors were sorted into a certain order. The title of the Laaksonen (2000) paper, for example, was 'Regression-Based Nearest Neighbor Hot Decking'; however, now the method would be described as 'nearest neighbor real-donor imputation when the imputation model is linear regression'. We therefore can see that a certain *near* or *nearest neighbour metric* is needed to select the best donor with an observed value that is to be borrowed for imputation.

Both the imputation tasks are first applied *deterministically*, as we will do in the first examples, but also *stochastically*. If stochasticity has been used in the imputation model, then the imputation task is automatically stochastic, but certain random numbers still must be used in the imputation task.

Stochasticity also can be added into the imputation task using appropriate random numbers. It is necessary to assume how the random numbers behave or their notional distribution; the most common assumptions are normal or uniform, but a lognormal distribution also is used for a ratio-scaled continuous variable. If the real-life data do not behave in this way, the imputation may violate the estimates. Stochastic imputation automatically means that there can be several imputed values, depending on the random choice. If the imputation task is applied deterministically, each missing value is replaced with one value. This is called *single imputation* (SI).

On the other hand, if a stochastic methodology is applied, this leads to an additional uncertainty in the estimate. The uncertainty can be handled using the tools of *multiple imputation* (MI). There is an introduction to MI in the last part of this chapter. At this stage it is worth mentioning that, if stochasticity is applied only for changing the random numbers, the multiple imputation is called *non-Bayesian multiple imputation*; however, if specific Bayesian rules are included in the tool, this is called *Bayesian multiple imputation*.

The imputed value of the model-donor method is simply either: (1) the predicted value of the imputation model (i.e., deterministic *imputation*), or (2) the predicted value plus a noise term of the imputation model (i.e., stochastic *imputation*). There are several tools for including this 'noise' term, and some of these are presented in the examples.

In general, this issue can be difficult to deal with thoroughly in imputations in which the imputation model is not robust. For example, when using a regression model, it is often *assumed that its distribution is normal,* with a mean equal to zero and a standard deviation equal to the root MSE. A problem is that there can be outliers in random values, consequently, in imputed values. This requires one to *truncate the outliers* in some way. Another option, which is less problematic, is to use a pattern of the *observed residuals* estimated for the respondents and then randomly to draw these residuals with noise for non-respondents. So, this strategy is a kind of a real-donor method.

12.4   Nearness Metrics for Real-Donor Methods

Main Case of Nearness Metrics
The most common metrics are derived from the *predicted values* of the binary regression model, therefore the link function should be chosen by the user. In the case of a stochastic selection, some random noise needs to be added, but there are various options for this. We do not go into detail about this here, but we want to mention a couple common tool from books on imputation by Rubin (1987, 2004):

- Classify the predicted values by their values into a certain number of categories, between 10 and 20, called *imputation cells*. These are relatively homogeneous and thus their values are close enough to each other.
- Randomly select one observed value from each cell to replace a missing value. This method is sometimes called *cell-based random hot deck*.

Observations of this kind of imputation cells also are called '*donor pools*'. There is thus a pool, and the imputation maker goes to it to borrow a good value to replace a missing value. Maybe it is good to create such donor pools in advance for imputing, but the values in this pool should at least be from the same period.

▶   **Comment** The most common nearness metrics that use the binary response propensity model work in the same way for all types of variables being imputed because observed values are borrowed from the respondents. The methodology can work well only if the distribution of these observed values covers the target population appropriately. This cannot be known for sure. Sometimes, it is possible to see that it does not work.

   Problems often are easier to recognize in business surveys, concerning large businesses. For example, it may be found that all or most of such businesses have not responded. When using real-donor methodology, it is not possible to get optimal respondents from whom to borrow the required values. The only option is to work with model-donor methods to try to find useful auxiliary variables in the model. The solution could be to motivate such businesses to give the best possible proper value.

Second Case of Nearness Metrics

The *other* rational strategy in many situations is to use model-donor imputation values (e.g., the *predicted values of a regression model*) taken from both the respondents and the non-respondents using the same nearness metrics. This thus means that we technically impute values for the respondents too, using the same strategy/model as for the non-respondents. The next step is to work in the same way as in the previous case to select either the nearest donor or a near donor, which is the usual method when there is a desire to randomise the procedure. Thus, the nearness metric may be the previous model-donor output:

- Predicted value of the imputation model (deterministic imputation of the entire dataset) or
- Predicted value plus a noise term of the imputation model (stochastic imputation)

To put this more clearly, we can work so that first we perform imputations using the model-donor methodology but for the respondents (observed units) in addition to the non-respondents (not observed). Now, we have a nearness metric that can be used to find the nearest neighbour (or a reasonably near neighbour) for each non-respondent from the respondents, and to borrow this neighbour's value for that unit. This also gives one the opportunity to compare the two strategies when estimating figures from the imputed dataset.

The second strategy for the nearness metric works relatively well for continuous variables, but as always performance naturally depends on the integrity of the imputation model. The same principle also works if the variable being imputed is binary (e.g., poor versus non-poor, unemployed versus employed, sick versus non-sick). In this case, the working model is binary, but the dependent variable differs in the response model. Thus, it is possible to use the two types of binary model for imputing the missing values of that binary variable (Laaksonen, 2016b).

12.5   Possible Editing After the Model-Donor Method

As is known, the real-donor methods give observed values that are (or should be) valid values. Consequently, nothing needs to be done before they can be used in estimation. On the other hand the model-donor imputed values are calculated, and there is no guarantee that they will be valid in all meanings. Sometimes they still can be used as such, but this is not always true. Some examples are as follows:

- If we wish to impute a value for Happiness from integer values lying between 0 and 10, then using model-donor methods means that the imputed values will be in decimals in most cases. No user would accept this. A simple solution, which is sometimes used, is to round these figures to integers, but this is not necessarily the best solution.

- The variable 'Happy' thus is categorical. In the case of a real continuous variable, post-editing also can be important, although its influence on the end results is not necessarily great. Nevertheless, most clients do not like to see, for example, income figures with several decimal places of the sort that can be obtained using model-donor imputation. To an expert such values also indicate clearly that they are imputed. Thus, if confidentiality is important, as it often is, rounding is a good solution; nonetheless, it is not clear what the best rounding is.

Mathematical rounding is not ideal, but statistical rounding that is carried out probabilistically is better. For example, if the value is 455.7, and the rounded values should be in the tens, the probability of rounding to 450 is (10–5.7)/10, and the probability of rounding to 460 is (10–4.3)/10. Mathematical rounding always leads to a fixed value of 460. This type of rounding also is called *aesthetic imputation*.

12.6 Single and Multiple Imputation

The point estimates of complete datasets that have been imputed multiple times are given in a similar way by both Rubin (1987, 2004) and Björnstad (2007), among others. The parameter being estimated thus may be any statistic of interest, including the mean, the standard deviation, the coefficient of variation, or a regression estimate.

To make the formulas simple, we denote the estimate by Q. Such an estimate is calculated from a complete dataset after each single imputation (SI). Thus, the estimate from a single imputed complete dataset is Q_l, and the respective variance is B_l, both calculated taking into account the sampling design and possibly adjusted weights as discussed in Chap. 8. The multiple imputation (MI) point estimate is thus simply the average of the L imputations:

$$Q_{MI} = \frac{\sum_l Q_l}{L} \qquad (12.1)$$

In the same way, the variance estimate is:

$$B_{MI\text{-within}} = \frac{\sum_l B_l}{L} \text{ where } B_l \text{ is a SI variance.} \qquad (12.2)$$

There are two alternatives for calculating the MI variance of the L complete datasets. The first term of the variance, called the *within-imputation* variance, is in both cases equal to that obtained from Formula (12.2), but the second term, the *between-imputation* variance, is larger in Björnstad's version:

$$B_{\mathrm{MI}} = B_{\mathrm{MI\text{-}within}} + \left(k + \frac{1}{L}\right)\frac{1}{L-1}\sum_l (Q_l - Q_{\mathrm{MI}})^2 \qquad (12.3)$$

The difference is in the term $k = 1/(1-f)$ in which f is the fraction of missing values or the non-response rate. This increases as the fraction increases. Rubin's formula does not depend explicitly on the number of imputed values. His Bayesian approach possibly takes this into account implicitly. Of course, it is not clear which is the most correct in each case. It could be considered that Rubin's formula works with Bayesian MI, and Björnstad's formula works with non-Bayesian MI; however, we will not state any definite conclusion about this, even though we do not present the details of Bayesian methods (see Rubin, 1987, 2004).

The MI thus requires a tool for a Monte Carlo type of simulations for SI to be developed. This means that each MI imputation should be close to the initial SI, but with a certain randomness added. Thus, the MI point estimate (i.e., the average of the single MI estimates) should be close to the respective SI estimate.

The *strategy* for applying a multivariate linear regression for model-donor imputation first *estimates* the model. Next, we compute the *predicted* values and then add to each of them a *normally distributed random* term with zero mean and a standard deviation equal to the estimated root mean square error (RMSE). It is possible to get the RMSE as an output using appropriate statistical software.

In other words, this non-Bayesian method is not difficult to implement. Because some stochastic predicted values may be very large, either positive or negative, we have truncated this standard deviation within the range $(-1, +1)$. This is one tool to make the *estimates robust*. The procedure removes some annoying outliers to keep the imputed data at an acceptable level. It is a good procedure in practice, unless a better strategy can be found. In the experiments we used this robustness correction before the imputation task, which is more objective than doing it after the task when incorrect imputed values can be found. In the end, these incorrect values are subjectively removed to a correct area, which is not a good strategy.

Nevertheless, plausible values are not ensured when making the model predictions robust. Some bad values, such as negative imputed incomes, still can be obtained. They can be removed into the minimum observed value. This is a simple solution but is not objective. Nevertheless, we use it later for method comparisons, and we call the results that apply this option 'results with constraints'.

This 'error-term'–based specification for MI in the regression models is logical. For each repeated imputation, a seed number is changed. The point estimates are expected to be close to the pure model-donor imputation, whereas the variance and the standard error, respectively, are expected to follow the uncertainty of the imputations in a correct way because they depend on the model fit. Thus, the better fit leads to a smaller (imputation) variance.

Example 12.1 PISA 'Multiple Imputation'

The literacy scores for reading, science, mathematics, and problem solving are not unique in the public micro dataset, but there were five 'plausible values' for each student in the PISA before 2015, and since then there have been ten values. These values are calculated from the results of several exam tasks that are not exactly the same for each student. This means that the score includes an additional uncertainty. The PISA group therefore decided to give five (or now ten) different 'plausible values' in the dataset.

When calculating the estimates, this can be considered as an additional uncertainty component. Nevertheless, the means and other point estimates without problems can be calculated as the average of the 'plausible values', as in the case of MI. The impact of the variation in the means because of those multiple values, fortunately, is not very large. This means that it is not catastrophic to omit the MI component. The graph in Fig. 12.1 shows these figures for some countries.

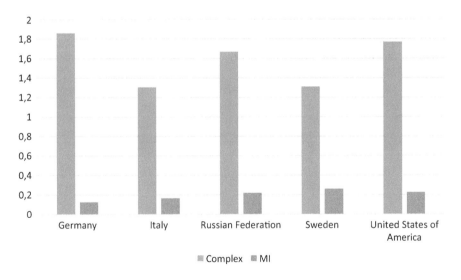

Fig. 12.1 The coefficient of variation of the mean estimate for problem-solving scores in the 2012 PISA, in percentages; 'Complex' uses three survey instruments (stratum, cluster, and weights) whereas MI is based on five plausible values

12.7 Examples of Deterministic Imputation Methods for a Continuous Variable

This section presents imputation results with deterministic methods first. The dataset is not completely from real life but is relatively similar to the initial data of the random sample of the Euredit test dataset (Laaksonen, 2016a; Wagstaff, 2003). We have, however, taken a sample of only 200 respondents to show the elementary methods more concretely. The variable 'Income' is the one for which 53 observations are missing (26.5%). Here we have only two auxiliary variables, the categorical Region, with five values, and the register income, which is fully correlated with the survey income (correlation = 0.97). This thus gives an opportunity to estimate a strong linear regression imputation model that can be used in the imputation task. We start from the model without any auxiliary variable, which gives the estimated constant term, and the average income of the observed values that can be used as such for those with missing values. This model-donor method, without any auxiliary variable in the linear regression model, corresponds to *mean imputation* in the standard literature.

We do not illustrate this simplest imputation by means of an illustration but show a graph when using a slightly stronger model in which Region is the only explanatory (auxiliary) variable. Now the *R-square* of the linear regression model is low, at 1.6%. If the average of each Region category replaces the respective missing values, the results are better. The scatter plot of Fig. 12.2 shows these values against the true

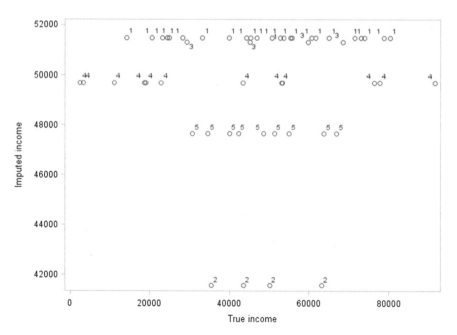

Fig. 12.2 Imputed values only with the deterministic model-donor method when one categorical variable (Region, with five categories 1, 2, 3, 4, and 5) is the auxiliary variable of the linear regression (i.e., cell-based mean imputation)

survey incomes. This method sometimes is called *cell-based mean imputation*. In most cases, we can see clearly how far those imputed values are from the true values. A method like this thus is not recommended. When the number of those cells or categories increases, the imputed values improve, but we do not take this further here.

Given that we have this extremely robust auxiliary variable, we naturally use it. We keep Region in the model as well. This gives much better imputed values, as also can be observed from Fig. 12.3. It is helpful to keep in mind that the register income is an extremely well-fitting auxiliary variable. Now the imputed values look rather good.

The previous imputation model is linear, but it is possible to use the same method with a logarithmic transformation that is very commonly used in econometrics. The model itself is similar, but the logarithmic transformations are as follows:

$$\text{the dependent variable} = \log(\text{survey\_income})$$

$$\text{the main auxiliary variable} = \log(\text{register\_income}).$$

In addition, the model includes the constant term and the categorical Region variable. Then the model is estimated, and the predicted values can be found. These predicted values accordingly are logarithms, not incomes, but after exponential

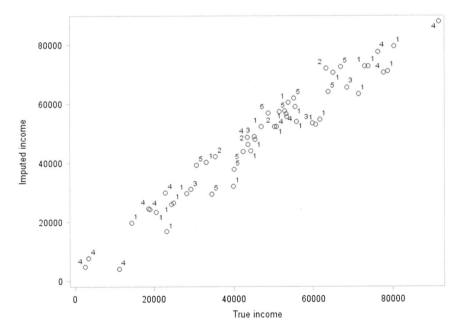

Fig. 12.3 Both the observed and the imputed values with the deterministic model-donor method when the Register income, in addition to the variable Region, is used as an auxiliary variable of the linear regression (i.e., deterministic regression imputation). The marks for Region are as in Fig. 12.2

transformation the imputed values can be obtained. Figure 12.4 shows the equivalent scatter plots for the linear case as in Fig. 12.3. They are not similar, but it is not possible to get the negative imputed values that might be found in the linear case if the model is as weak as in the present case; fortunately, we do not see such problematic values in Fig. 12.3 because the model is strong. The logarithmic transformation thus ensures that no incorrect values can be obtained.

We now continue to the real-donor methods, first, using the same imputation model as in the case in Fig. 12.3 (i.e., strong regression model). In this case, we estimate the predicted values for all units—both for respondents and for non-respondents. Consequently, it is important that these predicted values be derived from the same basis, even though we could use the observed values for the respondents. This would not lead to anything because now we finally have to use the observed values for the non-respondents.

These completely available predicted values are used as the nearness metrics, as illustrated in Scheme 12.2. This only shows one piece of the micro data. The predicted values, 'yhat_r', are first sorted, then the algorithm searches for the nearest respondent, and then takes that respondent's value for the non-respondent. The column 'yhat_r' also shows which value would have been taken in the case of the deterministic model-donor method (i.e., deterministic regression imputation). As we can see, all these values have figures after the decimal point and can be easily recognized unless we perform 'aesthetic imputation' (see earlier in chapter).

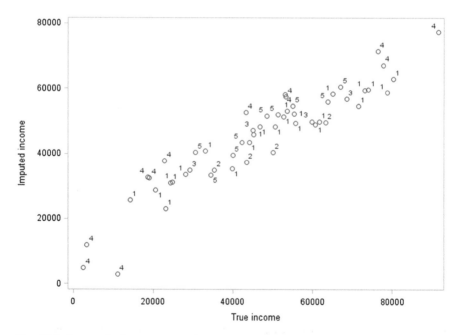

Fig. 12.4 Scatter plot between true values and model-donor imputed values with logarithmic regression

Obs	income _reg	income _survey	yhat_r Sorted	Nearest yhat_r	Imputed income
1	89068	97400	92706.81		
2	85142	84645	88726.79		
3	84784	82735	88363.86		
4	83052 .		88031.54	88363.86	82735
5	80245	76960	84842.05		
6	81441	79000	84324.62		
7	80508	79330	83378.79		
8	77804	77120	82711.33		
9	78679	79995	82174.86		
10	76728 .		79546.78	82174.86	79995
11	72882	71225	77721.61		
12	72876 .		77715.52	77721.61	71225
13	70944	74230	75756.94		
14	72421	81215	75180.52		
15	69832	65925	74629.64		
16	71860	77645	74611.80		
17	69649	76855	74444.12		
18	69622	73940	74416.75		
19	70064	67870	73441.33		
20	70184 .		72912.74	72845.43	67535
21	68072	67535	72845.43		

Scheme 12.2 Illustration of how to find the nearest neighbour for real-donor imputation when the deterministic linear regression model is used as the imputation model

Note that although Scheme 12.2 is for the linear regression method, it works for all other real-donor methods, except when using imputation cells or imputation classes. The other alternatives for the imputation model are: (1) linear regression with noise term (stochastic) and (2) response propensity model, deterministically or stochastically.

Scheme 12.2 is applied in Fig. 12.5. The scatter plot here is different from that of Fig. 12.4, but not very different. It can be seen that some observed values are used as imputed values more often than once.

Special Cases and an Example on Real Donors

- It is possible that there are two or more neighbours that are equally near. In such a case, the logical solution is to select one at random.
- It is possible that one observed value is the nearest neighbour for several non-respondents. This occurs more often if the proportion of missing values is large, or if the auxiliary variables do not give good predictions. It

(continued)

therefore is good to investigate how many times one respondent has been used as the real-donor and, if this number is large, to try some type of randomization. If no good solution can be found, the users should at least be told that the quality is not good.

We checked in the case of the method in Fig. 12.5 how many times each observed value had been used as an imputed value (see Table 12.1). Because the maximum number is three, and eight observed values are not used as real-donors at all, this case is not problematic.

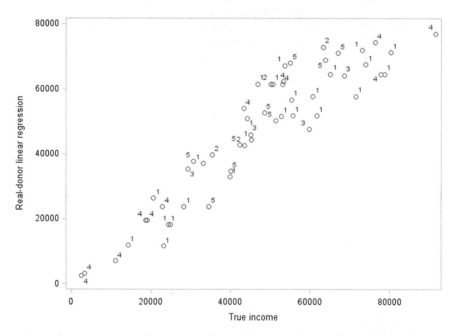

Fig. 12.5 Scatter plot between true values and real-donor linear regression-based imputed values

Table 12.1 Use of observed values as imputed values in the example of Fig. 12.5

Use of observed values	Counts	%
0	8	15.1
1	38	71.7
2	6	11.3
3	1	1.9
All	53	100.0

The real-donor method can be started from the logarithmic regression model instead. There are two alternatives here for the nearness metrics: (1) the logarithmic predicted values and (2) the exponential form of these. The order of the predicted values is equal, but the differences can vary. In Fig. 12.6 we choose the first alternative, which is easier. The results are not very different, but the variation looks to be larger for higher incomes.

The real-donor imputation methodology can be based on the response propensity model as well, in which case several link functions can be used. We present the results with the two link functions—probit in Fig. 12.7 and logit in Fig. 12.8. We find a relatively similar structure in these as in the earlier models, but some outliers were found—more when using the logit link. Most of these are for the same units. It is not clear how these outliers can be explained, but one explanation is that the response propensity is more difficult to predict with these auxiliary variables than with the survey income. Here, the latter model fits exceptionally well, but it is less predictable for response behaviour.

The scatter plots give some information about the performance of each imputation method, but they do not tell the whole story. Given that we know the true values, we can compare the diverse methods against them. Table 12.2 shows the results. It compares the results with four indicators that are at least important in the case of income. Income differences are measured mainly by the coefficient of variation but also with the minimum and the maximum. The mean is the third indicator that is commonly used for continuous variables.

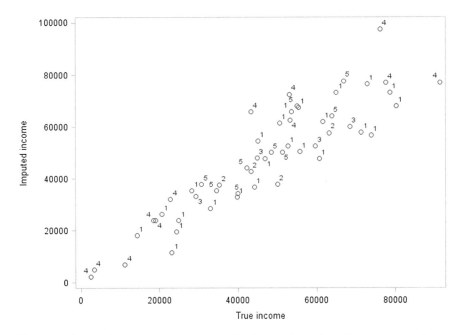

Fig. 12.6 Scatter plot between true values and real-donor logarithmic linear regression-based imputed values

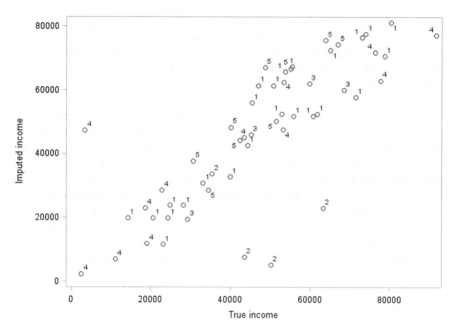

Fig. 12.7 Scatter plot between true values and real-donor imputed values with probit model

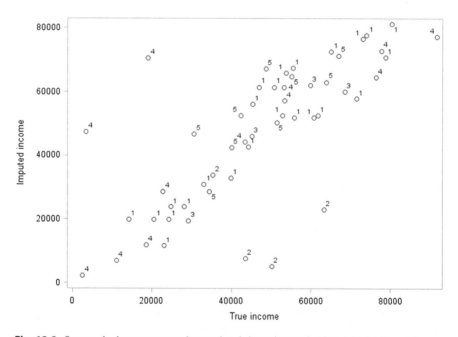

Fig. 12.8 Scatter plot between true values and real-donor imputed values with logit model

Table 12.2 Summary of the values imputed for the first dataset using different imputation methods

Imputation model and explanatory variables	Imputation task	Imputations	Mean	Minimum	Maximum	Coeff. of variation
TRUE		53	46,768	2475	91,615	44.8
Linear regression without auxiliary variables (mean imputation)	Model-donor	53	49,454	49,454	49,454	0
Linear regression with the explanatory variable Region	Model-donor	53	49,675	41,577	51,489	5.5
Linear regression, with Region and register income	Model-donor	53	48,112	4245	**88,032**[a]	41.8
Linear regression with Region and register income	Real-donor	53	**47,000**	**2360**	76,960	**43.4**
Logistic regression with Region and register income	Real-donor	53	**46,594**	**2360**	81,215	47.8
Probit regression with Region and register income	Real-donor	53	45,634	**2360**	81,215	49.3
Logarithmic linear regression with Region and register income	Model-donor	53	44,938	2962	77,375	33.6
Logarithmic linear regression with Region and register income	Real-donor	53	47,619	**2360**	**97,400**	**44.9**

[a] The two best methods according to each indicator are in bold type

First, we can see clearly how inferior method mean imputation is because it cannot say anything about income differences; however, the results might be satisfactory for some clients if missingness is low. The bias in income mean based on mean imputation is also large and the same is true for cell-based mean imputation. Now, some income differences can be found. All the results improve substantially when using the good auxiliary variable, Register income. There still are differences, and we can consider some methods to be unsatisfactory. Surprisingly, the model-donor logarithmic regression method is the worst of all. The reason is that it cannot predict higher incomes satisfactorily.

Real-donor methods seem to be best, although they are not always good. When using a response propensity model, the income differences are overimputed by a fair amount. If linear or logarithmic regression is the imputation model, the real-donor methods work well according to all indicators.

12.8 Examples of Deterministic Imputation Methods for a Binary Variable

It is good to repeat this sentence from the previous section: 'The most common metrics are derived from the *predicted values of the binary regression model* (then the link function should be chosen by the user)'. If the dependent variable of this model is the response indicator, the predicted values, or the response propensities, can be used for all types of single variable and even for a group of several single variables. In this latter case, the missing values are replaced by the observed values of the group. If the variables of this group are correctly related to each other, this real-donor imputation obviously works well. It thus does not matter which type of variable is being imputed.

Thus, we do not consider real-donor methods with the response propensity model in this subsection, but we look at other possible imputation methods in the case of a binary variable such as 'unemployed versus employed', 'poor versus non-poor', or 'sick versus non-sick'. If the variable being imputed includes more than two categories, it is still possible to impute one category as the binary variable, and then to continue toward the second category, and so on; however, this is not convenient. We do not present any details about this case in this book but specify a method for imputing a binary variable (see also Laaksonen, 2016b).

Model-Donor Methods
The first of these is *simple rounding*, which is sometimes used in practice. In this case, the predicted values are estimated using the binary variable as the dependent variable, and then these are rounded (1) to one if the predicted value is above 0.5 or (2) to zero, otherwise. The result might be improved when using its *adaptive version*—that is, when a normal distribution-based threshold is used when deciding whether the unit takes the value one or zero.

The third simple method also uses a threshold, but this is taken from the predicted values of the respondents. This method is here called 'Threshold from the respondents'. If the respondents and the non-respondents are similar, this method works well (given that the missingness mechanism is MCAR).

The fourth method, which also works better in the case of nonignorable missingness, follows a *Bernoulli approach*. In this case, the predicted values p_k of each unit k with a missing value are first estimated for the binary variable y being imputed. Then, a uniformly distributed random number within $(0, 1)$, u_k, for the same unit, is drawn. The imputed value for each k with a missing value is obtained as follows:

$$\text{if } u_k > p_k \text{ then } y\_imputed = 1, \text{ otherwise } y\_imputed = 0.$$

This strategy gives the model-donor imputed values with the desired link function. By changing the random seed number ten times, ten non-Bayesian model-donor

Table 12.3 Model-donor imputation results for the poverty rate based on Laaksonen (2016b)

True	0.249
Logit Bernoulli, 10 imputations	0.246
Probit Bernoulli, 10 imputations	0.244
Logit simple rounding	0.124
Logit adaptive rounding	0.184
Logit threshold from the respondents	0.164

multiply imputed values are obtained. This last method is not deterministic, but a single imputation result can be obtained by averaging the single imputed values.

The example is from a dataset in which the poverty line has been estimated from the income distribution. If the income is below this line, the person is coded with a one or as poor; otherwise, the person is coded with zero—that is, as non-poor. The mean of this indicator gives the poverty rate.

Table 12.3 presents the results of these four methods, and the true values for each. It has been shown that simple methods do not work because the missingness mechanism is far from being ignorable. In this case, however, the poverty indicators are relatively well predicted with a reasonably good set of the auxiliary variables. The last row conveys that the poverty rate of the observed values is much lower than the true value. Thus, without a good imputation method the poverty rate would be greatly underestimated.

12.9   Example for a Continuous Variable When the Imputation Model Is Poor

In the case of the examples of Sect. 12.7 with a continuous variable, all the imputation methods work relatively well, although not perfectly. If the pattern of the auxiliary variables is not as good as in these examples, the results cannot be expected to be good. The preceding first dataset is a small sample of a larger dataset that covers nearly 20,000 persons, 5315 of them (26.7%) with no observed income. We now illustrate imputation methods with that dataset but without any clear auxiliary variables, which is a more common situation in real life (Laaksonen, 2016a).

There are several categorical auxiliary variables here. The full list, which is used in all the imputation models, with the number of categories in each is as follows: gender (2), 5-year age group (11), marital status (2), civil status (2), education level (4), region (12), Internet at home or not (2), socioeconomic status (4), unemployed or not (2), and children or not (2).

All these auxiliary variables are statistically significant for income, with the best ones being gender, education, and socioeconomic status. Nevertheless, the fit is relatively low because no individual-level compelling variable is available. The R-square of the income regression model is 39%, while it is about 97% in the first dataset.

We initially concentrate only on point estimates, of which there are two in the test: 'mean income' and 'income differences measured with CVs'. This allows for comparison of both pure SI methods and MI methods, with the average of ten imputations being used as a point estimate.

The true mean income is $46,606, which is not far from the mean in the first example, and the mean income of the respondents is $52,857. This last average thus would be the imputed average if we were using 'mean imputation'; however, we do not present these results here and neither do we present cell-based mean imputations, which do not work well, as was found in the previous case.

We look next at the results of these methods, first presenting in Table 12.4 the performance of the single imputation methods when the imputation model is linear regression. This model-donor strategy may give impossible values because the values are calculated in a straightforward way. Of course, it is not known exactly which values are impossible, but it is certainly true that negative values are.

Several methods lead to values like these. They can be made robust simply by removing them so that negative values are winsorised to the minimum of the observed values, which is slightly above zero. There are other strategies for making the values robust, but we do not present them here.

Most averages are relatively close to the true value, but the income differences with CV are not, except for the MIs that have been made robust. This, unfortunately, makes the average worse.

Negative imputed values can be avoided using log-transformation. Because we found other problems when using these imputed values, we do not present this method in the chapter. The results are like the preceding when applying a good imputation model (see Sect. 12.7). The second group of results always gives plausible values because we borrow the imputed values from observed ones. Table 12.5 summarizes the findings.

Single real-donor methods work relatively well, and most are acceptable for both estimates, the best being the method using a probit link function; this is more or less as a result of good luck. Multiple imputation methods also are good for income differences. It is not easy to see why the logit MI method gives such an upward bias for the average. One reason is that in some groups there were not enough real donors to borrow from, and the values had to be borrowed from observed values that were too far away. This was not as problematic when using the other link functions.

Table 12.4 Single model-donor imputation results when the imputation model is linear regression

Method	Average	Rate of negative values, %	CV, %
True	46,606		65.1
MI Robust[a], No Constraints	46,142	5.1	71.8
MI Robust Constraints	47,380		65.1
MI Not Robust, No Constraints	46,576	8.4	57.5
SI	46,272	0.2	43.4

[a]'Robust' means normally distributed random terms within $(-1, +1)$; 'Constraints' means negative imputed values changed to the minimum observed positive value

12.10 Interval Estimates

It is possible to estimate variances for estimates when some values are imputed and no MI methods are used—thus, for singly imputed data. The basic component here is the imputation variance, which needs to be added to the ordinary sampling variance. This section just presents the results of MI-based variances.

The variances are calculated by applying both Rubin's and Björnstad's formulas (see Sect. 12.6). Given that the variances are not illustrative, the results are presented as the standard errors of the mean and as their relative versions, respectively. The mean here is the income average for the imputed values. It should be noted that the results are not automatically interpretable because the standard error depends on the mean and thus on its bias. We cannot know which standard error is true, but a kind of minimum standard error can be estimated from the true values. This mean is 416, and its relative version is 0.9%.

Table 12.6 presents the results of all the MI methods for the point estimates. The methods are sorted by their relative standard errors. This facilitates the interpretation of the interval estimates. It is not, however, automatic because the interval estimates are conditional on the average estimates. The table therefore also includes the averages. It is good to check how biased the estimate is when interpreting the interval estimates. The random real-donor method is a benchmarking method at this point. This is based on equal distances between all units, which leads to a random selection of the real donor to be used as an imputed value. It gives an average that is close to the mean of the respondents but therefore far from the true value.

Table 12.5 Single real-donor imputation results

Method	Average	CV, %
True	46,606	65.1
Logit SI	45,890	65.3
Logit MI	47,345	65.5
Probit SI	46,801	64.8
Probit MI	46,152	65.8
Regression[a] SI	47,264	65.9

[a]Regression means linear regression, which is now being used for a real-donor search

Table 12.6 Interval estimates based on the two alternative formulas for MIs

Method	Average	Standard error		Relative standard error	
		Rubin	Björnstad	Rubin	Björnstad
True values	46,606	416		0.90	
Random real-donor (benchmark)	52,922	613	666	1.16	1.26
Regression model-donor robust	47,380	598	650	1.26	1.37
Regression real-donor	49,341	644	693	1.30	1.40
Regression model-donor	46,102	642	699	1.39	1.51
Probit real-donor	46,732	676	722	1.45	1.55
Logit real-donor	46,713	841	877	1.80	1.88

Björnstad's formula gives somewhat larger standard errors. It could be best to use these because all the methods given here are non-Bayesian. Outside this exercise, we know that Bayesian methods using the same formula give a higher standard error than do non-Bayesian methods. This is because of an additional 'Bayesian' step in their calculations. In some cases, these steps lead to very biased point estimates (Laaksonen, 2016a). Nevertheless, we definitely cannot say which standard errors are best, although some users prefer smaller ones.

Weighting and Real-Donor Imputation Are Related to Each Other

The sampling weights are created for the respondents, and the estimates are calculated from the respondents as well. Real-donor imputations borrow the imputed values from the respondents. The number of times the value for each respondent is used again varies from zero upward. The real-donor imputed data thus resembles the weighting so that each respondent gives its own weight—this can be sophisticated, as shown in Chap. 8. 'Real-donor weights' may vary for each variable being imputed; in other words, this method is more flexible than the straightforward weighting method.

The weighting, or reweighting, works well if the pattern of values (i.e., values for the respondents) covers the whole target population adequately. It is then possible to adjust for the weights so that the estimates are as unbiased as possible. In the case of real-donor imputation the same opportunity arises. Nonetheless, this is not the case if the pattern of the observed values is not representative—for example, if extreme units are mostly missing. The only possibility then is to try a model-donor imputation methodology, but this requires auxiliary variables that can be predicted thoroughly.

References

Allison, B. D. (2005). Imputation of categorical variables with PROC MI. In *SUGI 30 Proceedings*. Retrieved February 2015, from http://www2.sas.com/proceedings/sugi30/113-30.pdf

Björnstad, J. (2007). Non-Bayesian multiple imputation. *Journal of Official Statistics, 23*, 433–452.

Carpenter, J., & Kenward, M. (2013). *Multiple imputation and its application*. Chichester, West Sussex: Wiley.

Chambers, R. L., Hoogland, J., Laaksonen, S., Mesa, D. M., Pannekoek, J., Piela, P., et al. (2001). *The AUTIMP-Project: Evaluation of imputation software*. Research Paper 0122. Statistics Netherlands, Voorburg.

Enders, C. K. (2010). *Applied missing data analysis*. New York: Guilford Press.

Laaksonen, S. (2000). Regression-based nearest neighbor hot decking. *Computational Statistics, 15*, 65–71.

Laaksonen, S. (2003). Alternative imputation techniques for complex metric variables. *Journal of Applied Statistics, 30*, 1009–1020.

Laaksonen, S. (2016a). Multiple imputation for a continuous variable. *Journal of Mathematics and Statistical Science, 2016*, 624–643. Science Signpost Publishing, Newark, DE.

Laaksonen, S. (2016b). A new framework for multiple imputation and applications to a binary variable. *Model Assisted Statistics and Applications, 11*, 191–201.

Laaksonen, S. & Piela, P. (2003). Integrated modelling approach to imputation. In *Euredit Project Documents. Standard Methods*, D512 StatFI. Retrieved October 2004, from http://www.cs. york.ac.uk/euredit/

Laaksonen, S., Rässler, S., & Skinner, C. (2004). Documentation of pseudo code of imputation methods for the simulation study. In *DACSEIS Project Research Papers under Workpackage 11.2 'Imputation and Nonresponse'*. Retrieved March 2004, from www.dacseis.de/deliverables

Lago, L. P., & Clark, R. G. (2015). Imputation of household survey data using linear mixed models. *Australian and New Zealand Journal of Statistics, 57,* 169–187. https://doi.org/10.1111/anzs. 12108.

Muñoz, J. F., & Rueda, M. M. (2009). New imputation methods for missing data using quantiles. *Journal of Computational and Applied Mathematics, 232,* 305–317.

Rubin, D. (1987). *Multiple imputation for nonresponse in surveys.* New York: Wiley.

Rubin, D. (1996). Multiple imputation after 18+ years. *Journal of the American Statistical Association, 91,* 473–489.

Rubin, D. (2004). *Multiple imputation for nonresponse in surveys.* Hoboken, NJ: Wiley-Interscience.

SAS/STAT 9.3 (2011). Help and Documentation, Users' Guide for the MI Procedure. Details. SAS Institute Inc., Cary, NC.

Wagstaff, H. (2003). Appendix B: data sets and perturbations. In *Euredit project,* vol. 2. Retrieved October 2004, from http://www.cs.york.ac.uk/euredit/

Summary and Key Survey Data-Collection and Cleaning Tasks

13

Good-quality surveys in all circumstances

This is a summary of survey actions and consists of a long list of steps and tasks in the order that is roughly the one followed in practice. For further details, please refer to the 12 earlier chapters.

(A) *Statement of the purpose of the study*, with a decision to use one or more surveys or registers to obtain the necessary empirical data. A survey can be a crucial tool for this purpose. The connections between the whole study and a specific survey should be determined as clearly as possible before going on to the next step.

(B) *Specification of the survey design* as much as possible. This specification is made up of all the following phases of this summary; however, a rough specification should be created at this stage. The most difficult tasks should be investigated thoroughly at this stage, but it is good to leave some flexibility in the design because it is not possible to know in advance how everything will

© Springer International Publishing AG, part of Springer Nature 2018
S. Laaksonen, *Survey Methodology and Missing Data*,
https://doi.org/10.1007/978-3-319-79011-4_13

work ultimately. An attempt should be made to predict or anticipate possible problems.

(C) *Determining the target population.* This should be done as precisely as possible and should be realistic. It is useful to consider first a *population of interest* and a *target group for the intended survey* that may be ideal but are not realistic in the strictest sense. Note that if there is a requirement to generalise the results, a decision needs to be made about the target population. If there is no intention to generalise, there is *no need* to go through the remaining steps in this summary.

(D) *Obtaining one or more frame populations* or sampling frames in order to approach the target population. These frames are the lists or registers that consist of the units of the target population at the last stage of the survey design. It is good to take any auxiliary variables from a frame that may be useful in the further steps of the survey. If a frame includes all the study units directly, this makes many things simpler; however, it is still good to note that the frame is not current for the time or period of the survey—that is, is more or less out of date. Therefore, it is valuable to try to get updates for the frame or frames. These are called *updated frame population(s).* It is good to try to update the auxiliary variables at the same time.

(E) *Deciding whether to use sampling.* Even if an attempt has been made to survey the whole population, it is good to meet requirements similar to those of sample-based surveys. It is mandatory to follow some survey methods if missingness occurs, as it does in all proper surveys.

(F) *Decision about sampling principles.* It is recommended that *probability-based sampling principles* be followed, but, if this is not possible, *nonprobability-based sampling* that is close to probability principles may be acceptable. The following phases of this summary are for probability-based sampling, but it is useful to follow many similar requirements in the case of nonprobability-based sampling, as much as possible. Case studies also could be used, but their generalisation to the target population level is difficult. Nevertheless, they are at least valuable for developing proper sample surveys, and as qualitative studies.

(G) *Planning and decisions about the survey sampling design.* This might take a great deal of effort because it requires many things to be considered. The basic target in this step is to decide what is a reasonable *effective sample size* and then to use this to calculate the *required gross sample size* for the whole survey as well as its subpopulations (e.g., strata). There are four main components that need to be considered: unit non-response, ineligibility, design effect due to varying inclusion probabilities or weights, and effect on design because of clustering.

(H) *Planning the data collection,* including: survey mode (e.g., single-mode, multimode, or mixed-mode), data-collection tools (e.g., mail, phone, face-to-face, web), addressing questions of confidentiality during data collection and when publishing the data and results, whether to have a cross-sectional or longitudinal/panel survey, estimation of costs, and budget.

(I) *Designing the questionnaire and preparing it* should be completed at this stage, but work on the task should be started at the beginning of the survey. If the survey is new, this may be the most demanding task. As part of the question-naire design, it is good to perform a *pre-test* or a *pilot survey*, and if possible, the survey process should be tested and taught at the same time.

(J) *Sampling and the creation of the first-order sampling design data file.* This file contains the gross sample units and the sampling design variables, and as many other useful auxiliary variables (i.e., macro and micro) as possible.

(K) *Decision about the time and length of the fieldwork.* The fieldwork should be performed at a time when potential respondents are most willing to participate. If the fieldwork is only short, there is less opportunity to be flexible and change things. If it is long, such as a period of three months, it is possible to use, a 'responsive design' that endeavors to motivate any gross sample groups that have not participated satisfactorily in the first half of the fieldwork period. A long fieldwork period also gives an opportunity to rectify, to some extent, any mistakes that are made.

(L) *Data entry* should be done as much as possible during the fieldwork. This gives an opportunity to check certain basic meanings of the data, using so-called *data pre-editing.* If the data entry is manual, the same basic editing can be done, but this takes more time and requires more resources.

(M) *Completing the sampling design data file.* The most important new variable from the fieldwork is the *survey outcome*—that is, who has responded completely and who has responded only partially or not at all. Naturally, the reasons for non-response, and other fieldwork experiences, should be documented in the same file if feasible. The sampling design data file may be completed with other auxiliary variables from registers and other administrative sources, as well as from the macro statistics. It also is possible to include some auxiliary information found by the interviewers, although this is not common.

(N) *Completion of statistical editing,* that is, examining how plausible the individual values are and looking at their relationships with the core variable values. If the values are not plausible, an attempt should be made to correct for them. It also is good to code the missing values and the reasons for them as much as possible (e.g., the value 'zero' is a real value but a missing value has a code: '−1' or '99').

(O) *Imputation of any missing and deficient values* that can be replaced with the best possible fabricated values, or proxies, so that the core estimates of the survey are more precise than without imputation (i.e., if they are left as missing values and the number of observations is reduced).

(P) *Construction of the sampling weights for respondents*, which should be the best possible by using the sampling design variables and auxiliary variables. These weights are needed if there has been an attempt to survey the entire target population but some missingness has been noted.

(Q) *Putting the file into a good electronic format* (e.g., SAS, SPSS, Stata, R, Excel). The survey micro data file basically is ready after the previous stage, but this step is needed in order for it to be used easily by all who will have access to it. The file should have good meta data so that each user can know quickly what each variable and its values (e.g., categories, ranges) mean. Para data for the variables of the survey process and the fieldwork also are useful. Survey information that cannot be included in the file should be documented in another way and should be publicly available.

The survey micro file for the respondents that is now available contains what are called the *cleaned survey data*. This file gives the opportunity to make correct estimations of the desired parameters and of the indicators of the accuracy of the parameters (e.g., standard errors, confidence intervals). The cleaned data may be of two kinds, with at least the following files:

– A file for the users of survey institutions
– A file for outside users, for which the best form is a public use file (PUF) such as the ESS or PISA

The latter file should be made confidential using anonymised identity codes and other statistical disclosure limitation methods.
It is important to *bear in mind* that no cleaned data file is completely clean, so it is still possible that some values and their connections are not plausible. Thus, they will need post-editing during the analysis.

Basic Survey Data Analysis

14

From raw data forward

This chapter includes basic survey data analysis, such as estimating frequencies, means, and statistical models, using 'survey instruments' but not going into most complex cases. The purpose is to give instructions for survey analysis using general statistical software, such as SAS, SPSS, STATA, or R, but without details about them. Examples using PISA and ESS are the main part here, some being derived from ESS-related test data as well (see Sect. 6.1). The chapter is primarily based on these examples. They do not cover complex samples, but such can be rather straightforwardly calculated using one of the software packages. The SAS, SPSS, STATA, or R software work well with the following sampling designs in cross-sectional surveys:

© Springer International Publishing AG, part of Springer Nature 2018   201
S. Laaksonen, *Survey Methodology and Missing Data*,
https://doi.org/10.1007/978-3-319-79011-4_14

- Simple or stratified random sampling
- Equidistance sampling, assuming that it corresponds to simple random sampling
- Unstratified or stratified two-stage cluster sampling

If the survey is longitudinal or panel-based, the respective solutions can be applied, but we do not present such examples here. The same applies to three- or four-stage designs. Fortunately, there are textbooks and articles available for more complex circumstances (e.g., Chambers & Skinner, 2003; Lehtonen & Pahkinen, 2003; Lumley, 2010).

14.1   'Survey Instruments' in the Analysis

The 'survey instruments' included are weighting, stratification, and clustering. The general software is easy to use because one only needs to give the variable indicating which of the three survey instruments is required, then run the program. If any of the instruments is missing, this 'box' does not need to be filled in, and the program will run correctly. The impact of each such instrument is presented in the following.

1. *Survey weights*

   The purpose of using survey weights is to *generalise* the results at the level of the target population (and its domain), thus to estimate the desired parameters as well as possible. If the quality of the weights is high, the bias in these point estimates can be expected to be minimised.

   Nevertheless, the estimates still can be biased in real-life situations. The objective is to select the weights that are the most advanced, as explained in Chap. 8. To develop these weights, the auxiliary variables from both the micro and the macro level are exploited as much as possible, including by calibration to margins that are accurate enough and useful for users. A careful check should be made of whether to use the analysis weights or the ordinary sampling weights. This is because the software packages do not necessarily work correctly in all cases. This problem does not affect averages or other basic estimates but is important for more complex estimates, including standard errors and design effects.

2. *Explicit stratification*

   The number of explicit strata should not be so high that there are too few primary sampling units (PSUs) and respondents to obtain sufficiently reliable estimates. Even though the minimum size of a PSU that can be used to estimate the variance is two, this does not mean that the estimates obtained from it are plausible. It is better to try to obtain more clusters and respondents. If post-strata are created to adjust for the weights, this variable should be used in the estimation in the same way as explicit strata.

3. *Clusters*

   The PSU clusters here are those used in the sampling design. It is beneficial if there are a reasonably high number of these. The PISA guidelines, for example, require that at least 150 schools should be drawn in the sample. That number varies greatly in ESS countries, often being higher but sometimes lower. This is more common if a two-domain sampling design has been used so that the clusters are only for rural areas.

Estimates
The survey estimates relate to either the points or the intervals. The best possible survey weights therefore give the least biased point estimates. The accuracy of an interval estimate depends on all three survey instruments: a variation in the weights increases the standard error, but not necessarily by much; good stratification decreases the standard error slightly; and clustering often clearly increases the standard error (see the discussion on DEFFp and DEFFc in Chap. 5). Without appropriate analysis for complex samples, it is possible that both the point estimates and the interval estimates are biased.

This chapter gives concrete examples in which the estimates are not completely different with or without the survey instruments, but in which it is possible to make an incorrect decision about the results. It is beneficial to include the best instruments for the data in the analysis. As we have learned, the public ESS data do not include two of the instruments (i.e., stratum and cluster). Thus, it is good to assess the impact of these. Fortunately, the cluster effect of small area PSUs is rather minor, so the ESS interval estimates are not dramatically below what they should be. On the other hand, the ESS-related test data include all the survey instruments and therefore help with an understanding of their impact (see examples in Sect. 14.2.3).

14.2   Simple and Demanding Examples

We turn now to the examples, which are in the following order:

- One-dimensional frequencies
- Two-dimensional frequencies
- Means and other distributional figures for ordinal-scaled and continuous variables
- Linear regression models
- Binary regression models

These are selected because they are used commonly in survey analysis.

14.2.1 Sampling Weights That Vary Greatly

It is often the goal to use a sampling design that leads to a small variation in sampling weights, which can be found from the design effects due to varying weights (*DEFFp*), as described in Chap. 5. It may be possible to achieve this even by using the anticipated response rates in stratified random sampling, if anticipation works well. A small variation in sampling weight also is good in the sense that a

Table 14.1 Percentages of elderly people without and with using weights

Age group	All weights are one	Ordinary sampling weights
61–70	37.5	60.1
71–80	44.0	33.0
81–90	18.5	6.9
All	100.0	100.0

less-qualified user can get quite accurate estimates without using the survey instruments perfectly. It should be noted, however, that standard errors may be too biased if the sampling is based on clusters.

On the other hand, proportional sample allocation is not rational in many cases. We are not referring here to business surveys where the sampling weights for the largest businesses are often very small (i.e., because there are a small number of such businesses in the frame), whereas the weights are substantial for small businesses. Self-weighting would lead in such cases to very biased estimates. Similar problems can be encountered in social surveys. We give an example of a survey of elderly people in which it was important to get enough respondents from the oldest age groups, even though those over 90 were not included in the target population. There was also a higher sampling fraction for males.

This allocation ultimately gave sampling weights for the respondents that vary remarkably. Table 14.1 gives the population frequencies by age group. It illustrates very well the bias in frequencies if weights are not used. Given that survey variables are also very age-dependent, the estimates also are biased in most cases unless the weights are not included.

14.2.2 Current Feeling About Household Income, with Two Types of Weights

This example is from Round 7 of the European Social Survey (ESS). It concerns subjective income, which is measured with four alternative categories as shown in the table. Statistics for two countries are given—Table 14.2(a) for Switzerland and Table 14.2(b) for Hungary. Selection of the countries is based on the design effects due to varying sampling weights (*DEFFp*). Chapter 5 presents some results from Round 6 for the DEFFp using the design weights; however, now we use the post-stratified weights, including the design weights, which are available in the public data. These design effects may be very different from each other. It is clear, however, that the post-stratified weights give estimates that are much less biased than those based on the design weights. Consequently, it is good to compare these two types of estimates—those based on the 'best' weights and those without any weights.

The two countries were selected because Switzerland has the lowest DEFFp (= 1.02), whereas Hungary has the highest (= 1.40). Table 14.2 presents the frequency estimates and their standard errors for each subjective income category. Thus, we have used one survey instrument, the best possible weight, that also gives

Table 14.2 Current feeling about household income, with two types of weights

Country and Category	Without weights		Best weights (post-stratified)	
	Percentage	Std error	Percentage	Std error
(a) Switzerland				
Living comfortably on present income	57.3	1.3	57.0	1.3
Coping on present income	31.9	1.2	32.0	1.2
Difficult on present income	8.5	0.7	8.6	0.7
Very difficult on present income	2.3	0.4	2,4	0.4
(b) Hungary				
Living comfortably on present income	6.4	0.6	5.3	0.6
Coping on present income	51.4	1.2	46.2	1.4
Difficult on present income	33.1	1.2	35.9	1.4
Very difficult on present income	9.1	0.7	12.7	1.1

Table 14.3 Means and CIs of subjective income with and without the sampling weights as in Table 14.2(a) and (b)[a]

		Mean	95% confidence interval	
Switzerland	Without	81.4	80.2	82.7
	With	81.2	79.9	82.5
Hungary	Without	51.7	50.5	52.9
	With	48.0	46.5	49.6

[a] The range of the subjective income goes from 0 to 100

the respective standard errors. Ordinary software without complex sampling tools does not give these automatically.

As expected, the Swiss estimates are quite close to each other without and with weights, the standard errors being equal to one decimal place. In contrast, the Hungarian estimates change considerably. The general line is that the best weights give higher frequencies for those who have more difficulties on their present income. This tendency is shown in Table 14.3, in which the means are based on a linear transformation into the interval from 0 to 100.

This result clearly shows how much higher the subjective income is in Switzerland than in Hungary. The difference is large with the best weights, but the Hungarian mean is significantly lower with these weights. This result is more plausible. We can see that, even when the weights are advanced, they do not always change any estimates completely unless the difference is clear; however, the target should be to go toward the least-biased estimates—for both point estimates and interval estimates.

14.2.3 Examples Based on the Test Data

We look next at two examples from the test data, using the adjusted weights created in Chap. 8. These weights are merged with the plain survey data for the respondents,

Table 14.4 Subjective income by its categories, with two weights

	Basic weights		Calibration after propensity weights[a]	
Category of subjective income	Low CI	High CI	Low CI	High CI
Living comfortably on present income	41.9	46.8	36.8	41.8
Coping with present income	40.1	45.1	42.9	48.2
Difficult on present income	9.5	12.7	10.8	14.6
Very difficult on present income	1.4	2.7	1.7	3.3

[a] Calibration margins are two genders, five age groups, and eight explicit strata (see Chap. 8)

Table 14.5 The 95% CI of the mean for some ESS variables using three weights

	Basic weight		Pure calibration		Calibration after propensity weight	
Variable[a]	95% CI		95% CI		95% CI	
Most people try to be fair, or take advantage of you	63.3	65.2	63.0	65.0	60.8	63.0
Trust in the legal system	61.6	63.9	61.6	63.9	60.0	62.4
Trust in politicians	43.5	45.7	43.4	45.7	41.2	43.5
Number of daily cigarettes	20.3	26.0	20.3	26.0	23.1	29.6
How happy are you?	75.1	76.8	74.9	76.6	72.9	74.9
Drinking alcohol every week, %	25.8	30.6	26.6	31.4	25.3	30.0

[a] The scale of all variables other than the one concerning cigarettes is from 0 to 100

as is illustrated in Chap. 6 (Sect. 6.1). The first example is for the frequencies and the second for the means. We use complex sample tools in both estimations, thus both the confidence intervals and the point estimates also should be less biased (Table 14.4).

The differences are relatively large with these two weights, resembling the changes for Hungary in Table 14.2(b). Thus, the non-respondents are coping less favorably with their present income than the respondents. The same trend is common in other surveys, but it is not always possible to investigate this because the auxiliary variables are bad, and the weighting methods are not good.

Next, we present a table that illustrates this problem more broadly. The same test data are used, but more variables are examined and one more weighting method—pure calibration (see Chap. 8)—is used. The calibration margins here also are gender (2 categories), age group (5), and explicit regional stratum (8).

Table 14.5 shows, first, that the confidence intervals are slightly higher when using the adjusted weights than they are when using the basic weights. The second point is that the estimates do not change very much when moving from basic weights to pure calibration. The importance of calibration margins therefore is not significant in the case of these estimates. The largest change concerns drinking alcohol, where the rate is slightly higher using pure calibration. Interestingly, when using the propensity weights before that, the rate is slightly lower.

In general, the impact of the adjusted weights is smallest for the variable 'drinking alcohol every week' when using the propensity weights before linear calibration. A similar tendency can be found in all other cases. That is, the basic weights lead to higher averages in the trust and happiness variables, whereas the number of daily cigarettes seems to be smaller when using these adjusted weights.

Some differences are even significant. On the other hand, it should be noted that the calibrated weights give correct estimates for their margins, thus by gender, the five age groups, and the eight explicit strata (regions), but nothing else is ensured.

Calibration Using the Test Data to Estimate Happiness

Chapter 8 includes reweighting methods, and we recommend using calibration as the final method if the calibration margins are really the true values or are close enough to them. This ensures that the margins are definitely correct, which often improves confidence in the estimates. We gave an introduction to calibration in Chap. 8, and recommended using the response propensity weights as the starting weights in calibration if the quality of the micro auxiliary variables was good.

Now we illustrate this situation using the test data, in which we use both the basic weights and the response propensity weights for the complete dataset (see Chaps. 4 and 8). Chapter 8 also includes the calculation of the post-stratified weights for the simple random sample (SRS) domain (see Sect. 8.3). Table 14.6 shows results of the type that can be used for calibration in most countries—that is, with three high-level category margins included: gender (2), age group (5), and regional stratum (8).

Table 14.6 is the example for average happiness, but corresponding results are obtained for the other estimates. The point estimates are ordered by their value. We can see clearly that happiness declines as more auxiliary variables are included. This is because unhappier people are less willing to participate in surveys. When using only these three margins, no weight is negative. We do not include the estimates

Table 14.6 Happiness averages using calibrated and other weights with three margins for the test data

Weight	Auxiliary variables	Mean	Std error
Basic	Stratum	7.596	0.043
Raking ratio after basic	Three margins[a]	7.581	0.043
Linear calibration after basic	Three margins	7.580	0.043
Sinus hyperbolicus after basic	Three margins	7.580	0.043
Post-stratified	Post-strata	7.477	0.047
Linear calibration after response propensity probit	Three margins	7.389	0.053
Response propensity logit	Section 8.4	7.385	0.053
Linear calibration after response propensity probit	Three margins	7.375	0.054

[a] The margins used were gender, age group, and regional stratum

Table 14.7 Happiness averages using calibrated and other weights with four or five margins for the test data, adding education and income to Table 14.6

Weight	Auxiliary variables	Mean	Std error
Raking ratio after basic	Four margins	7.348	0.056
Raking ratio after basic	Five margins	7.338	0.057
Linear calibration after response propensity probit	Five margins	7.303	0.059
Sinus hyperbolicus after response propensity logit	Four margins	7.286	0.059
Linear calibration after response propensity probit	Four margins	7.279	0.059

based on the probit response propensity weights because they are relatively similar to those based on the logit weights.

It is interesting, too, that the estimates based on calibration after the basic weights are about equal to those obtained with both raking ratio, linear, and sinus hyperbolicus calibration. Post-stratification decreases the average because of happiness differences by gender (i.e., females are happier, while males participate less in surveys). It also is interesting that the last three estimates are at the same level.

The impact of the linear calibration is minor when continuing from these weights to calibration. One obvious reason is that the same auxiliary variables are used in both. In practice, it is recommended that the two estimates of these, based on calibration, be used. The reason is that the margins are correct in this case. For example, if a user observes that the male–female ratio is not correct, he or she will not trust any of the estimates. Based on Table 14.6, the average happiness is about 7.38, not the result of 7.60 obtained with the basic weights.

We were able to continue the Happiness estimation because we also had Education and Income in the sampling data file (see Sect. 6.1). It was unfortunate that the linear calibration after the basic weights led to several negative weights. For this reason, we did not estimate anything with these weights. It is a good thing that the linear calibration after the response propensity weights gives the correct weights, although this is not ensured in all cases. Table 14.7 now includes the main results. The happiness average continues to decline although Happiness and Education are correlated. By contrast, Income does not have much influence after education. The estimates of the last two rows are the most plausible.

14.2.4 Example Using Sampling Weights for Cross-Country Survey Data Without Country Results

If the cross-country data include the ordinary sampling weights—that is, their sum is equal to the target population size—all types of domain analyses can be done using these weights. This is automatically possible for the PISA data, but not for the ESS data. Nevertheless, when creating the ordinary sampling weights, as presented in Chap. 8, the correct estimates can be calculated. Many cross-country analyses still can be done using the analysis weights, given that the statistical model includes the country as a control variable. Examples of this are given later in this chapter.

Table 14.8 Foreigner_Positiveness by religion in 21 ESS round 7 countries, sorted by the mean with the weights

Religion or denomination to which respondent belongs at present	Without weights			With weights		
	Mean	Low CI	High CI	Mean	Low CI	High CI
Judaism	51.4	50.6	52.1	50.1	48.8	51.4
Roman Catholicism	49.6	49.3	50.0	52.2	51.6	52.8
Not applicable	53.5	53.2	53.9	53.5	52.8	54.1
Protestantism	55.5	54.9	56.0	54.9	54.0	55.9
Orthodox Christianity	50.4	49.1	51.7	56.2	53.0	59.3
Eastern religion	63.2	60.3	66.1	58.4	53.0	63.8
Other Christian denomination	57.4	55.4	59.4	58.6	55.9	61.4
Islam	50.7	49.3	52.1	60.1	58.2	62.0
No answer	53.8	46.4	61.1	61.1	49.9	72.2
Other non-Christian religion	58.7	55.1	62.3	61.3	53.3	69.4
Refusal	56.5	50.8	62.2	65.2	53.4	77.1

Table 14.9 Foreigner_Poitiveness by education for 21 ESS round 7 countries, sorted by mean

Education	Mean	95% CI	
Very little	42.7	41.2	44.3
Low	46.9	45.7	48.1
Missing	47.3	43.8	50.8
Basic	50.0	49.0	50.9
Low university	51.5	50.5	52.5
Middle university	55.4	54.5	56.2
Master's degree	58.5	57.6	59.5
Doctoral	64.5	63.7	65.2

Here, we present two ESS examples in which the domain units can be in different countries. This requires one to use the ordinary weights, but we present the same results without any weights in Table 14.8. The dependent variable in both examples (Tables 14.8 and 14.9) is the variable created in Example 2.1 (see Chap. 2), called Foreigner_Positiveness, but the domains are different (i.e., Religion and Education).

The differences between the domains are quite clear. We will leave the interpretation to the readers. It should be borne in mind that some confidence intervals are relatively lengthy, which is very much because of the small size of the domains.

14.2.5 The PISA Literacy Scores

We have found that the PISA student weights vary by country in different ways although the DEFFp is rather low (i.e., around 1.1–1.2). This means that the estimates even without the weights give a rough understanding of the literacy and other scores, for instance. We illustrate this situation in Table 14.10 with an example

Table 14.10 Means and standard errors estimated without and with survey instruments for the PISA variable 'Problem solving'

Country	Respondents	Simple random sampling without weights		All survey instruments applied		Design effect (DEFF)
		Mean	Std error[a] of mean	Mean	Std error of mean	
Czech Republic	5327	528.3	1.2	509.0	3.2	6.7
Spain	10,175	488.5	1.0	476.8	3.9	16.9
Hungary	4810	467.7	1.4	459.0	4.2	8.8
Belgium	8597	513.6	1.1	507.8	3.2	8.7
Slovak Republic	4678	486.8	1.4	483.3	4.2	9.0
United Kingdom	4185	520.0	1.4	516.8	4.0	7.8
Israel	5055	456.4	1.6	454.0	5.2	10.0
France	4613	513.4	1.4	511.0	3.4	6.2
United Arab Emirates	11,500	413.0	1.0	411.2	3.5	13.8
Poland	4607	482.7	1.4	480.8	4.6	11.3
Estonia	4779	516.8	1.2	515.0	3.0	6.4
Austria	4755	508.1	1.3	506.4	5.2	16.7
Russian Federation	5231	490.8	1.1	489.1	4.2	13.4
Sweden	4736	492.1	1.3	490.7	3.3	6.3
United States	4978	509.2	1.2	507.9	4.6	13.6
Turkey	4848	455.6	1.1	454.5	4.2	15.2
Japan	6351	552.2	1.0	552.2	3.7	14.3
Korea	5033	561.1	1.2	561.1	3.8	9.3
Germany	5001	508.4	1.4	508.7	4.8	12.1
Ireland	5016	497.8	1.3	498.3	3.4	7.4
Norway	4686	502.5	1.4	503.3	3.7	6.8
Croatia	5008	465.4	1.2	466.3	3.6	8.6
Italy	5495	508.6	1.2	509.6	3.4	7.8
Montenegro	4744	404.9	1.2	406.7	9.5	64.7
Portugal	5722	491.6	1.1	494.4	4.1	13.0
Singapore	5546	558.4	1.2	562.4	4.7	15.1
Netherlands	4460	506.2	1.4	510.7	5.0	12.2
Canada	21,544	517.0	0.6	525.7	2.5	15.2
Australia	14,481	513.1	0.8	523.1	2.0	6.4
Finland	8829	510.5	1.0	522.8	2.3	5.3
Denmark	7481	481.3	1.1	497.1	3.5	10.8
Slovenia	5911	458.3	1.3	475.8	3.9	9.8

[a]The overall design effect, including all its components, is calculated from the standard errors. The countries are sorted by the relative differences between the means, with the top ones those for which the means go below when using the weights, and the bottom ones are those for which the change is in the opposite direction

that also includes the standard errors of the means with and without the student weights.

Seeing as the countries are sorted by relative change from the simple random estimates to the correctly weighted estimates, the table illustrates clearly that the change can go both ways. The mean score of the first country, the Czech Republic, is substantially lower with the weights, but in contrast Slovenia's score increases. Nevertheless, it is very clear that the order of the countries will not change dramatically.

The second, and more interesting, point is the substantial increase in standard error when using all the survey instruments. The overall design effect, DEFF, is a good indicator for this. Montenegro's DEFF is rather large, but it is quite moderate in all the other countries.

14.2.6 Multivariate Linear Regression with Survey Instruments

This type of regression works in the same way as tabulation or other basic estimations if the software package includes these instruments. There are a smaller number of such models in most packages, however. It is possible to use other tools in those cases, but we do not consider them in this book. The purpose here is only to present some basic information about multivariate statistical modelling. Because linear regression is used most often, we present an example from the 2015 PISA first. This illustrates the questions met in statistical modelling.

The dependent variable is 'Science literacy score' from the PISA study. In this example we include the following seven OECD countries: Germany, Finland, Sweden, Japan, Estonia, Korea, and the United States. The main thing of interest is not in comparing the countries but in looking for some explanatory variables that explain the variation in the dependent variable. The country, of course, is one such variable, but it can be considered as a good and necessary *control variable* in such models.

It should be borne in mind that this example is very technical; in other words, we have no subject matter theory to use in the model specification, but we try to show how the estimates vary between using a simple random-based model—that is, without survey instruments or a similar model with three survey instruments. The explanatory variables and their significance are shown in Table 14.11.

We can see that the goodness of the fit, R-square, is higher in the Complex model, but we are not going to interpret this further because it is not the most important observation. It is advantageous to recognise that most variables are quite significant by p-values in both models, but some differences can be found too. First, it is interesting that Subjective well-being is very significant in the SRS model, whereas it is far from significant in the Complex model, which is therefore the only one that can be trusted. This variable is created by the PISA team, and three dimensions are covered: 'one's reflective assessment of one's life (including the single "general life satisfaction" question); *affect*—an emotional state, typically at a particular point of

Table 14.11 Significance of the two alternative linear regression models for the science literacy score of the 2015 PISA survey for seven countries

Tests of model effects[a]	Degrees of freedom	F value		p-value	
		SRS	Complex	SRS	Complex
Model	30	246	86	<0.0001	<0.0001
Intercept	1	41,062	18,841	<0.0001	<0.0001
Country	6	191	57	<0.0001	<0.0001
Gender	1	41	41	<0.0001	<0.0001
Immigration status	2	189	18	<0.0001	<0.0001
Gender*Immigration status	2	34,001	42,980	0.0532	**0.1239**[b]
Grade	2	449	105	<0.0001	<0.0001
Environmental optimism	1	743	337	<0.0001	<0.0001
Parents' education	4	294	64	<0.0001	<0.0001
Noise in class	3	125	61	<0.0001	<0.0001
Parents' support	1	61	42,856	<0.0001	0.0046
Material wealth	1	16,438	35	**0.2281**	<0.0001
Subjective well-being	1	14,062	0	0.0066	**0.9408**
Late to school	3	216	69	<0.0001	<0.0001
Feels outsider	3	55	42,948	<0.0001	<0.0001
R-square		0.166	0.217		

[a]The SRS model is without survey instruments, whereas the Complex model is calculated with all three instruments
[b]The p-values in bold are special

time; and *eudaemonia*—a sense of meaning and purpose in life' (PISA, 2015; Martela & Steger, 2016).

The other slight difference is for the interaction between gender and immigration status. Because this is interesting in general, we present its details in Fig. 14.1.

Figure 14.1 illustrates the differences between the two models. First, we can see that the differences are clearer in the Complex model than in the SRS model. The Complex model plainly shows that the Science literacy score is higher for the first-generation females than for respective males, and that native males seem to be best qualified in science but the difference to native females is not significant. We do not interpret further differences between the two alternative models, as they can be seen in the graph.

We continue with some other regression estimates, but before that we compare the country differences without any model and when the model is used—that is, when those explanatory variables are used as control variables (Fig. 14.2). We can see that the differences almost disappear when the control variables of the model are included in the estimation.

Next, we present some results for these control variables. We start in Table 14.12 with the four continuous variables. The results are somewhat surprising. First, for Environmental optimism the sign is negative in both models. It seems that the

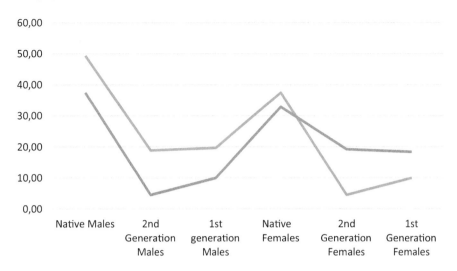

Fig. 14.1 Interaction estimates between gender and immigration status in the model of Table 14.11 (SRS = Blue, Complex = Red). The reference group is "Unknown status" = 0

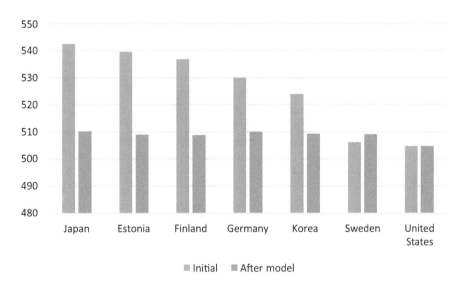

Fig. 14.2 Comparison of seven countries for the 2015 PISA Science scores with the initial scores and those estimated using the linear regression model in Table 14.11. The reference country is the United States

students with a good knowledge in science are less optimistic than those whose knowledge is not so good. The second surprise concerns Subjective well-being, which is positively significant only in the SRS model. The other estimates differ to some extent, with Material wealth being more important in the Complex analysis than in the SRS analysis.

Table 14.12 Regression estimates for the four continuous variables in the model of Table 14.11

Explanatory variable	Complex		SRS	
	Estimate	Std error	Estimate	Std error
Environmental optimism	−13.567	0.739	−11.267	0.413
Parents' support	2.289	0.807	3.742	0.478
Material wealth	5.923	0.998	0.749	0.621
Subjective well-being	−0.095	1.279	1.886	0.694

Table 14.13 Regression model for science literacy score of the 2015 PISA survey for seven countries

Education categories[a]	SRS		Complex	
	Estimate	Std error	Estimate	Std error
Parents' education[b] more than 15 years	49.41	5.84	58.05	6.47
Parents' education between 13 and 15 years	18.59	5.86	29.53	6.34
Parents' education between 10 and 12 years	6.24	7.07	6.62	6.33
Parents' education between 6 and 9 years	4.84	8.99	14.19	8,48
Parents' education below 6 years	0	0	0	0

[a]The reference group is those with the least education
[b]Parameter estimates are for parents' years in education

The educational background of the students' parents explains the science score ably, as expected (Table 14.13). If a parent is well-educated, then the science score of the student is better than if the parent is not. This main conclusion does not differ essentially according to whether the SRS or the Complex sample model is used. It is good to recognise that the three groups of parents with the lowest educational level do not differ significantly from each other.

The final categorical-level consideration concerns the two explanatory variables in Table 14.14. The impact of the variable 'Arriving late at school' is quite linear; the scores decline with the number of times the student arrives late; and the difference is minor between the SRS and Complex models. The second explanatory variable, Feeling like an outsider in school, is more complex. The result for the category 'Strongly agree' is as expected in the SRS model because it seems to decrease the science score, but this does not seem to be the case in the correct analysis, where it is insignificant. The best scores are in the middle categories; however, it is not easy to interpret this result.

14.2.7 A Binary Regression Model with a Logit Link

The last example is for logistic regression, with and without survey instruments. The data are from the 2012 PISA, but now we are interested in how well students know certain basic statistical terms that they are asked about in the questionnaire. The terms are 'Arithmetic mean' and 'Probability'. The student questionnaire gives the following alternatives for the answer:

Table 14.14 Regression model for science literacy score of the 2015 PISA survey for seven countries

	Complex		SRS	
	Estimate	Std error	Estimate	Std error
Arriving late at school[a]				
Never	45.76	5.01	43.02	2.49
One or two times	19.74	4.95	23.56	2.58
Three or four times	12.77	5.09	12.53	3.04
Five or more times	0	0	0	0
Feeling like an outsider in school				
Strongly agree	−1.27	4.90	−15.32	2.97
Agree	10.79	3.22	9.49	2.07
Disagree	9.93	2.23	9.52	1.26
Strongly disagree	0	0	0	0

[a]Parameter estimates are for two explanatory variables

1. Never heard of it
2. Heard of it once or twice
3. Heard of it a few times
4. Heard of it often
5. Know it well, understand the concept

Given that it is really very likely that the students know something about these basic statistical concepts, we create a binary variable so that if the student's answer is 5, then the variable 'Good statistical understanding' takes the value of 1; otherwise, this value is 0 (zero). That's why it is possible to apply either logistic regression or probit regression, and we chose the first of these. In this way, we will build a multivariate model for the 17 OECD countries.

The specification of this logistic regression model is that it is very easy to interpret. This leads to the requirement that a higher estimate means a high-level of plausible knowledge of the statistical terms. This is the same as the reference category, being 0, when the student gives the answer from 1 to 4, whereas it is 1 if the answer = 5.

The results are presented without country estimates, meaning that the country is a control variable. We are interested in other explanatory variables and their influences. Table 14.15 presents the general level results. There are two differences in the significance.

The model with survey instruments shows that gender is significant, meaning that females have a substantially better statistical knowledge. This is not found with the SRS approach, even though the sign is the same. The other difference is in school type—that is, whether the school is private or public. The SRS analysis clearly shows that statistical knowledge is significantly better in private schools, whereas this is not the case in the Complex survey case; this explanatory variable is not significant at all.

Table 14.15 Significance of the two alternative logistic regression models[a] for good statistical understanding from the 2012 PISA for the 17 OECD countries

		SRS	Complex
Effect	Degrees of freedom	p-value	p-value
Country	17	<0.0001	<0.0001
Family structure	2	<0.0001	<0.0001
Gender	1	0.0881	<0.0001
Public vs. private	1	0.0174	0.4311
Grade	5	<0.0001	<0.0001
Absence from school	3	<0.0001	<0.0001
Parents' years of education	4	<0.0001	<0.0001

[a]The SRS model is without survey instruments, whereas the Complex model is calculated with the three instruments

Table 14.16 Odds ratios from the two alternative logistic regression models for good statistical knowledge

	SRS		Complex	
	Low CI	High CI	Low CI	High CI
Five or more times vs. three or four times[a]	0.838	1.026	0.794	1.231
None vs. three or four times	1.157	1.317	1.155	1.532
One or two times vs. three or four times	1.023	1.173	0.949	1.318

[a]Absence from school is one of the explanatory variables
Source: The 2012 PISA of the 17 OECD countries

Many results are similar with both models. For example, if the grade is lower than the optimum, the score or the knowledge is lower than the optimum, whereas if the grade is higher, the score is higher. This means that the student has succeeded when moving up to an advanced class level. Table 14.16 gives an example for absences from school. Here we present the results as the 95% confidence interval for the odds ratios. We find that only the middle comparison is significant in the Complex samples model, whereas the last one in the SRS is significant as well. It therefore is possible to make an incorrect decision if one does not use complex sampling tools.

14.3   Concluding Remarks About Results Based on Simple and Complex Methodology

We can see various types of examples in Sect. 14.2. It is not clear in advance whether the results will give the same profile based on a SRS or a complex survey strategy with correct 'survey instruments' (see Sect. 14.1). Interestingly, we find very similar results quite often, but there are some exceptions as well. This means that it is best to use the complex survey methodology. It, of course, is possible to continue from the points presented here, thus to extend the analysis, including interpretation, as well as so that it helps policymakers and others with their problems.

References

Chambers, R., & Skinner, C. (Eds.). (2003). *Analysis of survey data.* Wiley Series in Survey Methodology. New York: Wiley.

Lehtonen, R., & Pahkinen, E. (2003). *Practical methods for design and analysis of complex surveys, Statistics in practice* (2nd ed.). New York: Wiley.

Lumley, T. (2010). *Complex surveys: A guide to analysis using R, Series in survey methodology.* New York: Wiley.

Martela, F., & Steger, M. F. (2016). The three meanings of meaning in life: Distinguishing coherence, purpose, and significance. *The Journal of Positive Psychology, 11*(5), 531–545.

PISA. (2015). *PISA, Questionnaire framework.* Retrieved January 2017, from https://www.oecd.org/pisa/pisaproducts/PISA-2015-draft-questionnaire-framework.pdf

Further Reading

Journals Much Focused on Surveys

Journal for Quantitative Methods and Survey Methodology. Methods, data, analysis. Mannheim: Gesis—Leibnitz Institute for Social Sciences. Retrieved from http://www.gesis.org/unser-angebot/publikationen/zeitschrift-mda/

Journal of Official Statistics. Statistics Sweden. Retrieved from http://www.degruyter.com/view/j/jos

Journal of Survey Statistics and Methodology. Oxford Journals. Retrieved from http://jssam.oxfordjournals.org/

Statistical Journal of the IAOS: Journal of the International Association for Official Statistics. Retrieved from http://content.iospress.com/journals/statistical-journal-of-the-iaos/

Survey Methodology. Statistics Canada. Retrieved from http://www5.statcan.gc.ca/olc-cel/olc.action?objId=12-001-X&objType=2&lang=en&limit=0

Survey Methods. Insights from the field. Retrieved from http://surveyinsights.org/?page_id=522

Survey Practice, The AAPOR e-journal with public opinion and survey research articles and commentary. Retrieved from http://www.surveypractice.org/index.php/SurveyPractice

Survey Research Methods. The European Survey Research Association (ESRA). Retrieved from https://ojs.ub.uni-konstanz.de/srm/

Survey Statistician. International Association of Survey Statisticians. Retrieved from http://isi-iass.org/home/services/the-survey-statistician/

Survey Textbooks

Allison, P. D. (2008). Missing data. Retrieved from http://people.oregonstate.edu/~acock/growth/NCFRgrowth/Allison,%20Missing%20Data%201.pdf

Bethlehem, J. (2009). *Applied survey methods: A statistical perspective* (392 pp). Hoboken: Wiley

Bethlehem, J., & Biffignandi, S. (2011). *Handbook of web surveys* (480 pp). New York: Wiley.

Biemer, P. P., & Lyberg, L. E. (2003). *Introduction to survey quality* (424 pp). Hoboken: Wiley.

Carpenter, J., & Kenward, M. (2013). *Multiple imputation and its application*. Chichester, West Sussex: Wiley.

Chambers, R., & Skinner, C. (Eds.). (2003). *Analysis of survey data. Wiley series in survey methodology*. Chichester: Wiley.

Christof, W., Joye, J., Smith, T. M., & Yang-chih, F. (2016). The SAGE handbook of survey methodology (720 pp). London: Sage.

Cross-cultural Survey Guidelines. Retrieved from http://ccsg.isr.umich.edu/

© Springer International Publishing AG, part of Springer Nature 2018
S. Laaksonen, *Survey Methodology and Missing Data*,
https://doi.org/10.1007/978-3-319-79011-4

Cochran, W. (1977). *Sampling techniques* (3rd ed., 448 pp). New York: Wiley.

De Leeuw, E., Hox, J. J., & Dillman, D. (2008). *International handbook of survey methodology* (549 pp). Retrieved from http://joophox.net/papers/SurveyHandbookCRC.pdf

Enders, C. K. (2010). *Applied missing data analysis* (370 pp). New York: Guildford Press.

Groves, R. M., Fowler, J. J., Couper, M. P., Lepkowski, J. M., Singer, E. & Tourangeau, R. (2009). *Survey methodology* (2nd ed., 488 pp). Hoboken: Wiley.

Heeringa, S. G., West, B. T., & Berglund, P. A. (2010). *Applied survey data analysis*. Boca Raton: Chapman and Hall/CRC.

Kish, L. (1995). *Survey sampling* (664 pp). New York: Wiley.

Little, R. J. A., & Rubin, D. B. (2002). *Statistical analysis with missing data* (2nd ed.). New York: Wiley.

Lehtonen, R., & Pahkinen, E. (2003). *Practical methods for design and analysis of complex surveys. Statistics in practice* (2nd ed.). Chichester: Wiley.

Lior, G. (2012). *Handbook of survey methodology for the social sciences* (520 pp). New York: Springer.

Lohr, S. (2010). *Sampling: Design and analysis* (2nd ed.). Tempe: Arizona State University.

Lumley, T. (2010). *Complex surveys: A guide to analysis using R. Series of survey methodology.* Somerset: Wiley.

Presser, P., Rothgeb, J. M, Couper, M. P., Lessler, J. T., Martin, E., Martin, J. & Singer, E. (2004). *Methods for testing and evaluating survey questionnaires.* Hoboken: Wiley.

Rubin, D. B. (1987). *Multiple imputation for nonresponse in surveys.* New York: Wiley.

Rubin, D. B. (2004). *Multiple imputation for nonresponse in surveys.* Hoboken, NJ: Wiley-Interscience.

Salant, P., & Dillman, D. A. (1994). *How to conduct your own survey* (256 pp). New York: Wiley.

Tille, Y. (2006). *Sampling algorithms. Series in statistics* (217 pp). New York: Springer.

Särndal, C.-E., Swensson, B., & Wretman, J. (1992). *Model-assisted survey sampling. Series in statistics* (695 pp). New York: Springer.

Valliant, R., Dever, J. A., & Kreuter, F. (2013). *Practical tools for designing and weighting survey samples. Statistics for social and behavioral sciences.* New York: Springer.

Research Articles Dealing With Surveys: Calibration and Weighting

Ekholm, A., & Laaksonen, S. (1991). Weighting via response modelling in the Finnish household budget survey. *Journal of Official Statistics, 7*(3), 325–337.

Henry, K. A., & Valliant, R. (2015). A design effect measure for calibration weighting in single stage samples. *Survey Methodology, 41*(2), 315–331.

Holt, D., & Smith, T. M. F. (1979). Post-stratification. *Journal of the Royal Statistical Society. Series A (General), 142,* 33–46.

Kott, P. S. (2006). Using calibration weighting to adjust for nonresponse and coverage errors. *Survey Methodology, 32*(2), 133–142.

Kott, P., & Chang, T. (2010). Using calibration weighting to adjust for nonignorable unit nonresponse. *Journal of the American Statistical Association, 105,* 491.

Laaksonen, S. (2007). Weighting for two-phase surveyed data. *Survey Methodology: A Journal of Statistics Canada, 33*(2), 121–130.

Laaksonen, S., & Chambers, R. (2006). Survey estimation under informative nonresponse with follow-up. *Journal of Official Statistics, 22*(1), 81–95.

Lumley, T., Shaw, P., & Dai, J. Y. (2011). Connections between survey calibration estimators and semiparametric models for incomplete data. *International Statistical Review, 79*(2), 200–220. https://doi.org/10.1111/j.1751-5823.2011.00138.x.

Lundström, S., & Särndal, C.-E. (1999). Calibration as a standard method for treatment of nonresponse. *Journal of Official Statistics, 15*(2), 305–327.

Särndal, C.-E. (2001). The 2010 Morris Hansen Lecture: Dealing with survey response in data collection, in estimation. *Journal of Official Statistics, 27*(1), 1–21.

Smith, T. M. F. (1991). Post-stratification. *The Statistician, 40,* 315–323.

Wittenberg, M. (2009). *Sample survey calibration: An information-theoretic perspective*. A Southern Africa Labour and Development Research Unit Working Paper, No. 41. Cape Town: SALDRU, University of Cape Town.

Research Articles Dealing With Surveys: Editing and Imputation

Chambers, R. (2003). Evaluation criteria for statistical editing and imputation. In *Euredit project papers*. Retrieved from http://www.cs.york.ac.uk/euredit/

Kong, A., Liu, J. S., & Wong, W. H. (2010). Sequential imputations and Bayesian missing data problems. *Journal of the American Statistical Association, 89*(425), 278288.

Laaksonen, S. (2003). Alternative imputation techniques for complex metric variables. *Journal of Applied Statistics, 30*, 1009–1020.

Laaksonen, S. (2015). *Principles of imputation methods, lecture material, social research*. University of Helsinki. Retrieved from https://wiki.helsinki.fi/display/SocStats/Laaksonen%2C+Seppo

Laaksonen, S. (2017). *Imputation methods, lecture material*. University of Helsinki. Retrieved from https://wiki.helsinki.fi/display/SocStats/Laaksonen%2C+Seppo

Laaksonen, S., & Piela, P. (2003). Integrated modelling approach to imputation. In *Euredit project documents. Standard Methods*, D512 StatFi. Retrieved from http://www.cs.york.ac.uk/euredit/

Schenker, N., & Taylor, J. M. G. (1996). Partially parametric techniques for multiple imputation. *Computational Statistics and Data Analysis, 22*, 425–446.

Statistical Solutions. (2016). Mahalanobis distance matching method. Retrieved from http://www.statsols.com/mahalanobis-distance-matching-method/

Research Articles Dealing With Surveys: Other Literature

A JOS Special Issue on Responsive and Adaptive Survey Design. Retrieved from https://www.degruyter.com/view/j/jos.2017.33.issue-3/issue-files/jos.2017.33.issue-3.xml

Al Baghal, T., & Lynn, P. (2015, Summer). Using motivational statements in webinstrument design to reduce item-missing rates in a mixed-mode context. *Public Opinion Quarterly, 79*(2), 568–579.

Beullens, K. & Loosveldt, G. (2016). Interviewer effects in the European social survey. *Survey Research Methods, 10*(2). Retrieved from https://ojs.ub.uni-konstanz.de/srm/article/view/6261#sthash.MwfsJ4w7.dpuf

Couper, M. P., & Zhang, C. (2016). Helping respondents provide good answers in web surveys. *Survey Research Methods: Journal of European Survey Research Association, 10*(1), 49–64. doi: 10.18148/srm/2016.v10i1.6273. Retrieved from http://www.surveymethods.org

De Leeuw, E. D. (2005). To mix or not to mix data collection modes in surveys. *Journal of Official Statistics, 21*(2), 233–255.

De Leeuw, E. D., Dillman, D. A., & Hox, J. J. (2008). Mixed mode surveys: When and why. In E. D. de Leeuw, J. J. Hox, & D. A. Dillman (Eds.), *International Handbook of Survey Methodology* (pp. 299–316). New York: Taylor & Francis Group LLC.

ESS Website: Europeansocialsurvey.org

Jäckle, A., Roberts, C., & Lynn, P. (2009). Assessing the effect of data collection mode on measurement. *International Statistical Review, 78*(1), 3–20.

Kim, J. K., & Riddles, M. K. (2012). Some theory for propensity-score-adjustment estimators in survey sampling. *Survey Methodology, 38*(2), 157–165. Statistics Canada, Catalogue No. 12-001-X.

Lumley, T. (2013). *Survey: Analysis of complex survey samples*. R package version 3.29. http://CRAN.R-project.org/package=survey

Lundquist, P., & Särndal, C.-E. (2013). Aspects of responsive design with applications to the Swedish living conditions survey. *Journal of Official Statistics, 29*(4), 557–582. https://doi.org/10.2478/jos-2013-0040.

Martin, P. (2011). *What makes a good mix? Chances and challenges of mixed mode data collection in the ESS*. Working Paper Series 02. London: Centre for Comparative Social Surveys, City University.

Martin, P., & Lynn, P. (2011). *The effects of mixed mode survey designs on simple and complex analyses*. Working Paper Series Paper No. 04. London: Centre for Comparative Social Surveys, City University.

PISA. (2015). PISA, Questionnaire framework. Retrieved from https://www.oecd.org/pisa/pisaproducts/PISA-2015-draft-questionnaire-framework.pdf

PISA. (2015). Retrieved from http://www.oecd.org/pisa/

Revilla, M. (2010). Quality in unimode and mixed-mode designs: A multitrait-multimethod approach. *Survey Research Methods, 4*, 151–164 Retrieved from http://www.surveymethods.org.

Robins, J. M., Rotnitzky, A., & Zhao, L.-P. (1994). Estimation of regression coefficients when some regressors are not always observed. *Journal of the American Statistical Association, 89*, 846–866.

Rosenbaum, P. R., & Rubin, D. (1983). The central role of the propensity score in observational studies for causal effects. *Biometrika, 70*, 41–55.

Index

© Springer International Publishing AG, part of Springer Nature 2018
S. Laaksonen, *Survey Methodology and Missing Data*,
https://doi.org/10.1007/978-3-319-79011-4

3

Printed in the United States
By Bookmasters